Steve and Cindy —

May you both find imagination, adventure, heroes, and dreams in these pages, and may they take you back to those days in your own childhoods when such things meant the world to us.

May those innocent children you were then, still live in your hearts and in your minds today.

Jack Osborne
12/15/07

Praise for
Makers of Mischief!

This is a **delightful and charming memoir.** Settle in and be transported back to those days when imagination, adventure, and life values were part of everyday life. Jack has done a **masterful job** of bringing back the essence of childhood memories.

—Judy Lawrence
Author, *The Budget Kit*

I was **mesmerized by the stories** and was reminded of the **lessons I learned** in my own youth.

—Tom Stinson
Owner, *Sinbad's* restaurant, San Francisco

Jack Osborne's childhood "mischief" stemmed from a constant desire for adventure, fueled by a rich imagination. He majored in "play," through which he and his neighborhood friends learned **valuable lessons** about how to make their dreams come true and **overcome the adversity** they faced.

—*Beacon Hill & South District Journal*
Seattle, Washington

The stories are **well crafted and entertaining.** The characters came alive, and I appreciated their imaginations and adventures. **Through them I was transported back to my own enjoyable childhood memories.**

—David Everitt
President and CEO, Everitt Companies, Colorado

Makers of Mischief is **a delight to the heart.** I found myself **laughing out loud** many times. Jack's humor and perspective in his storytelling are refreshing reminders of the great gifts we all enjoy of life and family.

—Don Hammond

Senior Pastor, *Communities of Hope Church,* San Jose, California

Makers of Mischief is an **inspiring** take on adversity, perseverance, and—most important—imagination. Jack and his brother spent their youth in search of high adventure, which they achieved through resourceful and creative play. Jack's "mischief" can teach all of us something about **making dreams come true.**

—Mikala Woodward

Rainier Valley Historical Society, Seattle, Washington

Jack Osborne has **a gift with words**—and the ability to use them for writing memories that **we visualize as we read.** I related to so many of the stories because I grew up at the same time.

—Beverly Stroebel

Author, *Full Sail: A 21ˢᵗ Century Cruise On Board The Mayflower*

Makers
of Mischief

Oh for boyhood's painless play
Sleep that wakes in laughing day
Health that mocks the doctor's rules
Knowledge never learned of schools.

—John Greenleaf Whittier,
The Barefoot Boy

Boyhood is a most complex and incomprehensible thing.
Even when one has been through it,
one does not understand what it was.
A man can never quite understand a boy,
even when he has been the boy.

—Gilbert K. Chesterton

Makers *of* Mischief

A "BOOMER'S" ADVENTURES
IN CHILDHOOD

A Memoir by

Jack Osborne

Books
Inc.

San Jose, California

Makers of Mischief is a memoir. This book is an account of the author's experiences growing up in Seattle, Washington during the 1950s. Some events appear out of sequence, and some names and identifying details of individuals mentioned have been changed. It is a fact that narrative based on over fifty years of memory is much easier to reproduce than dialogue. However, every effort has been made to capture the essence of those spoken conversations.

Published in the United States by

 **Books Inc.**

P. O. Box 5457
San Jose, California 95150-5457
www.makersofmischief.com
E-mail: makers@dreamawaybooks.com

Cover Design by Victoria Pohlmann
Interior Design using Bembo Font by Edward J. Kamholz
First Edition Production and Layout by Desta Garrett
Edited by Vicki Weiland
Bicycle image by Publitek Inc., Waukesha, WI
Photo enhancement by Robert Drewes,
  A Graphic Resource, Incorporated, St. Louis, MO

(excerpt) from *CAMINO REAL,* by Tennessee Williams, copyright © As "Ten Blocks on the Camino Real" (a one-act play), copyright © 1948 The University of the South. As "Camino Real," revised and published version, © 1953 The University of the South. Renewed 1981 The University of the South. Used by permission of New Directions Publishing Corporation, New York, NY.

Quotation by Linus from the comic strip "PEANUTS" by Charles M. Schulz (May 29, 1981), PEANUTS © United Feature Syndicate, Inc. Used by permission of United Media, New York, NY.

ISBN: 978-0-9798798-0-7
Library of Congress Control Number: 2007908545

First Hardcover Edition
Printed in Canada on acid-free, recycled (100% postconsumer waste) paper.

DEDICATION

For my daughters Amy, Erin, and Lindy.

You were my inspiration in creating this book.
The thought of surprising each of you with it
is what kept me going.

Love, Dad

CONTENTS

If I had my life to live over
I'd dare to make more mistakes next time . . .
I would take more chances. . . .
I would climb more mountains and swim more rivers. . . .
I've been one of those persons who never goes anywhere
without . . . a raincoat, a parachute. . . .
If I had my life to live over,
I would start barefoot earlier in the spring
and stay that way later in the fall.
I would go to more dances.
I would ride more merry-go-rounds.
I would pick more daisies.

—attributed to Nadine Stair

INTRODUCTION

MEMORIES . . . AND MISCHIEF

One objective for the harvesting of memories is enjoyment. It is common for people of all ages to daydream, and to relive moments simply for the fun of it.

Some of my earliest memories have come from my childhood experiences during the early 1950s when I enjoyed a close relationship with my younger and only brother, Doug. Now in our later years, we continue to share intimate time together. On occasions, we find ourselves looking back at the two young boys who *lived* every moment—from the time we awoke at dawn, until we safely ignored the monsters under our beds for another night of dreams.

Our dreams fueled our imaginations, and our imaginations channeled our adventures, each limited only by the length of the day . . . and our abilities to dream. Our world was what we made it to be. If we didn't like the way it was, we simply imagined something different and everything was OK. We had our special heroes—whether real or imaginary—to protect us, not only from the villains and bad guys who stoked our fears, but also from the reality of our daily-life environment. Our imaginations and our heroes carried us through all of our adventures—safely I might add. Heroes, by example, teach that life's obstructions and difficulties are simply temporary annoyances, although this view is always easier to appreciate when the danger has passed.

1

These are personal stories of Doug and me, and our neighbor-hood pals of the time. I have tried to capture our perspectives when we were pre-teens. In telling of the stories, sometimes great lessons in life emerge in the narrative. On such occasions, I have **emboldened** these passages in order to highlight the significance of those realizations.

The primary focus is on young boys, but girls were always among us. We children all shared the common experiences of early radio, the advent of television, escapes to the movies, and living in a changing post-World War II America.

The most startling realization from writing my memory journeys back to my childhood is that the little boy I was then still lives, thankfully. And that we all *can* find our boyhoods and girlhoods—those innocent people we were then—striving for expression and helping us dream again . . . if only we let them.

That young boy is with me when the difficulties of adult life overwhelm. He still provides me with the magical escapes to overcome and live another day. He still dreams, and those dreams charge my imagination leading to all of the pleasures and adventures I enjoy now. He makes me aware that we all need heroes, regardless of how young—or old—we are.

I never want that little boy—that *Maker of Mischief*—to leave me. Precisely because he is by my side and in my heart, *I* am still a "maker of mischief" today.

Whether we were alive then, or were born later, that period nevertheless is a part of our make-up today. We, our country, and all of our lives today were defined in part by that decade in our history. Yes, whether we now understand it or not, we *all* were children in . . . or *of* the 1950s.

Doug (right) and me, 1952.

THE 1950S

America prior to 1950 simply wanted to be left alone. This attitude came from her history, way back to her beginning. She was founded by people—Pilgrims—who wanted to live their lives in peace. If America had a motto for her first 330 years after Plymouth Rock, it would have been "Live and Let Live." But the rest of the world saw things in America it liked. It saw a country with enormous natural resources and an almost unlimited ability to grow and expand. It saw a people who had a deep reservoir of character and human strength, a foundation of moral and spiritual values, and a strong work ethic. The rest of the world saw America as a non-aggressor, but it learned when conflict came she was someone to have on your side after "choose-ups."

This "personality" of America existed through the first half of the 20th century. She continued to develop, but had a semi-isolationist mentality. Contributing to this was her geographical location; she was separated from the older world by two large oceans. Good fortune also had placed her with no aggressive contiguous neighbors. She was content to live and let live.

But some of the world favored exploitation and domination. Two "world wars" ensued in the first half of the 1900s. In both wars America resisted entry, but once committed made the difference; she helped gain victory and preserve the peaceful order. As a result, America grew in stature and became the world's big sister/brother, a role she never sought, but also never overtly denied. The world looked upon her as a "can-do" nation and she saw herself that way too.

By the end of the Second World War, America had a level of internal morale and positive self-image that was unparalleled in her history at any time. She had emerged from her shell to finally see herself as a country of major influence on the world stage. But with leadership comes responsibility.

In 1950 hostilities erupted in Korea. What began as an intra-country civil war expanded into a major conflict as powerful allies supported their ideologies. America, now a "player," defended democracy (South Korea) halfway around the globe. But the Korean War became a torturous nightmare for America. The costs mounted (almost 55,000 Americans killed, with thousands more wounded!) and she struggled for meaning and identity. America faced a pragmatic *and* moral dilemma. She couldn't be (and didn't want to be) the world's "protector," but she also couldn't allow the expansion of communism. She asked herself, "What role could/should I play in the world community?" She spent most of the 1950s trying to answer that question.

In 1952 America elected Dwight D. Eisenhower as her president. "Ike" and his wife Mamie were effective caretakers to shepherd America through that dilemma and the uncertain 1950s. He was everybody's lovable grandfather and she was the perfect image of the American housewife in that period—domestically capable, sweet, motherly, and always supportive without controversy.

Then on October 4, 1957 everything changed. America suddenly was dragged into the second half of the 20th century, almost against her will. That historical turning point was the surprise launching of "Sputnik"—the first man-made satellite of the Earth—by the U.S.S.R. ("Russia"), who was America's (North) Korean, and now

"Cold War" atomic adversary. Sputnik demonstrated that if Russia had a rocket powerful enough to send a satellite into orbit, then that same rocket conceivably could also lob a nuclear-tipped warhead onto any American city from the other side of the world. That impressive leap in technology single-handedly changed the world's geopolitical dynamics in an instant. The race for world leadership now was on, and America had no choice but to join up and run hard.

The decade of the 1950s was the transition period—from "old" America as an uncertain and sometimes reticent country of major *potential*, to "new" America as a fully-committed *world leader*.

Life was not *easier* in the 1950s. Society experienced diseases without cure, organized crime, social injustices, racial segregation, military conscription, the threat of nuclear annihilation, and economic upheavals, to name a few examples. It still was a difficult time for families to simply maintain, and there never was a "free lunch." Survival and happiness could never be taken for granted.

And yet . . . there was something special about that time. There was a general confidence in institutions, including governments. There was respect for service organizations and *anybody* in uniform. Someone's "word" meant everything. There was a perspective that things were "good" and could only get better; upward mobility *was* possible. Technology *was* our friend and it *would* improve our lives. Things worked! Kids felt secure playing on the streets and fields of America or riding a bus, alone, clear across town and back. Their moms didn't worry about such things. It was a golden age for Hollywood and entertainment. Church (and God) had more of a presence in our lives, and society in general. There was almost . . . an *innocence* in the way people approached life. It was, in short, *life in a simpler time*.

Like the rest of America, Seattle had been changed dramatically by the Second World War. Due to its access to the Pacific Ocean, its prior military presence, its industrial and manufacturing capabilities (Boeing Aircraft and others), its history as a commercial port, its great natural resources, and its moderate weather, Seattle became a strategic location for mobilization and industrial efforts to support America's war effort in the Pacific. Its resident and transient population grew dramatically immediately prior to and through the War.

There was a great displacement of population from America's mostly agrarian heartland to Seattle and other West Coast cities. Thus Seattle and the surrounding region during the 1940s became a significant defense-based economy. There were occupations in, and in support of, the military, and there were also civilian jobs crying to be filled. Things boomed!

My family was drawn into this dynamic, actually sucked into it would be a better expression. My mom, my father, and I (as an infant), found ourselves uprooted as sharecrop farmers in the sugar-beet fields in northern Colorado, and relocated to become part of the military activity in Seattle. My brother Doug was born as the War ended.

Once the War was over, the size of the standing military was dramatically reduced and most of the non-career soldiers and sailors were recycled back into mainstream America. However, for much of the large population who had been displaced *into* the War, the path *back* was not simple, or desirable. Many now ex-servicemen and their families either didn't want to return to their rural roots in the central states, or for various reasons those paths no longer were open. Once you've seen the big city, the bucolic fields lose their allure. And those self-sufficient family-owned farms had begun to disappear due to post-War economics.

For many, such as my father and mother, this was the case; they, too, were "in transition," and it was painful. They lacked the education, the skills, and the training to compete in a non-military *and* non-agrarian life. As such, they were betwixt and between.

When I was almost four years old and my brother was almost two, my mom and dad divorced. She found herself with two small children and no job. Her domestic work in the War was no longer needed, plus opportunities were not prevalent for women in the working force, as they are today. She was stuck: she had no money, no promise, no opportunity, almost no hope. One of life's earliest lessons was: **It is very difficult, without help, to rise above what you do know or to migrate into something you don't know.**

The man who became our stepfather was similarly displaced. And, in that time, in their situation, one place where such poor and desperate people converged was in the government housing projects. This is where we came to live, almost without choice. We remained there for half-a-decade, during my pre-adolescent boyhood, until we completed our own transition into something better.

That is where my brother and I spent our formative years as young boys. Neither he nor I then had an understanding of all of the dynamics influencing our lives. The "projects" was where we were, and where we experienced life during that period, the first half of the 1950s. The approximate half-mile radius around our home in south Seattle was our world. It was all we knew.

We had the same needs and desires as boys everywhere: to play, to discover, to win in our competitions, to always have fun, and to dream about our futures. We learned to do all of those, and more, in the projects—our world within a world.

We made it our own special place.

—Jack Osborne

The Rainier Vista federal government housing project in south Seattle, circa 1950.

A pair of "mischief makers" readying for Halloween fun.

Jack: "They'll never know who we are!"

Doug: *"I* don't even know who we are!"

PART ONE

LIFE IN THE PROJECTS

1

THE PROJECTS

Having been poor is no shame, unless you are ashamed of it.
—Benjamin Franklin

I have enough money to last me the rest of my life,
unless I want to buy something.
—Jackie Mason

I was born in Denver, but I spent my early childhood in Seattle in the 1940s and early 1950s. The hows and whys of that move had to do with the Second World War, "The Big One," as my Uncle Johnny, my mom's brother, called it even though he never served. My mom was a welder in the shipyards during the War, and Uncle Johnny cared for me and my younger brother Doug, when she worked.

Our dad, however, did go to war. Mom rarely talked with Doug or me about him, unless to say something angry or bitter. Neither of us remember our dad before he went overseas, and he never came home afterward. Oh, he survived; it's just that he never came *home* again. There was a messy divorce and we never saw or knew our real dad.

My mom remarried when I was about four years old. I don't know how that came about; the man who became our stepfather simply began living with us one day. My mom and step-dad thereafter had a daughter, Cindy, who was born exactly on my fifth birthday. Mom always told everybody Cindy was my twin, and that Cindy had simply taken her time in the delivery. The fact that Doug was born between Cindy and me merely was a complication, I guess. That was my family.

We were terribly poor. We kids knew we were poor because it was a continual lament from our parents. And we heard the fights, saw the drinking, and often were on the receiving end of their ongoing frustration—both verbally and physically—from life in that condition. But we didn't fully understand the extent of what being poor meant because we were kids. All of our friends were also poor. We were not unhappy about it because we had no comparison; it was the only life we knew.

Indicative of our poverty, we lived in "the projects" in the section of south Seattle called "Columbia." The projects were government-subsidized housing, what today might be called "slums." Actually, there were two types of projects in that area. There were what we kids called the "good" projects, which were cream-colored *duplexes* with patches of lawn (mostly weeds) here and there. And, there were the "old" projects, which were *four-plexes* that looked like Army barracks, with unpainted weather-worn siding, no lawns, and graveled streets without curbs. We lived in the latter: the "old" projects. We had one source of heat in the whole house, which was a coal-burning stove in the kitchen. To maintain a tolerable temperature we had to keep a fire of coals burning in it almost all day.

One memory I have of that stove is that it was customary for my mom to get up early and light the coals to heat the house. Then she would go back to bed for half-an-hour or so. One Sunday, when I was about eight years old, I came into her bedroom after she had returned to bed. She asked me to do her a favor and "put some water on the fire." She meant that I should heat some water in a pan on the top of the hot stove.

Misunderstanding her, though, I poured water into a pan, lifted one of the circular iron lids in the stove-top, and poured the water onto the fire, thus dousing it. Needless to say, this action became the subject of retold stories well into my middle age and always was good for many laughs at family gatherings.

But, back to the coal. Burning coal meant that we also needed a place to store the coal. Every family in the "old" projects had their own coal bin out by the street. It was a square box, about five feet on a side, with a large hinged door at the top for filling and a little door on the lower side for removing the coals. One of my twice-daily chores was to go to the bin, shovel out some coal into a pail, and bring it into the house regardless of the weather. I still remember the always prevalent unique smell in the neighborhood from the burning coal. That smokiness hung in the perpetually gray, drizzly sky of what was typical Seattle weather for most of the year.

Our project "unit" in our four-plex was small for a family of five. There was an entry/kitchen, a "living" room, a bathroom complete with a tiny tub, and three tiny bedrooms. Cindy had her own room, and mom and dad also had a bedroom. All rooms were stuffed with minimal and basic furniture. Doug and I shared a bunk bed in our bedroom; he was on the top, me on the bottom. There was another twin bed in our room, used by Uncle Johnny when he occasionally "crashed" at our place. It was shoved against one wall and our bunk beds were shoved against the opposite wall, thus providing barely enough space to walk between them.

Doug and I, exercising our imaginations at all times, took this closeness as an opportunity to play *Tarzan* (a popular movie hero of the time) jumping off the cliff or over the waterfalls. Or sometimes we were paratroopers; the fact that we lacked chutes was a minor detail. We climbed up onto Doug's bunk and then jumped off and across, usually accompanied by screams for emphasis. These were daring leaps best attempted when mom and dad were away from the house. We always landed on the twin bed with bounces.

This was great fun and we could have jumped forever. However, there is always a limit, beyond which you push things too far. This came when we imagined we were the *Lone Ranger* and *Tonto* (popular television heroes of the time) jumping off a balcony together and onto our waiting horses below.

"Yiiieee!" we yelled, and then fell the five feet, making perfect simultaneous impacts into our imagined saddles. Except that the backs of our "horses" cracked with a huge BANG and splayed out their sides. The bed frame completely broke apart! I bounced into the wall and Doug landed on the floor. Instantly, we went through the quick cycle of emotions familiar to every child everywhere when a play activity doesn't go as planned: excitement from the conception, thrill from the anticipation, apprehension from the possible danger, exhilaration from the doing, fear/pain from the unexpected result, and panic from the consequences.

We were in panic mode! What would we tell mom? *Think!!!* We both wished with all our might we could go back to that "balcony" and never have jumped, but to no avail. Our horses' backs remained broken. We never did concoct a satisfactory story on that one. We knew mom would not buy the argument that we both accidentally fell off Doug's bunk at the same instant and were luckily saved from harm by fortunately falling onto the single bed. We also doubted she would believe that *Gorgeous George*—professional wrestling's bad guy of the time—had come into our room and torn it up against our wishes. We were in a pickle with no solution.

We finally decided to just ignore it. "Yes mom, we see it's broken, but we have no idea how it happened. Maybe Uncle Johnny had a really bad dream!" That was our story and we stuck to it. We received a week's detention in our room as punishment, but to us we simply imagined we had been locked in a dark cave by *Ming the Merciless* (an evil Saturday matinee movie character). We were trapped against our will, but somehow we would eventually escape.

We could turn anything into an adventure—even household furniture or appliances.

We had a washing machine on wheels that was permanently placed in the bathroom. It had a top-loading tub with an agitator that swished the clothes in the water back and forth. When the washing and rinsing was finished, all manually controlled, the clothes were removed from the tub and threaded into a pair of rollers to wring out the water as they passed through. I was talking with mom one afternoon while she was doing this. Distracted, her hand became caught in the rollers. Once caught, there was no escape.

The rollers devoured her hand, her wrist, and then her arm. Past her elbow, and up toward her shoulder they rolled onward! The rollers exerted great force, and she screamed, as much from fright as from pain. I was also scared by her shrieks. Finally, I jerked the electrical plug from the wall socket. She couldn't dislodge her arm, as she was awkwardly bent over the washtub. I ran out of our unit to get help from our neighbor. Mom's arm finally was freed, but it was bruised and purple for weeks. I never again talked with her when she wrung out clothes in the wash.

Thereafter Doug and I gave the washer an "animated" soul. We imagined that an evil and demonic spirit had entered that washing machine, and it became an object to be feared whenever we went into the bathroom. We knew it was devilishly waiting for us to turn our backs so it could grab us with its drain hose, then feed us through its rollers, and eat us alive! Nights were the worst. We even used to scare Cindy by telling her we would feed her to the washing machine if she displeased us in any way. This usually produced her scream of "MOOOMMM!" followed by a self-pitying cry. Doug and I would be "forced" back into our "cave" by the monster's accomplice (mom) to scheme and plot our next escape.

If washing clothes was a chore, drying them was even more difficult. The challenge was the weather. To us, Seattle seemed to have only two seasons: summer when the sun shone, and the rest of the calendar year when it rained or drizzled often.

We had a clothesline in our front yard, between the house and the gravel of the street. The drooping lines were suspended between two large "T's" planted into the ground. The washed and wet clothes were hung on the lines with wooden clips. The hope was there would be a break in the drizzle, maybe even with the sun coming out for a few hours midday, enabling the clothes to dry. The reality was that often they were brought back into the house still wet and then laid out across the beds and the backs of the kitchen chairs and table. Even when the clothes finally were dry, they were so stiff they risked breaking when folded.

One day dad brought home a super new invention. It was a clothes drying rack that was folded. When he pulled it "open," much as one would pull an accordion, the legs popped out along with three wooden dowel-like racks on each side and at different elevations. Each parallel dowel became a horizontal rod over which wet clothes could be draped. When opened, the rack was about four-feet wide, four-feet tall, and less than a couple of feet deep. This was one of the niftiest things we had ever seen, and it solved most of the drying issues. Mom could unfold the rack in the kitchen, near the coal stove, and then drape the wet clothes across the rods. After a few hours, everything was suitably dry for another display of wet clothes.

It worked so well that dad brought another rack home and soon we had an obstacle course of drying racks and wet clothes in the (already tiny) kitchen. Shortly thereafter, we had a third such rack, now occupying the nearby "living" room. We had wet clothes drying everywhere. We loved them, though, because not only were our clothes noticeably warmer (and dryer) when we put them on, but also the racks, with clothes laid out, contributed to our play. They stirred our imaginations and became tools for our in-the-house hide-and-seek games.

They also were perfect hiding places for us, or dens for the wild animals we imagined we became. This was always best done when mom was out of the house for a while, notably Saturday mornings (wash day) when she went to buy groceries.

One Friday night Uncle Johnny stayed over. He was about five years older than mom, but he was closer to us in temperament than to being an adult. The next morning after mom had washed and laid out all of the wet clothes on the racks, she left for the grocery store. Dad also was gone. Doug, Cindy, and I thought it would be a good time to play pirates and forts, and somehow we talked Uncle Johnny into being the head pirate.

I climbed inside one rack (fort), Doug and Cindy entered another, and Uncle Johnny somehow managed to get inside the third. We shouted pirate commands at each other and threatened each other with great bodily harm, in between our laughter. Uncle Johnny picked a pair of dad's boxer shorts off of his rack and pulled the elastic waist over his head to now display an outlandish pirate's "hat" on his head. We all laughed even more. I then had the brilliant idea to fire a cannonball into Uncle Johnny's fort. I picked a wet T-shirt off of my fort, wadded it up, and tossed it into Johnny's fort, smacking him in the face. More laughter by everyone. This really was fun!

To get even, Uncle Johnny lifted up his fort and began moving toward us, peeking out between the hanging underwear on his racks. We feigned fear, screamed, and tried to lift our forts too. I was able to get mine off the ground, but Doug and Cindy's wobbled unsteadily. Onward Uncle Johnny came. We screamed more. I tried to turn my fort but it was unsteady. Clothes swayed every which way as I peeked out between them.

I saw the head pirate, with the shorts on his head, coming closer to "destroy" our forts. I lurched with another scream, and then stumbled. I fell into Doug and Cindy's fort, which caused them also to fall, and like tumbling dominos we all fell into Uncle Johnny's fort. All three of our forts, with us inside, now were splattered on the floor, with wet clothes scattered here and there. We screamed in almost delirious laughter.

Suddenly, the front door opened! It was mom!! She was the *Wicked Witch of the West*, who hated laughter . . . and fun . . . and pirates and forts . . . and most of all, intensely hated seeing her freshly washed clothes now scattered all over the (dirty) floor. She instantly doused all of our fun with her shrieking. The party was over. We kids were banished to our rooms for the rest of the day. Doug and I both received a swat of her hand across our butts, although Cindy escaped with only a scolding. Uncle Johnny was banished "forever" with the stern admonishment from mom to, "Grow up!" Why would anyone *want* to do such a thing, Doug and I wondered. Uncle Johnny was gone for two weeks but then returned from his banishment; apparently his sentence had been commuted by the warden (also mom).

Life returned to normal, and the drying racks never again were forts, but still they remained an obstacle course for other games when mom and dad were away. The pirates were temporarily retired, but we never forgot the head pirate with his boxer shorts hat.

In our house, food was an ongoing medley of whatever was available. Our meals were basic and bare subsistence. We lived on foods that were inexpensive. Mom often made a stew, which she called "slumgullion." It never tasted the same twice because it was created from boiling together in a large pot whatever saved leftovers were around. Elbow pastas and a potato or two were thrown in to give texture, or "body."

Occasionally, large lima beans were the "mystery" ingredient. We rarely had meat, and it always was the cheaper cuts called "ground round," which may have been ground *anything*, for all we kids knew. I used to joke with Doug that some nights we had "ground square" or "ground triangle." We often had cheap roasts cooked in a large pot with vegetables added. Once in a while we had pork chops as a special treat. I never had a steak until I was age thirteen.

We had more than our share of various pastas. Also, macaroni and cheese appeared more times than we liked. One protein we did have was fish. Fish from the Puget Sound (salmon and halibut mostly) was plentiful and cheap. Additionally, mom, dad, and Uncle Johnny often fished for trout in the local rivers and lakes. It provided inexpensive recreation as well as food for the table.

One thing we never had was butter. It was too expensive. Instead we had something called "oleo." This was a non-dairy product that was purchased in one-pound white slabs. When cold it looked like a white brick, but when warmed to room temperature it could be spread around somewhat like butter. But it was white! To make it more visually pleasing and "butter like," it came with a small packet of orange-colored powdered dye.

If so inclined, and my mom was, when the slab was warmed and in a bowl, you could break open a packet of the powdered dye and then mix it into the oleo block. This was one of my regular chores. Doing this produced a bowl full of something which looked like butter, but lacked the flavor of the real thing. Doug and I imagined mom thought it important to have the "butter" look in case our school principal just happened to drop over for dinner some night.

Another food cost saver we endured for the first couple of years in the projects was powdered milk. This was a white powder that came in a box. It was then mixed with water to produce a liquid that looked like milk, except it tasted more like white water. And the water came from the tap. In those days there was no "bottled water." Water was something you poured and drank straight from the tap. And it was "free," hence the cost of powdered milk was significantly cheaper than real milk, although not nearly as satisfying.

Fortunately, we always received free six-ounce cartons of whole milk in school every morning as part of the Seattle Public School's nourishment program. We never refused our school milk. One of our great treats was when we occasionally visited our Grandma Pearl, our step-dad's mom, for Sunday brunch. In our mind she was rich because she always served us kids homemade pancakes with real maple syrup, real butter, and as much chilled whole milk as we wanted. It took little to make us happy in those days and Grandma Pearl had the recipe.

THE BEST SPAGHETTI IN THE WHOLE WIDE WORLD!

One special dish I'll always remember was mom's spaghetti. As non-Italians, you wouldn't think spaghetti would be the great family treat, the great cooking memory from my childhood, but it was. There never was spaghetti like my mom made, and I've never tasted anything like it since I left home! She made it about twice a year, usually on holidays.

She would casually make an announcement about a couple of weeks in advance to properly pique our interest and get us salivating. It became a topic of conversation for the two or three nights before the cooking began. Mom never had a recipe; it was all in her head. She never used measuring spoons or cups. She just added whatever felt good to her at the moment. She was like a witch concocting a secret brew, except it always became the most flavorful and tasty sauce you could possibly imagine! How she did it was a mystery, every time.

It originated as a thin and watery base with large chunks of tomatoes floating in a giant pot. She began with about three or four gallons of liquid. As the hours went by she added herbs, spices, onions, and greens . . . and eye of newt and toe of frog. Naw, not really, but who knew what she put in? Slowly the liquid cooked down, filling the whole house with tantalizing aromas that would permeate every room, and every towel or washcloth. It cooked for almost two full days.

At night she let the coals go out in the stove and everything sat, distributing flavors. Then with morning, the heat again was applied and more secrecy was added throughout the second day. The buildup was almost more than we could take. In the last few hours she turned her attention to making a plain French bread loaf into marvelous chunks of garlic bread. These by themselves almost brought tears to our eyes when we first chomped into a slab.

The last accompaniment was the salad. Mom sliced iceberg lettuce heads into quarters and then lavishly poured a homemade dressing over each quarter. The dressing was a magical composition that was also indescribable. It was similar to a cross between a great Thousand Island and a Caesar. She began with large jars of mayonnaise and ketchup, then added various dollops of mustards, sauces, and who knows what? It had random chunks of unknown tasty bits floating through it, which made our mouths water.

By 4:00 PM we all were delirious in anticipation, knowing we had another hour to wait; mom's spaghetti dinners were always served precisely at 5:00 PM. That was the routine. We all purposely skipped lunch so we could stuff ourselves at dinner. The last half-hour was spent cooking the spaghetti, the last magical ingredient. Where she found the pasta I also do not know, but it tasted nothing like the plain pasta I have had since.

When we finally sat down, and dinner was served by mom

with a flourish, it was a true family feast and celebration. Uncle Johnny always showed up for that dinner, and sometimes one of mom's other brothers, Uncle Joe, also came. I ate and ate until I couldn't move, under the possibility that I would lose it all. It was glorious.

Then near the end, mom would rise, and suddenly produce from a cabinet a homemade apple pie, which in itself was a masterful delight. Out would come the ice cream, and my uncles and step-dad would gorge themselves on dessert. I always had to wait until later when I finally had some spare room in my tummy to squeeze in a thin sliver of apple pie. Doug and I went to bed those nights simply stuffed, lying on our backs, afraid even to move. It was heaven. And mom always made far more than we could eat. We always looked forward to leftovers the next night.

To this day, I have never had another spaghetti dinner like those my mom made. Her homemade spaghetti twice a year made all of the slumgullion in between worth it!

THE "GREAT OUTDOORS"

One of the things I remember most vividly about life in the projects are the wonderful adventures Doug and I shared together outside, in the great outdoors. Once we left the house, we entered another world of imagination and play. There were various courts and streets within the projects, each with their own local "gang." They were not tough gangs like today, fighting for turf. Rather, they all were adventure "clubs," sharing experiences with each other, but with serious competition.

Our school, Columbia Elementary, was a three-block bike ride. We whiled away countless days and weekends on its playgrounds, all year around. Our bikes brought us another couple of blocks further from our school to downtown Columbia, an inner-city single street of shops, stores, places to eat, alleyways, and other play locations.

A favorite spot was the "dime" store, as we called it, which had a "soda counter" in it, where we climbed up on stools attached to the floor. The stool tops swiveled and were covered in red Naugahyde®. We could order a soda, or "pop" as we called it, for a nickel, or an ice cream scoop for a dime. Another form of heaven was when mom treated me with a quarter so I could go in there, climb up on a stool, and order my favorite—a chocolate malt or milk shake—as though I "owned the joint."

I also remember that in the store they had pneumatic tubes at the sales counters, which led to a room up on the second floor. When the saleslady (it was ALWAYS a lady) made a sale, she put the money and a sales ticket into a shuttle, stuck it in the tube, and it was whisked away with a big sucking sound up into that room above. One of my fantasies was to someday go up to that room and see them counting all of the piles of money. I also remember the guy behind the soda counter was called a "soda jerk"—I don't know why; that's just the way it was.

The dime store was across the street and down a ways from the Columbia Theater. Every Saturday, all of us kids rode our bikes to the movie theater where we spent almost the entire afternoon sharing our lives with our heroes, and stoking our imaginations with dreams of their adventures.

Being poor, and without the toys that today's children have, we had to find enjoyment through our imaginations, and we did. *We lived for adventure every single day and realized it in our play.* We invented and made our own toys. We created anything, from contraptions and endeavors which could occupy us for a few moments, to whole rapturous experiences that could go on for months and take on lives of their own.

One of the latter was the "haunted house," which was three blocks away in the other direction from the school. This was across from the "woods," the territory that separated the projects from civilized society—those streets with sidewalks. The "woods" actually was a large city block of overgrown weeds, with giant "castles" of blackberry bushes and sapling cedar and pine trees. The haunted house, and the endless mythical wars that we fought in the woods before getting to it, were the preoccupations of countless bands of scruffy kids, such as Doug and me, for years.

The Skate Key
Making Fun from Almost Nothing

One enjoyable plaything for kids at this time was roller skates. There were two types. The first were expensive skates which had very nice rollers (four per shoe) with ball bearings. These were permanently fastened to the bottom of boots, which were then laced onto the foot. These skates, in our minds, were for rich people, movie stars who occasionally skated in the movies, and the people who earned their livings in the "Roller Derby" (a popular sport of the time).

The only skates we ever saw, however, were made of cheap metal rollers fastened onto a metal platform which then was clamped onto a shoe. The most important parts were two metal prongs near the toes which came up and over the sole of your shoe to clamp into the top of the sole, and hold the skate securely against the bottom of your shoe. Since these skates were designed to fit many shoe sizes, the toe prongs were adjusted by turning a bolt on the bottom of the metal platform upon which the rollers were mounted.

The tool which allowed this adjustment was the "skate key." It was critical, because without it you couldn't make adjustments and thus couldn't get the skate to fit tightly against your shoe. Skating was difficult enough, but without both the skate and your shoe "being one," it was almost impossible.

Doug and I had one skate between the two of us. Not one *pair*, one *skate*. We had found it one day in an alleyway in downtown Columbia. It was either lost or discarded by its previous owner, neither case mattered to us. It was ours now. Interestingly enough, the ever precious skate key was also tied to the buckle, thus making this one skate useful. We both could share its use as long as we had *the magic key* to make adjustments. We used it much as modern day youths use skate boards. We bolted the skate onto our right shoe with the key, and then pushed into a run with our left foot. When we had enough speed, or were lucky enough to go downhill, we balanced our whole body on our right leg. The balancing act was critical because we were not skating on flat or smooth surfaces. The rocks, cracks in the roads or the sidewalks, or the potholes, all made it interesting.

Every skate run was an adventure, even those which ended in crashes and tumbles. Remember, too, we never had elbow or knee pads, or protective helmets. Regardless of the apparent danger of perhaps breaking our necks, we never, ever considered a crash as a sufficiently important deterrent to having as much fun as possible. We would jump on that one skate, gain speed, and then wobble all over using our outstretched arms much as high-wire walkers use their long poles to maintain control.

That one skate was another example of the ways we found our fun by using whatever object or circumstance happened to come into our lives—and then adding a little imagination. And the best part: the price was right! Free was better, and often it was all the money we had.

BICYCLES
WERE OUR CHARIOTS TO ADVENTURE

Life is like a ten-speed bicycle.
Most of us have gears we never use.
—Linus from the comic strip "PEANUTS"
by Charles M. Schulz (May 29, 1981)

In spite of how poor a family might be, the one undeniable possession a boy had to have in the 1950s was a bicycle. *Our bicycles were our chariots to adventure!*

My first bicycle was an old fat-tire Schwinn®, and it was my most prized possession. Uncle Johnny gave it to me one day, and I thereafter accepted one of my earliest beliefs in life, that **miracles do happen**. My brother received his first bike on his sixth birthday, also from Uncle Johnny. Both of our bikes looked like they had been through the Second World War, and somehow had survived.

At one time in its life my bike had been red in color, but that was a millennium before it came into my possession. Now it was scratched and scarred, with dappled rusted metal here and there. It was not a full-sized bike with 26″ tires, but it worked fine for me. The wheels were straight and the sprockets and chain were in great shape. The bike had a fender over the back wheel, but the front wheel fender was missing. This was a problem when I rode in the Seattle rain because the front tire threw water up onto my clothes. I often came home with a dirty, vertical stripe bisecting my body, much to the wrath of my mother. It cost money to wash clothes. I had an abundance of mechanical skills and took pride in maintaining that bike to the best of my ability. My second and third most trusted possessions were my crescent wrench and a can of 3-IN-ONE® oil.

One aspect of owning bicycles in the projects was the existence of "the Code," and every kid, both girls and boys, in our neighborhoods knew of the Code and its meaning. Since living space was always at a premium in the projects, there was no place to park the bicycles inside the house. And, since every boy had a bike, and since nobody had any spare money for extravagances like locks, and also since everybody knew everybody else's bike, we all just dropped them on the ground outside our front door stoops.

The unwritten code of conduct was that a guy's bike was sacred, regardless of how beat up it might be. The rule was that you left another guy's bike alone. It was much like the general understanding in the old Westerns where one cowboy never bothered another cowboy's horse. If they did, the result was a hangin', without due process. "Miranda Rights" did not exist in the Old West! The same was true in the projects.

Our bikes were different from bicycles of today in that they were very simply constructed. They had one large pedal sprocket, one rear wheel sprocket, and only one gear. That gear was "forward." They had no shifters, derailers, or linkages. They also had no handlebar brakes. The brakes were applied by the pedals. If you wanted to go forward, you pushed the pedals around in a forward direction. If you wanted to stop, you applied pressure to the pedals in a reverse direction and a brake was applied to the rear wheel. That was it; very simple and straightforward.

But I longed for another. I had lascivious dreams for the ultimate machine: a Schwinn® Phantom with "Typhoon Cord" white sidewall tires, a shock absorbing spring above the front wheel forks, shiny chromed wheel covers with a light built into the front wheel fender, a rack over the back wheel, and wide, shiny-chromed handlebars. That bike had everything and was the epitome of riches to me. I knew I would have "arrived," if and when I could ever buy one of those, and brand new too, no more second (or more) hand for me. But my lusts were unfulfilled and I was never able to acquire one during the years when it was important to me.

There was one other standard accessory that was associated with every bicycle and every bike rider, regardless of how poor one might be. And that, almost magical accessory, was a deck of playing cards. What, you might ask, is the connection? Well, from our view, bikes were not meant to be objects of stealth—they were our imaginary motorcycles, fighter aircraft, race cars, and hydroplanes. Bicycles were much more than mechanical conveniences to provide transportation. They were also extensions of our imaginations leading to adventures. And what all of those vehicles possessed was *noise*. There is just something about young boys and noise—they go together! It was difficult for us, at our age, to do anything quietly—just ask our moms. Riding our bikes was no exception.

The cards were used to make noise, and make it they did! The way this worked was that we attached one card to each side of the bars that held the back wheel fenders onto the bike. This was accomplished by using a spring loaded wooden clip that mom used for hanging clothes on the outside clothesline for drying. Thus the back wheel had two cards stuck in between the wheel spokes, which then flapped against the spokes as the bike was ridden.

The flapping produced the sound of our imaginary engines. The faster we rode, and the newer the cards, the more noise. It was so simple! Our heaven was having new cards in the spokes, and going down a hill as fast as we could pedal, with both gravity and the wind at our backs adding to our speed (and noise production). I always imagined my red marauder as being a P-51 Mustang fighter skimming across the treetops spraying machine gun bullets at will against the imaginary enemy ground forces below.

We cherished our own set of cards and used them, two at a time, until we had worn through the whole deck. We then prayed for another new deck to appear as a surprise gift at our birthdays or Christmas. The cards were never consumed at random; there was a preferred order of use. The most valuable cards in the deck were the Kings—black over red always. Then came the Jacks, then the Queens, then all of the numbers. I know now that Queens are above Jacks, but when we were young boys, that was not the case.

The fact that I was a "Jack" meant *those* cards were even more precious to me. I saved my Jacks for the most important battle-winning sorties, when I needed the most "horsepower" (noise) to pull out of the dive just before I launched the giant bomb under my fuselage. That bomb blew up the last remaining bridge, thus trapping the enemy and thwarting their escape across the river. *Good* prevailed, and *our side* was saved—all because of those two playing cards jammed between my wheel spokes in ways that old man Schwinn never designed.

It was all made possible with our playing cards . . . and our imaginations.

Uncle Johnny.

Seattle Junior League skaters in 1952.
We never saw any of them in our alleyways.

One of our concrete alleyways
for "skate adventures."

The washing machine "monster"
—just waiting to eat an arm . . .
or a sister! According to television and magazines, this is how
a typical American housewife
dressed every day in the 1950s.
Not our mom—she wore a dress
only on Sundays and holidays.

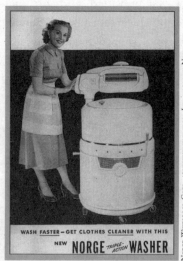

WASH **FASTER**—GET CLOTHES **CLEANER** WITH THIS
NEW **NORGE** _TRIPLE ACTION_ **WASHER**

2

THE ALDERWOOD COURT GANG

Friendship is the hardest thing in the world to explain.
It's not something you learn in school.
But if you haven't learned the meaning of friendship,
you haven't really learned anything.
                                                    —Muhammad Ali

Our gang of ragamuffins was all of us boys who lived on Alderwood Court. In early 1952 that was my brother Doug and I, Jackie Richey, Jackie's brother Bobby, Ronnie Landers, and Freddie Roberts. There were always about six of us at any point in time. The other Courts in the "old" projects had similar gangs. The composition of the gangs changed regularly because tenants of the projects were somewhat itinerant. A family could move in the middle of the night and be gone, without any warning. And, just as suddenly, there would be another family living in that location. We were used to change.

My family, though, lived in the projects for over five years, and I suspect now that somewhere, in some bureaucrat's office, we were silently being tracked as "record holders" for project stability. That does not mean we always paid our rent ($40 per month), just that we stayed in the "old" projects far longer than most other people.

DOUG AND I

Doug and I definitely looked like gang members of the time. We always wore T-shirts and jeans; we never enjoyed color-coordinated or matching outfits. When I say "jeans," I mean just one pair. That was the extent of our play wardrobe, and those clothes were purely functional. Typically, we wore them until they disintegrated.

We each also had another pair of pants for special events. Those "dress up" pants were always "salt and pepper" cords. They were, as the name may imply, made of black corduroy with flecks of white woven in. I have not seen pants like those for years, but I have old pictures of us standing ramrod stiff in them, our Sunday best, with pained looks on our faces waiting to take them off. They were held up with clip-on suspenders. Looking at those pictures now, Doug and I realize just how dorky we looked, but for some reason our mom liked that look. What could we say?

We had two pairs of shoes in our wardrobes. The "dress-up" shoes were usually purchased (always on sale), or sometimes were donations from other families. Somehow, if they were within two shoe sizes, we made them work; more socks did wonders. I wore my good pair until they either saw so much action they evolved to become play shoes, or they were still good enough to pass along to Doug and become his dress-up shoes. Our play shoes were often old "tennis" shoes. Where this term came from I never understood because our tennis shoes were as far removed from an actual tennis match as we were from living in Beverly Hills.

I remember wearing "tennies" that were black high-tops and which always seemed to have about 16,000 miles of rough service in them. The laces had multiple knots, and at least one of them wrapped around my ankle a few times to take up the "extra." Even when my feet were ready to explode out the sides, I knew I could still get another thousand miles out of the pair before complete destruction. All of the rubber on the front toe coverings usually was worn smooth. I would now love to find some of those shoes, bronzed as reminders of the way things were then, but alas, I know that never happened with our level of poverty.

A belt, which I wore for most of this era, also was a thing of beauty. It was cinched tightly around my wisp of a waist and the tail hung down my side almost to my knee. Either it was something I had found and made work, or else mom had bought one belt for my entire lifetime and I simply had not grown into it yet!

Doug was always dressed in an equally desperate condition.

Our childhood hair style was called a "butch." Later I heard it referred to as a "crew cut." These haircuts were perpetrated upon us by mom. She had found an old manual shaver in a junk pile and it had become her barber's tool for our monthly touchups. It was operated by squeezing the handles together sideways against a spring. The problem was that the handles had to be squeezed rapidly with vigor to have even a chance of a good cut, and about halfway through one head mom's hand and arm muscles would tire. Additionally, the shears were dull (maybe that's why they had been discarded).

As a result, we never looked forward to our haircuts because the shaver always pulled our silky fine straw-blonde hair, rather than cutting it cleanly. This then precipitated wrestling matches with the barber, and stern admonishments to "Sit still, dammit!" Neither Doug nor I could get through a monthly session without at least one of us bawling, even when I was as old as twelve.

Doug was a smaller version of me, without quite the mischievousness that I possessed. He was an easy-going kid, who was very cute and likeable. He was thin with a light build like me, but was destined to grow up a little shorter and generally smaller than me. But, whereas I was more of a spontaneous doer, sometimes at high risk, Doug was more thoughtful and cautious. He was quieter in personality than me, but that was just a mask for a brilliant mind at work inside that little head. It was not until much later in life that I came to fully realize just how smart he actually was.

JACKIE

Neither Doug nor I were leaders of the gang. That title belonged to Jackie Richey. A year older than me, he was taller and also stronger than the rest of us. He was a kid of average build, not thin and wiry like me. He had pale white skin with freckles over his arms and across his face. His eyes, blue in color, were small and beady. But he had one thing that distinguished him—his hair. He had a full head of thick, roan-colored waves that looked like a reddish mop. And his mother cared less about haircuts, so Jackie's hair was long and often fell over his forehead.

I imagined that if I had his hair, I would wear an Indian headband like Tonto, the Lone Ranger's friend, but Jackie always let his hair flow freely. I don't think it mattered to him that it flopped around, and he did take some pride in it. I'm sure that without being aware of the psychology, he nevertheless vaguely understood the natural instinct among male pack animals that hair was equivalent to virility and position, and, thus, the more you had the better. This was something my mom never understood.

Jackie gained the leader's position by seniority to some extent, but mostly because he had what today would be called "attitude." This 'tude extended beyond cocky and into the realm of occasional meanness. I was convinced he was a future "JD." This was our abbreviation for "juvenile delinquent," and it was a term that had some meaning on our block. Somewhere, we knew there was a home for kids who seemed to have a bent toward nastiness. I knew it was just a matter of time before Jackie Richey would "graduate" to that home, and be gone from our gang.

Jackie, as impossible as it seemed, was even scruffier than me. My clothes were occasionally washed and I did take a bath, usually nightly. But Jackie and his household apparently had an aversion to water because rarely was there any smell of freshness to any of the Richeys, or what they wore. He, too, had one pair of pants. They were not jeans, but rather some form of dark khaki. There was an Army surplus store a few miles from the projects and I had seen pants like that when I happened to rummage around the store with my step-dad. The khaki pants were next to the web belts with canteens. I had no interest in the pants, but I dreamed about having one of those canteens in case I happened to get stuck in the woods for days; at least I would have enough water to survive.

Jackie's pants always had a mixture of stains that would challenge a modern day forensic technician trying to identify clues. And his shirts were equally camouflaged with various spots and smudges. They looked as if, when eating, he had tried to pass the food through his shirt on the way to his mouth. But none of this bothered Jackie, or his mother for that matter.

Jackie had a unique signature in the way he wore his pants, and it was not the rope he used for a belt or the granny knot as the tie. No, it was his right pant leg, which was always rolled up to his knee. Presumably, he had rolled it up the first time he had put on the pants and had never bothered to let it down again. Now a mixture of dirt and various unknown spills had rendered that pant leg permanently creased into those folds.

The reason for the roll was that Jackie's bicycle did not have a chain guard. That was a small, formed metal piece attached over the top of the large chain sprocket, which prevented the pant leg from catching in the chain as you pedaled. Apparently, Jackie had once done that, thus taking a tumble that opened up his wrist. Jackie, not being too stupid—although there was some debate about that—figured he would never risk doing that again. He would go through life with his right pant leg rolled up to his knee, in case he had to make a fast getaway without time to adjust his pants.

There was one additional trait Jackie had that was unnerving, even to us kids. He seemed to have an excessive interest in fire. He loved fire more than the way I loved my comic books or my slingshot, almost the way I loved my bicycle. He always had matches and was not afraid to use them, so to speak. His highlight of the year was the Fourth of July when he tried to light every incendiary object he could find.

We all loved the Fourth of July because back then we had real fireworks. There were no restrictions and, even with the little amount of money all of the projects' denizens had, somehow we could put on a fireworks show that would give Walt Disney envy. We had rockets, firecrackers, cherry bombs, Roman candles, etc. And we had the best time setting them off—especially Jackie.

One year when Jackie was ten years old, he "accidentally" set off a Roman candle he was holding. All of us in the street discovered it when a flaming red ball of fire swished through the air sideways, about three feet from my ear, and magically entered the open kitchen door of our next-door neighbor's house. A second later another one flew up against the side of our house. There were great shrieks from the parents, and kids flew in all directions.

Doug and I ran behind our coal bin and peeked around both sides to watch hot blobs of fire emerge every couple of seconds from the cane Jackie waved. Finally, he was grabbed and disarmed. He vociferously claimed it was an accident, right up to the time his dad's open palm crashed into the back of his head. Jackie was dragged home for even more whipping and was grounded for a week after that. But we kids all knew that deep inside he enjoyed it immensely and considered it a fair price to pay for the joy of having a flame-spitting armament in his hands, even for a few moments.

BOBBY

Jackie Richey had a brother, Bobby, who was about the same age and temperament as Doug. Whereas Doug and I looked somewhat alike, Jackie and Bobby Richey looked nothing alike. Bobby had straight "dishwater" colored hair, also coarse but short. He had brown eyes and more of an olive-shaded skin.

One day Bobby decided to play coal miner. The "mine" was the coal bin out by the street. With Doug as his accomplice, they forced open the lid so that Bobby could climb up and tumble inside the half-full bin. Then the lid was dropped down again. Doug stayed outside to play "rescuer" in case of a "cave in" or if Bobby couldn't get out. Also, he could talk with Bobby through the walls. Once inside Bobby found a dusty, stifling space that was as totally dark as . . . well, a coal mine! His plan was to dig himself out through the small door at the bottom. He had no light or shovel, so his means was by hand and by feel.

Although Doug was outside, he also had some risk. If he were seen talking to the bin, he knew he would look like a fool. And, if they were discovered, he also knew he would be branded the instigator. All of us kids, and our parents too, knew that in a comparison of intelligence between Doug and Bobby, Bobby would get the "short end" of it, if not be judged an outright idiot. Doug would then be assigned the blame for such a "stupid thing to do" in grown-up talk. One of our life's early lessons was: **If intelligent people associate with idiots (or fools), the idiots will be forgiven, but not those who "should have known better."**

Eventually, after significant struggle, Bobby emerged from the hole at the bottom. His white T-shirt, blue-jeans, and reasonably clean skin going in, now were "Ace of Spades" black. Chimney sweepers were cleaner. Bobby looked as if every square inch of his skin and clothes had been spray-painted flat-black with an aerosol can. However, the whites of his eyes were piercing in contrast. He easily drew gasps from Doug, and a few other kids who were clued in about the "Big Mine Escape."

To Bobby's credit, he "took his medicine" without implicating Doug, thus preserving the tentative peace between both sets of parents. It took a week's worth of baths for Bobby's skin to again approach Caucasian. His clothes were goners and disappeared with the next garbage pickup. Despite the lameness of the caper, Bobby gained some respect among all of the neighborhood gangs because of its uniqueness. A parent might judge the escapade as stupid, but that never was a deterrent for any of us kids. Our imaginations were attracted by the perceived adventure.

RONNIE

Ronnie Landers was the athlete of the gang. I yearned to be a great baseball player because I had "baseball blood" in my veins. I lived it, slept it, and dreamed it! I loved baseball and played it every single day (even rainy ones) after school with whoever showed up. But even in the single digit ages it was apparent that some kids were more talented than others. As much as I wanted to be the star player of the universe, Ronnie was a better fit for that title. He naturally could do things that none of us other kids could do, me especially.

This bothered me for a long time, and I carried a bad case of envy for Ronnie's skills. He excelled at athletics so effortlessly, and I had to try so hard to achieve, well, mediocrity. It was another of those hard lessons we learned—that merely wanting something intensely was not enough. **If you were not born with it, you may never excel to match your dreams, and the best thing would be for you to find another "ball game" which suits you better.**

Although Ronnie and I were the same age, he was slightly

smaller than I, and noticeably smaller than Jackie, but he could darned near hit the cover off a ball. And he could hit to a location on the field at will—wherever the fielders were not. Where that power and that ability to control the ball came from was a mystery. I was envious, but Jackie was unnerved by it to the point of anger. There were many times when Jackie left the game screaming at Ronnie. Normally, the gang leader would assert his position over the underlings with physical prowess, but even Jackie knew he was no match for Ronnie.

If Jackie tried to run Ronnie down and pound him good, he couldn't because Ronnie was too elusive and could outrun him. So Jackie would resort to yelling and cursing, things he practiced often, and ultimately would leave because he could not dominate Ronnie and be the best. To Ronnie it didn't matter, as he was not interested in being the leader. He was not a fighter, and he was confident he could avoid any danger with his legs. I liked Ronnie Landers very much and always wanted to be on the same team as he, because I knew we would win.

One memory I shall always have of Ronnie was his dad. One night he and one of his drinking buddies from the next Court over in the projects were loading up on six packs of "Olys." That's what everybody called Olympia Beer®. After a number of beers, Ronnie's dad conjured up the brilliant idea that they should go trout fishing right then. Night fishing! This was not very smart, though, because of the darkness, but also because trout season was not yet open. And, they decided to use cheese for bait, which further was not very smart because it was illegal. And, to compound the brilliance of this plan, the place where they would fish was a place where they most surely would catch fish, namely the Washington State Fish Hatchery. Now there was a plan! And, after another couple of beers apiece, they enacted it.

Ronnie's dad, and his buddy, didn't come home again for three months. After scaling the eight-foot high chain-link fence surrounding the Hatchery, and falling down the other side, splattering their fishing gear 'roundabout as gravity helped their descent, they found themselves greeted by the Hatchery's security force. Failing to

convince either the blue suits, or the judge, of the intelligence of
their plan, they were thrown into the slammer. It was the talk among
our neighbors for weeks. Even people at our strata of existence
could discern the stupidity of these actions.

For a while Ronnie carried a double-sided cross about this incident regarding his dad. On one side, he definitely achieved some
level of playground notoriety, but the downside was that it was
such a bonehead idea, even to us kids, that for him actually being
related to his father became a dubious distinction. Ronnie's dad
finally returned, but after a couple of months we never saw him
again because he took a trip to the "big house." Something about
an armed robbery. . . .

Freddie

The last gang member at that time was Freddie Roberts. He,
too, was about my age, but that was where the similarity ended.
Whereas I was skinny as a pole, Freddie was slightly on the pudgy
side, not fat, just a typical endomorph, although that was not a term
I learned until much later in life. Freddie was just roly-poly Freddie.
He could not run to save his life, and as such was always the last one
remaining during the baseball "choose-ups." By default he always
went to a team as a leftover. But he had a good disposition—there
was nothing too distinctive about any aspect of who he was. He
was a great "filler" person in any group.

I came to know many such Freddies as I progressed through high
school, college, and eventually the real world. There are maybe more
Freddie types among us than we appreciate. We need them too.

Freddie's value to the group was that he was funny and always
had snacks, which he shared without keeping tabs. His family was a
little more stable than most on our street, as his dad worked regular
hours and they occasionally went to church. He was the only boy
in his family and he had two sisters. Gangs in that time were for
guys only, but his sisters always wanted to tag along.

Jackie Richey would have none of it, and that was that! I was
not too keen, either, on his sisters hanging around, but Jackie was
the authority and he spoke for all of us. Freddie could always come,

though, because he made us feel better about ourselves. We liked him for his congenial nature, and he was happy simply to be one of the gang.

For all of the shortcomings of the projects, we still had the things that mattered. We had people who cared for us (parents, relatives, teachers, etc.), sufficient clothes, warm beds, food in our tummies, mobility (bicycles), sports, and best of all—friends. Neither quantity nor quality was important to us. Our lives were much simpler. And, the enjoyments we gathered in our existence, to a very large extent, were defined by our friends—our Court gangs and the other kids from school. This was our network, and it fulfilled much of our needs.

From our friends came our sense of belonging. We fought occasionally, but we also cared . . . and we shared. We shared, without judgment, all of our hopes and fears—and our dreams and adventures. We longed for play and engaged daily. We grew, and we learned, with each other. And we allowed our imaginations the freedom to overcome any limitations placed upon us by our environment.

My family: Mom, our step-dad, Donn, Cindy, me (what a manly chest!), and Doug.

"Salt and Pepper" cords, and suspenders.

Cindy, Doug, and I having one of our favorite treats; Kool-Aid® popsicles homemade by our mom. Notice the black "tennies." How about those cuffs?

RANIER VALLEY HISTORICAL SOCIETY, SEATTLE, WA

The "old" projects in which we lived.

One of the four-plexes in our projects. The visible center door is where Jackie Richey lived. Notice the coal bins near the street. The man in the picture is my Uncle Joe. This picture was taken on Labor Day in 1952.

3

MYSTERY IN THE WOODS

Don't look back. Somethin' might be gaining on you.
—Satchel Paige

The cure for boredom is curiosity. There is no cure for curiosity.
—Ellen Parr

One morning Ronnie Landers, my brother Doug, and I were playing dodge ball on the school grounds before another day of classes. Before the bell rang, Freddie Roberts rushed up to us, full of excitement, and said he had found something really strange. He said he and his cousin Sid had been over at the haunted house the previous night before dinner. They had been there on a double-dare by some ruffians from Cedarwood Court, another street in the projects. The Cedarwood JD's had dared him that he couldn't ring the doorbell of the haunted house.

Well, none of us guys on Alderwood Court could let a double-dare go unanswered; otherwise it would be all over the playground within a half-hour. So Freddie told us that he and his cousin Sid, along with the Cedarwood guys as witnesses, met at the far side of the woods. There was a narrow street there and the haunted house was across that street. There was a severely weathered picket fence around the house, with a gate leading from the fence to the front porch. Near the gate were some large bushes, suitable for hiding behind.

Freddie and the group ever so carefully crossed the street and crept up to the bushes. They stared toward the porch and front door of the haunted house. Even from this distance they all were filled with fear.

Freddie somehow, against the greatest trepidation on his part—and I still admire him for this—opened the gate, snuck up on the creaky porch, and rang the doorbell. He then bolted back to the bushes as fast as his chubby, uncoordinated legs carried him. Then all of the boys ran for their dear lives across the street and to the safety of the woods. Freddie ran like he was toting a backpack stuffed with bowling balls, so the possibility of being caught by someone, or *something*, coming out of the haunted house must have terrified him. But they all made it to the woods and disappeared inside to safety, as surely as if they had been engulfed in London fog.

No ghost, or adult for that matter, would ever try to find their way through the blackberry patches in those woods. They were so thick that even *Brer Rabbit* would not have wanted to be thrown into them. But we kids knew all of the secret paths because we had accumulated miles of scratches on our bare arms as tuition for the education.

After hiding inside the brambles, so as to judge the coast was clear and let their hearts recede back into their chests, Freddie was released from the double-dare by the Cedarwood JD's. The Cedarwood guys left and took a different path across the woods to their section of the projects, presumably to regale their colleagues with tales of *their* bravery.

Then Freddie came to the "strange" part in his story. As he and his cousin Sid made their way back across the woods, there was a small open field near the large street bordering the projects. In the midst of that open field they saw something none of us had ever seen before—a large metal barrel! To us kids, who had covered every square inch of our homeland territory and knew it as intimately as the Sioux Indians knew every rill and valley of the central Plains, this was big news!

This was a mystery of the highest order, and within minutes of relating it to me, the discovery was also related to Jackie Richey. As was his expected response, he tried to discredit it as a joke. Since he had not found the barrel himself, it was of lesser importance. But this was too weird and too impossible to discredit. There was a large foreign object, a metal barrel, now in our territory! Where did it come from? What did it mean? What was in it? There seemed to be a hundred questions in our minds, and our imaginations raced as the bell called us to class.

During the free times at school that day, the discussions among all of us Alderwood Court gang members centered on only one subject, the barrel. Clearly, further examination and discovery was necessary. We spoke in hushed tones among ourselves so as not to tip off others who might beat us to the prize. We counted the minutes until school ended and then we all blazed out to our bikes. We jumped on and rode off *en masse* just like a posse in the Saturday afternoon movie matinee Westerns.

It was four blocks around and through the projects until we reached the big street bordering the woods. At the first open opportunity, we dashed across the street as a wheeled herd, and dove onto the trail toward the now famous open field area. We crashed through the weeds, rounded some blackberry bushes, and then slid to a halt. There it was, in front of us, finally, just as Freddie had said!

We all dropped our bikes and crowded around the object of our attention. It was like the scene from a much later movie, "*2001: A Space Odyssey*," where the moon colonizers find the black monolith. Just like them, we too stared in wonder, with each of us trying to contemplate the enormous significance of this object, which had perhaps dropped out of the sky, for all we knew. It was painted as black as that monolith and held us in a similar trance. The only difference was that our "monolith" lay on its side. One of us would approach it for a touch, and then back off to savor the moment. Wow, look at it, we all thought.

Jackie took charge and tried to roll it over. There was a spot on the bottom where a label had been at one time. Now the remains were only partially readable because the left side of the label had disappeared. It said:

_____micals Corp.

_____**GER**

_____able

We were perplexed. What did that mean? It was as if we had just discovered some archeological wonder. We knew this was a huge clue, but in our excitement and competitiveness to one-up each other with the solution, we could not decipher the code. Jackie, Ronnie, and I struggled to turn the barrel upright. It was not particularly heavy, as it seemed to be empty, but it was unwieldy. We finally tipped it up, and then stepped back to admire it again. All six of us stood there, captivated by the most exciting thing we had come across in as long as we could remember—at least a week. And what did "_____micals Corp. ..._____**GER** ...and _____able mean?" Hmmm?

Now that it was standing upright, we noticed that the barrel had about a two-inch diameter fill hole near an edge on the top horizontal surface. There was a cap screwed into the hole. The inside of the cap had formed edges that must have been made to fit a special tool for opening the cap. But we didn't have that tool, so our minds collectively churned on how to get that cap out.

We *had* to know what was inside the mystery barrel! Doug and Freddie looked in the brush for a stick we could use as a lever. But Bobby Richey had the answer. He always carried a pocket knife, which he produced with a large grin. He was so proud he could contribute in our time of need. Jackie grabbed it from his brother's hand, flexed open the big blade, and began to dig inside the cap, pushing and squirming with his fingers.

We all stood near, our mouths wide open in suspense, as if we were watching the world's best safe-cracker ply his skill on a WELLS FARGO premium model. Suddenly, the cap moved slightly. There was hope! Our eyebrows danced and our heads bobbed as we all tried to observe the action. Then it moved again and began to unscrew slowly.

There was a *hisssssssss*, as gas escaped the cap. The exiting air smelled like gasoline, although not exactly. It was a smell with which none of us were familiar; it smelled quite sweet, yet pungent and sharp. Doug commented on how stinky it was, and we all gave silent assent to his adjective. The cap finally came off and Jackie pushed it across the surface. Now we all took turns smelling and trying to look into the innards of the barrel. The smell was definitely intense and very solvent-like. But it was so totally dark inside that we couldn't see anything deeper than the rim of the hole.

I wished more than anything that I could pull a flashlight out of my pocket and be the hero for the moment, but I only had a pink eraser. But Jackie brought out of *his* pocket the next best thing, something he always carried . . . matches! The other guys let out whoops and hollers of excitement about this, and I must admit that my first reaction also was exhilaration. But it took about five seconds for some mental caution to displace my celebration. I could not pinpoint it in my mind, but it had something to do with the similarity of the barrel's smell to that of gasoline.

Something tingled in my mind about whether this was such an excellent idea. I have since learned that whenever I get that unknown tingle—that "sixth sense" of concern I guess, for lack of a better identifier—that **I should pay more attention to my "sixth sense" and let it override the other emotional aspects of my mind.**

It was about then that I detected Doug having the same tingle. He had tempered his excitement and now had an expressionless look on his face. I looked at him and he looked at me, but neither of us spoke. I knew those gears with the big cogs, the ones labeled "caution" and "reason," were turning slowly inside his head. I also knew his naturally quiet personality was creating a conflict between saying something and just going along. Finally, softly, he asked, "What if it catches fire?"

Jackie bullied back, "You dodo. It's made of metal. It's not gonna burn!"

I don't think that's what Doug questioned, but he said nothing more. Then we both again were caught up in the mystery of what was inside the barrel. We shoved our caution to the back corners of our minds and joined the others in the impending thrill of discovery.

But who would look first? Ronnie said we should draw straws. Right, like that had a chance! Freddie said that since he had found it, he should be able to look first. Neither Doug nor Bobby was tall enough to look over the barrel without finding something to stand upon, and that was not going to happen either. I was about ready to make a claim, against my better judgment. However, Jackie, bless his "me first" soul, squelched the debate by proclaiming that since they were his matches, and since he was the gang leader, he was going to look first! And that was it!

We all crowded around Jackie as close as we could so as to vicariously enjoy the first look. Jackie took out one of the wooden matches and sparked the phosphorus tip on the side of the box. It burst into flame. He leaned his head near the edge of the hole. I pushed my head as close as I could to the side of Jackie's head. That didn't leave much room for Ronnie or Freddie, as they also jockeyed for position. Doug and Bobby each had resigned themselves to the fact that they would receive the details from the taller lookers and they formed the second row. Then Jackie slowly and deliberately brought the match closer, passing it between his ear and my forehead, trying to position it so as to throw some level of illumination inside. . . .

FWWWOOOOOMMMMM!!!!!!!!!

Instantly, a deep blue flame with yellow tinges at the tip erupted from the hole. It roared straight up into the air about four feet in length. The rocket blast burned for just an instant, less than a second. But to all our collective sense organs a few inches away, it seemed like an eternity. Everything in our brains now ran at "warp" speed, but everything in our bodies reacted in super slow motion.

The intense brightness of the light overpowered our eyes with a blaze of brilliance. The roar of the ignition was deafening, being so close to our ears. But it was the heat that did the damage. Immediately, we felt what seemed like 1,000 degrees of pain on our exposed skin. Before we could even move, the rocket self-extinguished, but when we did move, it was with "all systems go!"

We all exploded backward, knocking each other over and rolling around on the ground. All of our excited inquisitiveness pre-match, had been flushed from our consciousness post-match, as if someone had hit a delete switch. And all of those happy boyish feelings had just as instantly been replaced with the most intense and painful fright imaginable—the kind of fright that people who fall to their death must feel before they hit the ground. We were terrified, and even that cannot adequately describe it. We acted almost frantic in our fright—screaming and crying, and shaking like mini-earthquakes had been unleashed inside all of our bodies.

Almost at the same time the smells registered in our brains, and they were a repulsive mixture. Dominant was the remnant odor from the flame itself. It was an aroma similar to an electrical fire combined with burning automobile tires. It was putrid. Worse, in fact overpowering, was the unique smell of burning hair. We all discovered that this particular smell is instantly recognized by the human mind, as if it were part of Mother Nature's basic programming to alarm us.

Jackie screeched to "high heaven" because it had finally registered in his mind that his right hand was in great pain. A few seconds later, he also realized his head hurt. We looked at him and saw that the thumb and two fingers on his right hand were brilliant red and blistering. But it was his hair that caused all of us to recoil in shock! Most of it on the top of his head was gone! Vaporized! The torch-like flame had burned a cylindrical path at a slight angle to the centerline of his head, right down to his scalp. Remaining were charred tips, with a sooty white appearance. There also were regions which had not burned but which now curled grotesquely from the disfiguring heat. Jackie's scalp showed the same redness as his right hand.

We screamed, "Your hair's burned! It's gone!!!"

He rubbed his left hand over his scalp and reacted with horror. We then noticed that his right eyebrow was also missing, as well as part of his left. My hair also was singed locally, but, sporting a butch and being naturally blond, it was not such a ghastly sight. My eyebrows, too, were singed and the skin on my forehead suffered a mild burn.

By now huge tears streamed down Jackie's cheeks and he sobbed like the dam broke.

As the fright ebbed, the relief of still being alive was replaced with the pain of the injuries, combined with the fear of his parents. He could possibly hide a burned hand, but he could never hide the fact that he now missed half of his hair, especially with his original adornment. Even if he wore his baseball hat, sometime over the next three months he knew he would have to take it off and his parents would then notice half of his hair was gone.

"Oh no," he shouted. "My mom's gonna kill me!"

I knew he was correct, and I feared that I, too, was in for it. Once this news would erupt back home, there would be momentary relief that Doug and I were not hurt seriously, but then I would get spanked hard just for general principle. The *"that'll teach you to never do that again"* spanking was coming, and I knew it. We slowly picked up our bikes and rode home, not as conquering heroes, but more as tired old veterans, just happy to have been spared.

I did, in fact, get the spanking I expected, although since it was applied with the bare hand and not the cedar switch that my mom kept handy for such disciplinary occasions, it was not as bad as I feared. I was happy that the relief for our general safety was greater than I expected. Doug escaped a spanking, but did receive the stern admonishment to never be as stupid as his brother.

Jackie and Bobby trudged into their house across the Court after delaying outside a number of minutes. They wanted to put off the inevitable as long as possible and conjure up some plausible explanation which made sense to a ten-year-old. I'm sure a scenario they considered was that aliens had unexpectedly landed, seized him as a hostage, and diabolically burned him and his hair because he would not divulge the location of the coal mine—the source of our energy.

Ultimately, Jackie and Bobby gave up and entered, resigned to their fate. Even in our house we could hear the shrieks from their mom, followed by Jackie's screams as a belt was applied without mercy to his posterior. The bare skin on his right calf also received a couple of lashes just for emphasis.

By this time, Doug and I had been exiled to the bedroom we shared, where we whimpered in self-pity. As the cacophony emanated from the Richey household, we both peeked out the window by raising the roller shade slightly from the bottom. Suddenly, the door to the Richey's house flew open and Jackie's mom headed straight for our house, dragging Jackie along by the scruff of his neck. He was a pitiful sight, screaming at the top of his lungs, his feet barely touching the street. She shouted strange words that all ran together—"sonofabitch," "gawdawful," and "dammitohell" were some of her combinations. I swear, steam came out of her blouse she was so mad.

The two of them thrust up onto our front stoop. Without a pause, she hit the door with her shoulder and turned the knob all in one motion. She burst into our kitchen and threw Jackie into the center of the small room. The shocking sight of him momentarily distracted my mom and step-dad from the fact that our house had been forcibly entered. My mom's mouth fell open as she stared at Jackie, but no words came. Even my truthful explanation of what had happened, prior to my licking, had not prepared her for what her eyes now saw.

Then Jackie's mother lit in and accused me of leading her son to the devil himself. Doug and I cowered in our room, a few paces away from the kitchen. We were not going out of that bedroom, nooo sirrr! Not on our lives! But our ears grew as large as radar disks. We could have heard a moose bellow in Alaska at that moment. Jackie's mom erupted. Apparently, everything that had ever happened to Jackie, and the whole Richey clan for that matter, had been caused by other people, including us. She now had endured enough of it! Her limit had been reached; this hair incident was the last straw!

Doug and I finally came out of hiding. We decided we had to see this; a confrontation like this did not happen every day, and certainly not in our kitchen! We slowly crept down the short hallway to the edge of the kitchen. As curious as we were, we also were concerned that if we stuck our heads out too far we could accidentally get hit by a flying sauce pan, should one suddenly become airborne.

My mom was a fighter—after all she had been a welder—but for some reason she didn't reply in kind. My step-dad was too over-whelmed to do anything either. They just looked at her, and then at Jackie, and then back at her. There was momentarily the kind of silence where you think you can hear your own blood course through your veins. Doug and I carefully peeked around the corner, me standing, he on his knees. We probably looked like two heads stacked on top of each other. Then the tears began to roll down the cheeks of Jackie's mother. Finally, my mom said, well, she could at least try to make him a little more presentable. She went to a cupboard and retrieved her hand shears; the barbershop was open!

Jackie was placed on a stool, still sobbing, and my mom went to work. We all stood around watching the remaining red tufts fall on the floor. By the time she finished, nearly all of Jackie's hair was gone. A very short butch remained. Skin was now exposed which had never before seen the sun. Jackie cried through the whole ordeal, but at least the pain in his hand distracted him from the hair-pulling of the shears. When finished, Jackie's head was movie-screen white except for red stubble and a reddened patch of burned skin.

My mom slathered some oleo on his head as well as his fingers, and offered to take him to the hospital emergency room, but Jackie's mom declined. They left, and Doug and I used that as an opportunity to slink back to our bedroom, quiet as church mice.

Jackie wore a bandage on his right hand for a couple of weeks. In a few months, when the school year was over, his hair had grown out evenly and he looked somewhat normal again. That was not the end of the Jackie Richey saga, but at least the neighborhood was quiet until June.

It was not until years later that I realized a true miracle had occurred. It was not that Doug and I actually grew up and merged into mainstream society as contributors and reasonably upstanding people. It was not that my parents and Jackie's parents did not have an all out war. No, it concerned that specific incident with the barrel. The miracle was that we all were not killed, as would have been the case had the barrel exploded, rather than contained the explosion and dissipated the pressure through the fill hole.

No one ever determined what the barrel contained. And none of us went back to the clear area in the woods for a few weeks. When we did, we discovered that the barrel was gone. We had no more idea where it went than from where it came. It was merely an object that entered all of our lives and provided us with a vivid experience which still blazes in all of our memories. I certainly know it does in Jackie Richey's mind, wherever he is.

The only picture I have of The Alderwood Court Gang
(as blurry as it is).

IN THE BACK ROW FROM LEFT TO RIGHT: Freddie Roberts, Ronnie Landers, me, Jackie Richey (after the haircut—notice the "Hoppalong Cassidy" shirt).

IN THE MIDDLE ROW LEFT TO RIGHT: Bobby Richey, my brother Doug (notice the suspenders), a cousin of Jackie and Bobby (in front of me and hidden).

IN THE FRONT ROW LEFT TO RIGHT: My sister Cindy, an unknown Cedarwood Court kid (notice the diamond shirt which is just as dorky as some our mother made us wear), an unknown girl, another unknown Cedarwood Court kid (again, notice the suspenders).

4

THE LAST STRAW

'Tis the last straw that breaks the camel's back.
—French Proverb

As the weeks went by after the barrel incident, Alderwood Court returned to a normal level of activity. There were the occasional drunken parties and the family fights now and then, which sometimes extended to the street where the outcast would hurl expletives into the night. And the gang returned to its typical level of imaginary play and occasional mischief. Nothing special, just stuff within the noise-band of life in the projects. But my mom overcame her out-of-character sympathy for Jackie Richey's mom that night of the shearing, and returned to her normal state of bashing everything about the Richey's. From her perspective all of the Richeys, and Jackie especially, were no good. Jackie's mom also destroyed the *détente*, and yelled at us every once in a while, just for good measure. The "Cold War" was on again.

One warm afternoon late in June my mom took my brother Doug and me, along with our sister Cindy, to an old city park near the projects which had a shallow but large concrete wading pond. Many kids from the projects played in the water in the summer because it was free, and because kids just have a natural affinity for water. If it happened to be dirty water, that was even better!

As was our custom, whenever Doug and I were not riding our bicycles or were away from the house, we always left them in the

53

front yard next to our front door stoop. But when we returned from the pond some hours later, my bike was gone!

Disappeared! Vanished!! My prized possession, stolen!!!

I was crushed and cried for most of that night. My mom alternated between anger that someone would do such a thing, to hope that maybe it was not actually stolen, and then back to anger when she thought of the cost of replacing it. A kid could not live without a bicycle from a parent's point of view too, not only because it was part of Nature's basic rights, but also because a bicycle gave the kid mobility, as in out-of-the-house and away from hanging around mom all of the time whining about this and that. Bicycles emancipated mothers as much as they did their sons. Some girls also had bikes, again, more for the needs of the mother, but for all boys they were standard issue. Boys were just more aggravating under foot pre-television. Ask any mom.

Well, the word spread like wildfire that my bike was missing. This was big news, and a violation of the fundamental Code that no one ever touched someone else's bicycle. Every kid in the projects was on alert to spot it. I wanted to believe there was a reward offered, but we had no money. The only reward was that every kid knew if he found my missing red Schwinn®, he would instantly become a hero, and could earn enough good points to carry him until Christmas.

A few weeks went by and I was desperate. I had to walk everywhere and I hated it. I borrowed Doug's bike occasionally, but then I just transferred my plight to him; he was then "grounded." My mood sank, because it was clear we could not replace my bicycle.

Then one late afternoon when I was trudging home from a ball game, kicking a can ahead of me through one of the fields behind our Court, I saw my brother riding his bike down the trail toward me. He was stirring up dust and obviously in a hurry. When he neared, he braked and slid to a stop. He had a grin on his face as if he had learned he had received a special dispensation to never dry dishes again. You see, our chores were that every night after dinner I had to wash the dirty dishes in the kitchen sink and he had to dry. We both hated it, and I hated it more when he often, merely in spite, returned a washed dish back into the sink claiming it was still dirty.

Anyway, the dust had not even settled when he blurted out, "I found your bike!" I was shocked, and instantly elated. My heart soared!

"How? Where? When? Is it home?" My mind raced without waiting for answers. "Let's go get it," I said, and off we went, him riding and me running beside him.

We came up behind our four-plex. Each of the four-plexes was built on a foundation with a slightly elevated floor. That's why we had to climb a couple of stairs on our front porch to enter the house. This meant there was a crawl space under each four-plex. The crawl spaces were accessed though square doors about three feet on a side. The crawl space doors were on the back of the buildings in the middle of the structures. None of us kids had ever been in the crawl spaces because they were always locked with padlocks on big hasps. Also, since the doors were at ground level, they were usually overgrown with weeds and were not easy to reach.

Doug led me to the crawl space door behind our building. By this time I was ready to burst with the anticipation of seeing my number one asset again. But Doug kept trying to quiet me. I could not understand why he was so deliberate. He looked around to check that we had not been seen and then said, "It's in here, under the house." I was surprised, but I could see that the weeds had been flattened in front of the door. Also the padlock was gone, but the hasp was still closed with a stick jammed in to hold it shut.

I ran over, fell to my knees, and pulled out the stick. With a struggle the two of us pulled the door open enough to look inside. We squinted into the darkness and waited for our eyes to adjust. There, about ten feet away was my bicycle, lying on its side next to the foundation. We crawled under and drug ourselves around the plumbing and across the damp dirt.

I excitedly said, "Let's get it out of here and go home."

"No. Don't touch it," Doug said.

"Don't touch it. Are you crazy? It's mine and I'm getting it out of here."

Doug said, "Yeah, but wait a minute. How did it get in here?"

"I don't know, it looks to me like someone dragged it in," I said. "Let's go."

"No," he persisted. "Who dragged it in here?"

We stared at each other. Neither of us had the answer, but suddenly my mind caught up with Doug's mind and had his same curiosity. It finally dawned on me that whoever had dragged it in, knew it was there. And it was very likely that the only ones who shared that secret were Doug and me . . . and the thief!

There was pause as we sat on our knees for a few moments, thinking about this.

Doug said, "Let's set a trap."

"Yeah . . . but what?" I asked.

"I don't know right now, but let's get out of here before we're caught," he said.

We scurried out, closed the door, tried to put the weeds back somewhat, and left.

As we ran around the side of the four-plex, I asked him how he had found it. He said he was back there checking out how dry the grass was and happened to notice the weeds near the door were trampled down. Closer inspection revealed the door could be opened, and then curiosity took over and he found it. Then he came to find me, without telling anybody.

I must explain that the grassy hill immediately behind our house had a good slope to it and in the winter a great crop of tall grasses grew on the hill. 'Long about the end of June the grasses began to dry out and when they browned and dried thoroughly, all of us kids spent days sliding down the hill on pieces of cardboard, or anything else we could find that was slick. It was great free fun and we did it until we wore the grass down to the dirt.

We went around to the front of our house. Doug dropped his bike near the front stoop and we sat and leaned back against the coal bin. We picked up gravel and threw it into the street as we talked.

Doug said, "If there was a reward maybe the thief would return the bike to get the reward. That always happens in the Saturday movies."

"But we don't have a reward," I said.

We stared into space for a few moments.

"We have our allowances," Doug said. "Let's go talk to mom, but don't tell her about the bike. She'll want us to get it now if she knows."

We went in the house and mom was cooking dinner. We hung around in the kitchen with her and chatted as nonchalantly as possible. Finally, I spoke.

"Um, mom . . . Doug and I have been thinking about my bike. We want to offer a reward because that always works in the movies."

"You know we don't have any money for a reward," she said, predictably.

"Yeah but . . . we've decided that we'll give up our allowances for a month, and the money could be the reward," I said. The previous year mom had begun to give each of us a weekly allowance. She gave me forty cents and Doug thirty cents. We used some of this money to go to the movie matinees every Saturday afternoon. Giving up our allowances for a month was a huge sacrifice for us, but it was worth it.

Doug's mouth was in the shape of a small "O" as I slowly worked this logic to mom, and he nodded his head in assent. We waited for the response.

"Four weeks, huh?" she said.

I said, "Yep. How much is that?"

She thought for a moment, to draw out the suspense, and finally said, "Two dollars and eighty cents between the two of you . . . OK, I'll do it. Do you think that will be enough reward?" Heck, we had no idea, but the thought that now we actually had big bucks to set the trap was almost more excitement than we could contain.

The next morning we put out the word through our gang that Doug and I wanted to have a pow-wow just before lunch with all of the kids in the projects. The lure was that we had a "big announcement." A pow-wow was something we saw in one of the Saturday movie Westerns where all the Indian tribes put aside their differences and came together for a big meeting. The Indians sat around in their teepees, smoked peace pipes, talked about the Iron Horse, and played Canasta—stuff like that.

Sure enough, just before lunch we had dozens of kids in our

front yard. Jackie Richey pressed for answers about what this was all about, and he was a little agitated because if something was not totally of his thinking and under his control, he didn't like it. I said loudly, so everyone could hear, that we were now offering a reward for the return of my bicycle. Of course, the first question everybody wanted to know was how much?

I said, "Two dollars and eighty cents!"

That was met with oooh's and aaah's and instantly had their attention. I know $2.80 seems like nothing today, but in the summer of 1952, that was a lot of money, especially to sub-ten-year-olds. Ronnie Landers asked where this money came from; meaning how believable was it that the reward really was there to be paid. I said, our mom had agreed to give it to us! Well, that was it, instant credibility. Every kid knew that parents were strange people, and just when you least expected something, they could surprise you. If they said "No" on something, it didn't necessarily mean no, but if they said "Yes" on something, it always was a done deal. So this was money in the bank! There was excited chatter by all, and then everybody drifted away for lunch.

Doug and I ate lunch quickly, washing down our PB&J's (peanut butter and jelly sandwiches) with Kool-Aid®, and rushed out the door. We ran around to the side of the four-plex bordering the big street. This was opposite the side where the paths cut between our four-plex and the one in which the Richey's lived. Nobody walked on the short side because on this side of our building the hill fell away to the street and became very steep. Since there was not a steady stream of kids walking here, very high weeds and grasses grew up the slope and also next to the building. We crept along the wall through the waist-high grasses, toward the back corner. Once there, we laid down on our stomachs and slithered forward, side-by-side. We stuck our heads around the corner and then looked to our right, and down the length of the back side of our house. By moving the grasses and weeds, we could see the opening to the crawl space, where we had been last night. And we felt fairly comfortable that we probably could not be seen. We imagined we were Indian scouts waiting for the buffalo hunters to come by. We waited . . . and we waited . . . and we waited more. We squirmed and fidgeted. The grass was sticky, and occasionally ants and earwigs crawled across our arms. But we didn't leave. We were determined.

Finally, after more than an hour, we heard someone coming from the direction of the crawl space door. We tensed up to get a good view, much like a mother lion before she charges. Who was it? We could not make him out because the grass blew across our lines of vision. Slowly, the figure came closer. Then I recognized the telltale sign! The figure had his right pant leg rolled up! It was Jackie Richey!!! Doug punched me in the side and I pushed his hand away. Still we waited until he arrived at the door. Then he stopped and stood for a few moments, and looked around casually. He approached the door, took out the stick, pulled it open with a big heave, and disappeared inside. We stayed hidden. After what seemed like three days, but which probably was not more than a minute or more, Jackie emerged from the space, pulling my bike out behind him.

That was it! We had seen enough. We both jumped up and ran down the back-side of the building. We had taken about five steps when he turned around and saw us coming. He froze.

I yelled, "Jackie, you big SNOT!"

He took a step backward out of surprise and fell across the bike. As he tried to regain his stance, I was upon him. I hit him in his face with my right hand and tackled him with my left arm around his waist. We rolled around for a while in a great donnybrook, me sweating and grunting, flailing with anger, and him cussing furiously—he always had a foul mouth. He put some good hits on me, and he took a few too. Doug stood near the side of us and whenever he had a good shot he planted a kick into Jackie.

I initially had the advantage of surprise and momentum, but Jackie was stronger than me and his strength began to prevail. I was on the bottom and screaming in frustration. Doug jumped on Jackie's back and was more of a pest to him than anything, but it gave Jackie two of us to deal with. We wrestled around and all began to tire. Jackie finally freed himself from the both of us and took off running. We slowly rose and tried to catch our breaths. I had a scrape on my cheek that was bleeding, a sore ear, and a lip that was swelling. Doug had a sore ankle, too much kicking perhaps.

Doug summed it up for both of us, "The trap worked. That rotten piss ant, Jackie!"

I picked up my bike. Doug and I walked it around the corner and over to our front yard. I was so happy to have my best friend back, but I just let it fall over on its side, as we climbed the stoop and went inside. Mom was shocked to see us, and we told her the whole story, amidst an occasional whimper, as I now was feeling soreness and pain.

As she listened, she became incensed. Finally, she had heard enough and she picked up the phone. I looked at Doug and he looked at me, and we both shrugged as if to say, "I dunno." She dialed the operator, and when the operator answered mom said she wanted the police. *The police!!!* Doug and I stared at each other and our mouths dropped open. Oh, no, we thought, the police are coming!!! We're in really big trouble for beating up Jackie! Our ears were in rapt attention. We heard mom say she wanted to report a robbery, and that we had caught the robber. She wanted a squad car at our place immediately. After a few more words, she hung up, still fuming. Doug and I were stunned and didn't know what to do or say. The cops were coming to talk with us. Oh, my gosh! This was big stuff.

About fifteen minutes later, sure enough, a patrol car made its way down Alderwood Court and stopped next to our coal bin. We were outside waiting for it. And, as soon as it entered the projects, every other kid that saw the car ran behind following it, and other moms peeked out their doors. Two policemen stepped out. They were surrounded by a throng of open-mouthed scruffy kids of all ages, and some moms, wearing hair curlers, aprons, jeans, food spattered blouses, wailing infants on their hips. What a scene! Everybody was there except Jackie and his mom.

My mother lit into it about the Richeys, and told the whole story of the missing bicycle, and how Doug and I had caught him with it red-handed, when he was the only person who knew where it was. And on and on. . . . Then her arm straightened out and her finger pointed straight at the Richey's door. All eyes clicked in that direction, and then the whole troop moved toward the Richey's. One policeman knocked on the door and called for Jackie and his mother to come out, which finally they did. Jackie stood there like he was facing an Inquisition Council ready to burn him at the stake, and we knew he had the matches. How ironic? He denied it. He was not really the thief, he just happened to find my bike! Of course nobody was buying it, especially the cops. Jackie's mom was her naturally defiant self, claiming this was all a neighborhood conspiracy.

Finally, one of the policemen said that he had heard enough, and he went for his handcuffs. The other pulled out his billy club, just in case. In case of what I had no idea, but I was scared and I wasn't even the one to be handcuffed. The cop said they were going to arrest him and take him "downtown," unless he confessed and told the truth. Well, that was all it took. Jackie caved. Again, giant tears streamed down his cheeks. Between sobs he admitted that he had stolen the bike and had hidden it under the house. He really hated me and wanted to "get even"—for what was not explained. He bawled and bawled. The policemen put their cuffs and billy club away and admonished him and his mother. He was free to go, but if they ever again heard any complaints about Jackie Richey, he was going to be taken away and severely punished. The mob accompanied the police back to their car, and watched them climb in and drive away. There was much milling about and examining of the bicycle, along with comments of our bravery and tales of the fight, which by now had become as big as Lewis versus Dempsey. Slowly, the group dispersed, and Doug, and I, and our mom went into our house for dinner.

When the police decided to let Jackie go, and we all walked away from their yard, Jackie's mom grabbed him by the ear and dragged him into their house. We were not even halfway back to our house when we heard his screams as the whipping belt tore into his posterior. The screams were louder than normal, but there was not a tear of sympathy from any of us. Finally, the lashing subsided and Jackie's wails were muted as he obviously had been banished to his bedroom with the door shut.

As a final justice, the next day we discovered that Jackie had a boil on his butt that afternoon, and when his mom whipped him, it broke the boil open and they had to take him to see a doctor later that evening. Then we were sympathetic because we knew the beating must have hurt him beyond description. I felt badly for about five minutes, but then began to worry about Jackie's next move to gain retribution.

But I never had to worry about it. The whole Richey family disappeared about two nights later, like most project tenants, and we never heard of them again. My mother made reference to Jackie for years, as she was convinced his ultimate destination was a reform school somewhere. I could not dispute it, because I always knew he was a legitimate JD.

One thing I very much appreciate now, as I look back on this event, was just how calm and analytical my brother was during the whole sequence. If it was not for him, we probably would not have found my bicycle, and we certainly would not have caught Jackie. Finally seeing my bike again, I was happy and excited to grab it and get out of there, but Doug figured there was more going on and we had opportunity if we just played it right. That was pretty good thinking for an eight-year-old. I told you he was smart! I'm still impressed, and I observed that understated calmness and correct perception of the situation many more times from him as we grew up and became adults.

Oh, and by the way, with Jackie now gone from the neighborhood, the position of leader of the gang was vacant. I thought it was Divine providence that I should step in and fill that position, and I did since there was no argument from the others.

5

A Magical Afternoon

Baseball is 90% mental, the other half is physical.
—Yogi Berra
The Yogi Book: I Really Didn't Say Everything I Said

Sometime after Jackie and Bobby Richey and their family had moved in the middle of the night, another family moved into their unit in the four-plex adjoining the one where we lived. I always wondered how people came and went so quickly in the projects. Was there a waiting list for these places, or did another family just happen to show up when word was out that a house was vacant?

Anyway, moving into the Richey's old place was the Owens family. They had two children, Spike and Jenny. They were twins and a few months older than me, all of us almost ten. However, it became apparent that the only things they had in common were the same parents and the same birthday. Spike was a little shorter than me and fit well between Doug and me in body size. He had light brown hair that had a natural wave and was trimmed regularly (by his uncle who was a real barber) so it was never allowed to grow long. His eyes were green, and he had a small nose that appeared to be turned up at the tip. He always seemed to be well mannered and polite, and never tried to bully his way with the rest of us. What a refreshing change he was from Jackie Richey.

My mom liked him instantly, and I did too. Now that I had inherited the gang leader's position it was obvious that Spike Owens would never challenge my role. His attitude was to let someone else lead. Spike and I became instant playmates and the more he was around, the more fun we seemed to have together. Freddy Roberts and Ronnie Landers also liked him, as did my brother Doug. Spike was in the middle of the pack so to speak, in about everything. He was an OK student in school and was OK on the playground. He was not a natural athlete, but knew the games and could complement any team as a position holder. He was not the guy you wanted at bat with the score tied late in the game, but you also didn't have to worry that he was going to make a mistake in a tight situation and take you out of the game. He fit in well and his greatest wish was to be just one of the guys.

Jenny, his twin, was another matter. She actually was bigger than Spike and more closely approximated my size. In fact, she was very similar to me—a little taller and a little skinnier than Spike. Her hair was also wavy, although it was slightly more blonde than her brother's and it also was longer, over shoulder length. Most of the time her hair was braided in two pigtails. Her skin was more on the fair side and her eyes were more toward the bluish hue. She also was well presented in that her clothes were cleaned regularly. Being poor too, like the rest of us, neither of the Owens had many dressing options, but whatever they wore always seemed to begin the day clean. By night time, though, considering all of the mayhem we kids could cram into a day, it was expecting too much of us to still be clean.

She also was generally likable, but in spite of all of the good things about her, she had one big problem from the beginning—she was a girl! She desperately wanted to be in our gang, but, of course, no girls were allowed. Sorry, that's just the way it was. Guys only! Besides, what would the other gangs from the other Courts think of us if we let a girl into our innermost playing circle? We would forevermore then be known as the "sissy" gang.

But Jenny persisted. She hung around us all of the time and tried to unobtrusively worm her way into our activities. Still, we continued to push her out. She rarely wore dresses, only on Sunday mornings. The rest of the time, she dressed like us guys, and if it for one of us. She also rode a boy's bike, like Spike's, and she would show up on our rides. When we tried to ride away from her, though, something became apparent—she could ride like the wind. She didn't ride a bike like any other girl we knew. She also never played with dolls or did many of the things other girls did. It finally dawned on us that she rarely played with the other girls. She always wanted to be with us.

This wasn't a problem for Spike, because he was never jealous of Jenny and they were close as brother and sister. Whereas Spike had a more mellow temperament, Jenny was far more competitive in everything and wanted to be the best. She always challenged Spike, and, more often than not, beat him at whatever the challenge was. To most brothers this would have been degrading and demoralizing—to have your sister take you down—but for Spike, to his credit, he never let it get to him. He was much like Ronnie Landers in temperament, but nowhere near the athlete Ronnie was. But it bothered me, because I felt as the gang's leader I had a tradition to uphold. After all, it didn't matter how good she was, the fact remained she was still a girl!

One day, however, there was a big baseball game in the projects between us on Alderwood Court and the kids from Cedarwood Court, as well as Pinewood Court, near the other boundary of the projects. Jenny often came to the ball field and rolled around in the grass off the playing field watching the action. She was also there this day.

I should say that when I loosely speak of playing baseball we usually played with whatever type of ball was available. Most generally we kids played with softballs. These were a little larger than an actual baseball and were, as the name implies, a little softer. Ours typically had rubber covers on them and thus were all-weather too. An actual "baseball," though, was not only slightly smaller, but also much harder than a softball. Hence, among us kids, we referred to an actual baseball as a "hardball." The lingo of the time was that if we were going to play "baseball," we were actually going to use a softball. But, if instead we said we were going to play "hardball," now we were talking real baseball. This was more of a man's game, because we definitely had a much better chance of getting hurt playing hardball.

This particular day we were taking a step up and playing hardball. As I said, it was a big game with more players in attendance. We began with us Alderwoods on one team, and all of the Cedarwoods on the other. The Pinewoods divided equally between us. It was a spirited game and as the sun continued to fall in the sky, the game was tight in the late innings and could go either way. Then three of the Pinewood kids on our team decided that because the score was tied, it was a good time for them to quit because they would be late for dinner and their moms would be unforgiving. This was a dilemma, because nobody wanted to stop the game and there was still plenty of daylight left. Doug and I were willing to risk being late for dinner; after all, this was far more important.

Ronnie said, "What're we going to do? We can't play three short."

We all stood there kicking our shoes in the dirt, trying to come up with a great solution. The problem was none of us wanted to split up and rearrange the teams. Yes, the game itself, in the grand sense, was important, but it was Alderwood Court versus the ruffians from Cedarwood Court, with a few Pinewood Court guys thrown in for the merriment. None of us wanted any of the Cedarwood guys on our team, and the remaining Pinewood guys didn't want to change.

Just then, we heard a voice say, "I'll play." We all turned toward the voice and saw that Jenny had stood up and was walking onto the field from beyond third base, her pigtails bouncing with each step. We all, in unison, looked incredulous and smirked and gestured as to the ridiculousness of this possibility. A girl had never played before and we were not about to break tradition now!

She kept walking and again insisted, "I'll play. I can play this game."

We laughed. How stupid! A girl playing baseball! And besides, this was hardball.

"You could really get hurt," I said.

She said, "Maybe, but I still want to play, and I know I can. Let me play!"

At this, a couple of the Cedarwood guys laughed and said they had won the game because we obviously had to forfeit. They slapped themselves and had a great sport of the supposed "victory."

I said to the Cedarwood guys, "Hey, hold on! . . . C'mon, give us a time-out for a minute."

I looked at Ronnie, Freddie, Spike, Doug, and the last Pinewood guy. I said, "I don't like this idea, what do you guys think?"

Ronnie said, "Umm . . . uhh, I dunno. We need some help. Maybe she can play somewhere while we're fielding, just to give us another person on defense and get us though this inning, until we come up (to bat) again." I knew that Ronnie, being the very best player on the field loved to play baseball, or hardball, or whatever, just as much as I. Although he did not exhibit a competitive spirit on most things, he always put that aside on the diamond where his physical skill was matched only by his desire to win, especially to beat the Cedarwoods.

I said, "Spike? Freddie?"

Spike said, "I dunno. She's my sister. I don't want her to play either because I don't want any girl playing hardball with us, but I have to go home with her and hear about it all night. She's always pickin' on me at home about us not letting her do things with us!"

Freddie, the least qualified athletically, said, "Yeah, I don't like it either. But I don't want to stop the game, and I don't want to lose. Maybe with two players short we'd still lose, but I don't know how we can play three short. No way!"

Then my brother Doug said, "Why not let her play? What difference could it make? We could lose anyway, and it won't matter. But at least she might help us in the field, like Ronnie said."

I said, "Yeah but . . . if we let her play now, *we'll have to let her play again!*" We all stared at each other, realizing the gravity of this predicament. There were big stakes here.

After a pause Doug shrugged his shoulders and again said, "Let her play. Who knows how it'll turn out? If she plays, it helps our chances."

I turned to Jenny, who by now had walked up behind us. I said, "OK. You can play. But if you get hurt, it was all your idea."

The Cedarwood guys then let out big hoots and hollers, and one of them began chanting, "Sissy. Sissy. Sissy." I was ready to go smack him good, but Ronnie said, "Naw, don't bother. You knew they weren't going to like it." The razzing continued, as they were now assured of certain victory, and it would be over soon. They were confident.

Suddenly, something dawned on me and I said to Jenny, "You don't have a mitt. How are you going to play without a mitt?"

She said, "I can do it. I promise. I won't get hurt."

Ronnie said, "She can't play outfield without a mitt. The safest place for her is third base. She won't get any fly balls, and few grounders are hit there. And she probably won't interfere with much there." The full logic of his arguments didn't completely sink into my mind, but I agreed.

We took the field again, with Jenny standing on the dirt near third base, hands on her knees, looking like she was ready for anything. I thought, Right! Now with Jenny as the third baseman, er . . . basegirl, a thought which curdled my brain, our infield was set with Freddie at second. Actually, we rarely played with a first baseman, and we always altered the rules whereby the ball, when hit, had to be fielded and thrown to the pitcher before the runner arrived at first base. This constituted an "out." Since there was no actual first base—or any base for that matter—this always led to arguments on close plays about "safe" versus "out," but we tried to get around it by allowing that "ties go to the runner." Since Freddie couldn't run well, but his hands were not too bad, we always put him in the infield. He generally roamed an area from the first base foul line to about second base. Then we typically had a shortstop that covered from around second base to close to third base. But now we didn't have a shortstop because he was one of the Pinewood guys who went home.

We were weak in the infield coverage especially with Jenny at third base and Freddie at first-second base. I was pitching and, as such, I would have to be ready for any infield grounders. Ronnie covered most of the outfield, along with Doug in right field. The last remaining guy from the Pinewood group was in left field. The team at bat always did their own catching, and the pitcher called balls and strikes. As long as everybody accepted it, the scheme worked.

We resumed the game. When it had stopped, the Cedarwoods were at bat with one out and a guy on second base. We all knew that if the runner on second base scored, we would trail and that would probably be the game, unless we also could do something in the bottom of the inning. I thought we had to keep the guy who was on second from scoring.

The batter came up. He was a big strong guy, and at twelve years of age was more than two years older than most of my team, and me too. He seemed as big as a fourteen-year-old! He batted right-handed, with power. I gulped and threw the ball. He let it pass and I called strike one. He gave me a sour look but didn't argue. He just screwed his tennis shoes into the home plate dirt.

I threw two more pitches that were definitely balls. Then I threw another strike, only this one was swung at late. The ball took off in foul territory toward first base. Doug chased it down and threw it back to me. Two balls and two strikes was the count. The big guy screwed himself down into the dirt some more. I looked at all of my team and they were ready and staring in. Even Jenny looked OK near third base. I pitched a strike to the inside of the plate.

The big guy swung and his bat crashed into the ball with power. The ball left the bat as a blur, going about a hundred miles an hour. And, it headed on a line drive to Jenny's left side. My immediate thought was, darn, he smoked it, and the guy on second will score. I never thought of Jenny because I knew the ball would be by her in a heartbeat; it scorched as it headed on a beeline.

But then, the most amazing thing happened! Jenny jumped out toward the ball with incredibly quick reflexes. With the best hand-eye coordination I had ever seen in a kid, she put both hands on the ball—remember, a hardball practically screaming, "Don't even think of touching me." As the ball smacked into her hands with pain-making force, she stopped it almost effortlessly and held onto it. All of us were stunned! All I could think of was how much her hands must have stung because she didn't have on a baseball glove. The last thing any of us expected was that she could catch a hardball with her bare hands, especially one that truly had been smashed.

Then, the second most amazing thing happened! The runner on second base had left the bag on his way to third base, certain that the mightily struck ball was a sure hit and he could score the go-ahead run. When Jenny caught the ball in front of him, he immediately "slammed on his brakes," because now he knew he was in "no man's land," and according to the rules he had to return to second base before being tagged with the ball. From his view, this was a fairly easy thing because Freddie was out of position to take a throw at second base. And Jenny was a girl. Yes, she had the ball, but everybody knew a girl couldn't throw or run. Or, so he thought. As he turned to return to second base, Jenny had already taken off on the fly.

The runner saw her coming and put his legs in motion. But to our total shock, he was no match for Jenny. It was as if she had extra running gear. She was all grace and fluid motion. He was "dead meat," and we all knew it as it unfolded before our eyes. She ran him down and tagged his back, with him still a good eight feet from the bag!

Double play! Side over, no score, still tied, Alderwoods coming to bat!!! Yeah!!! Everybody was excited and they chattered as if they had just seen a legend occur. How'd she do that? Who knew? Wow, that was something! Even Ronnie said he could not imagine making a catch like that, and with bare hands! And the run down—how could a girl move like that? Freddie right then was prepared to trade Jenny every toy he had if she could only give him some of her speed and quickness. Jenny beamed. There was mumbling and grumbling from the other side as they took the field. They knew they had been robbed by two unbelievable plays.

We were now up to bat. One of the three guys who had left the game was supposed to be our first batter. What should we do? We all looked at each other.

Doug said, "Why don't we let Jenny bat now."

I said, "Naw. What if they throw at her? What if it hits her? What if she gets hurt?"

Before anyone could answer, Jenny said with all confidence, "I can hit, and it's my turn anyway because I replaced the kid who was next up!"

Silence. We all looked at each other. Finally, Doug shrugged and said, "Yeah, let her bat." So I said OK.

Jenny picked up the bat and approached the box. The other team saw her coming to the plate and they all hollered and chuckled.

"Easy out. Easy out," someone said.

Jenny stepped to the plate to bat right-handed with the bat resting on her right shoulder. She took a couple of practice swings, like we all did. As we watched her ready herself, it occurred to me that her practice swings were not herky-jerky and awkward as I expected from seeing other girls swing bats. Her bat motion was fluid, and moved smoothly through the strike zone. I thought, Can I be seeing right? Can she actually hit too?

The pitcher was into his motion and delivered a fastball as hard as he could throw. I'm sure he thought that no girl our age had ever seen a ball thrown that hard, and surely she would be scared stiff after having this one swish by close to hitting her. Except that, he didn't hit her, or even come close. Instead, the ball hung slightly outside of its intended path, and was right over the plate.

The bat came off Jenny's shoulder and arced into a swing all in one smooth motion. Everything became a *blur*—the motion of the bat, the movement of the ball, until both collided in the same space at the same instant in time. Something had to give. The bat continued through its arc across the plate. The now struck ball instantly flew in the opposite direction as if fired from a machine. It soared higher and higher toward deep left-center field, farther than any of us imagined possible. It was far over the outfielder's head as he turned to chase it. He ran as well as he could, certainly knowing that he had a tough play to recover the ball and get it back into the infield before she could take too many bases. His only hope was that she, being a girl, couldn't get to third base.

But, at the strike of the ball, Jenny took off. She showed that same speed seen in the rundown earlier. She was blazing! How could a girl run like that? She approached second base about the time the fielder got his hands on the ball. As he turned to throw, she was already past and on her way to third. Third base was no longer an issue. Jenny had her mind set on home plate and there was no other consideration. She rounded third and headed home moving her legs and arms in synchronized smooth motions. As she bore down on home plate, the ball was in the air. But it was too late. She beat it easily and tagged the general home plate area with her left foot as she went by.

Pandemonium! We all yelled and jumped around as if it was the last game of the World Series. It was such a great feeling. We were shocked, and surprised beyond belief, and also wonderfully happy. Just amazing! I have to admit that I was one of the most surprised guys there. It never occurred to me that I would see such demonstrated athletic skills at our age, unless from Ronnie, and especially coming from a girl! It just shocked me to realize that Jenny was our hero. She had won the game for us, almost single-handedly, because both sides decided to quit after that home run. Everybody on the other side was deflated after her homer, and all of us were hungry and tired anyway—everybody except Jenny, because I'm sure she floated all of the way home that evening.

Doug and I continued to talk about it with mom and our step-dad over dinner that night and mom was very interested. Previously, she had never seemed to give even a single serious thought to our baseball antics, but this night was different. As we entertained her with our enthusiasm for what we had seen, she realized, as did we, that something special had happened that afternoon. And it was not that our side had prevailed in a game of play. It was not even that a girl had shown some of us boys something special. Rather, we all came to a realization, which Doug and I have held for the remainder of our lives: **It is unfair to pre-suppose anybody can, or cannot, do anything. It is unfair to categorize people for any reason.** Just when you do, somebody comes along and smashes apart that imaginary box you had put them in with your pre-judgments. Even if they happen to be _____. (Fill in the blank. In this case, fill in "a girl.")

That afternoon Jenny became a member in good standing of the Alderwood Court gang, much as I never thought such a thing could ever happen. She always played baseball, and "hardball," with us after that, and participated in most of our daily doings and shenanigans. She was fun to have around, and she contributed to all of our lives in ways we never expected.

6

THE DRIVE-IN MOVIE

There is only one thing that can kill the movies,
and that is education.

—Will Rogers

In addition to our boyhood movie adventures *inside* the theater at the Saturday matinees, we also enjoyed other movie experiences, occasionally involving some of our heroes! As a family in the early 1950s we regularly went to the "drive-in" movies on Friday nights. Drive-ins were movies shown *outdoors*, projected onto a large screen standing upright in a huge parking lot. You watched the movie while sitting in your car. The cars parked on short slopes elevated toward the screen. The slopes were arranged in concentric arcs with the screen as the focal point of the arcs. In between were flat areas where the cars could drive until the driver found that certain desirable spot to pull up onto the slope and park.

Next to each car was a stand upon which rested two cheap speakers of very poor audio quality, one for each car parked on either side of the stand. Once parked, you retrieved the speaker from the stand and then hung it on the inside of your window. Thus you had the movie's "sound" inside your car! You could adjust the volume with a scratchy dial on the speaker. Many hours later when the movie was over, and presumably people were either dead tired or worn out (to be explained later), the projector began flashing warnings on the giant screen to: *"Please remember to replace the speaker on the post when you leave the theater."*

Of course, the warning was not always 100% successful, as every evening there always seemed to be at least one fool who tried to drive away with the speaker still hanging on the inside of his window. Naturally, something had to give—sometimes it was the speaker cable with a snap, in which case the driver had his very own speaker as a souvenir. Occasionally however, it was the driver's window that surrendered with the sound of smashing glass. People recognized that sound and thought, There goes another idiot.

Rarely, however, did anybody who had this happen stop; to do so meant you suddenly became a visible embarrassment. If you did stop, you might as well have had a large sign painted on your car that read, "I am a complete idiot. Make as much fun of me as you want!" Instead, these people continued driving out the gate, onto the highway, and all the way home as if to say, "What window? No, it was that way when I came in. Oh, the speaker . . . that was always in here."

At the drive-in, once the projections began, cartoons were shown first, then previews of coming attractions, and then the feature movies—usually *two* movies, with an intermission in between. The drive-in also had two more items: before the movies there was a "review" of current news, plus a short feature titled "Industry on Parade." This often highlighted how steel ingots were smashed into train tracks, or how tin cans were filled with strange looking goop dispensed in plops from machinery while the cans whirled through guided channels before being automatically sealed. These "shorts," as they were called, were intended to stir our nation's pride in our ability to produce goods and expand our economy. Presumably, the rest of the world wanted to buy those cans with that goop. Guys always thought the machine stories were really "hep." Years later the word became "cool." Gals usually cared less.

The drive-ins mainly appealed to people in their twenties and thirties. Rarely did patrons in their forties (or older) go because people that age tended to no longer have kids of pre-teen ages, and they generally could afford the real theaters.

Most drive-ins have since disappeared. Ours, the "Duwamish" in south Seattle, is now history. However, in the 1950s, drive-ins were big—they were places where lower economic families, such as ours, went for very cheap entertainment. There was something for everybody. At the Duwamish, directly in front of the screen's base was a playground area for children. There were slides, swings, "jungle-jims," "monkey bars," and other playground structures for entertaining kiddies like us until dusk.

It was common to see kids of various ages, up to about twelve, running around in the play area wearing pajamas. The reason was that not too long after the movies began, many of them would fall asleep. My brother Doug and I never wore our pajamas; we thought that was too "baby-like." The twelve-year-old guys we saw in pajamas could never have been members of our gang even if they had lived on Alderwood Court. By definition they would have been disqualified. However, I'm not sure that some of those twelve-year-olds in pajamas didn't actually grow up to own companies and employ the rest of us. But we had no visibility into the future. From our view, wearing pajamas at the drive-in was just too sissy, or was something girls did.

The entertainment for the dads was to play with "Spotty." Spotty was a little spot of intense light that was projected onto the screen about the time it became dark enough to see the spot, but before the cartoons began. As Spotty darted over the screen, he was "chased" by men operating spotlights on their cars.

Many of the unmarried patrons and all of the hot-rodders had cars with spotlights. You could not have a hot-rod those days without also having a spotlight. Not many "family men" had spotlights, and we certainly never had one on our Willys Jeep Wagon. We could tell, however, that our step-dad wished for one with all his might. We knew, if given the chance, he would avidly become another drooling idiot trying to chase Spotty.

Of course, none of this Spotty stuff appealed to women at all, unless the female was a "rodder's flame" and was enamored with every single thing her man did, including this banality. Our mom never sat through this. She was usually in the "snack bar" building loading up on tubs of popcorn which she carried back to the car and passed around once the cartoons began. Our step-dad always said something like, "You missed it," and she always feigned great pathos and drama at having been so unfortunate as to miss Spotty.

By the way, the hot-rodders were usually the crowd we kids all called "greasers." This was long before the Broadway production, of *Grease*, and then the movie starring John Travolta and Olivia Newton-John. The implication, of course, was that these guys had long hair for the period and it usually was held in place by some applied viscous liquid which made their hair look oily, or "greasy" in worst cases. The old joke was that someone's hair "needed an oil change."

We also called these hair-do's "DA's," which stood for Duck's Asses. If someone had a "DA," then their hair was long, greasy, and was combed back on the sides, meeting in the back of the head in a way that presumably resembled the rear end of a duck. All the greasers had DA's, leather jackets, hot-rods, and spotlights . . . and they smoked cigarettes. That's just the way it was.

Their cars were "customized," which meant the back ends were generally lowered, they had no hood ornaments or door latches, and sometimes they had very strange paint jobs. They also had mufflers that tended to rumble instead of being quiet. These were called "glass-packs." Fake fire coming out of the engine compartment was big, and "pin striping" was also big. Presumably, these helped to make your car look not only really hot and dangerous, but also "bitchin'," a word commonly used by all greasers. I always wondered about the fake fire . . . like why? If your car really had fire coming out of the engine compartment, that should have instantly been a clue, even to a Neanderthal, that something was amiss, and, if you didn't check it out soon, you would not even have a car!

There was also the matter of the pin stripes. I could appreciate the artistic skill required to apply the lines without wobbling, but I also wondered how anybody ever developed that skill. Where did one go to learn how to apply pin stripes? Even by the time I entered high school, many years later, pin stripes were still prevalent and still a mystery to me.

Our step-dad wanted all of those things, but to have them required two things: foolishness (he had), and money (he did not have). He often wistfully brought up the subject of "customizing" our Willys Jeep Wagon, but mom, true to her focus on every penny, tolerated none of that nonsense. She could not see the value of having no door latches, let alone fake fire. I think this was a major disconnect between family men and women of that period, at least for the next fifteen or twenty years.

One day, however, dad finally gave in to one of his cravings. If he couldn't have a spotlight to chase Spotty, he was at least going to get "glass-packs" installed on our Willys Jeep. He did, and was in mom's "doghouse" for weeks thereafter. But he was in heaven! Now he was able to pull up next to a hot-rod at a stoplight and "rev" his engine, showing off his muffler rumble, an act which I'm certain he thought struck fear into the heart of every hot-rodder around.

For most of the hot-rodders we saw on Friday nights, there was a reason for going to the drive-in, other than seeing the movies. Let's see . . . if you were young, had raging hormones (which with being "young" was redundant), didn't have your own place to live but had a car, could park somewhere with relative safety of not being bothered, where it was night, under the pretext of doing something civilized and acceptable (like going to a movie), then, hey—the drive-in movie fit the bill. Thus, scads of young couples, in addition to families like ours, streamed into the drive-ins to see a good evening of wholesome entertainment. I'm certain this was the plan. But eventually, after Spotty had run his course, the cartoons and shorts were over, it was finally dark, and the movie began, it sometimes happened that the movie became of secondary importance and the young couple's hormones took over.

One night, Doug and I were front row "witnesses" to this fact—"up close, and personal," as the saying goes. The memorable events of that night will be forever blazed into my childhood memory of the drive-in movies.

Even though it was dark once the movies were on the screen, it was still possible to partially see into cars parked next to you and in front of you. On this particular Friday night there were fewer cars than normal, and there were open spaces between the cars here and there. Although I always sat in the back seat, I used to scrunch up on the front of that seat and lean my arms and shoulders onto the back of the front seat so that I could have a better view out the windshield, and also could get a better panoramic view around us.

There was a hot-rodder's car in the ramp in front of us and slightly to the left. Sometime after the first movie began, the couple inside moved from the front seat to the back seat of that car. I didn't think much about it, but I did notice it nonetheless. Mom punched my step-dad in his side and smiled, although no words were exchanged. Over the next half-hour or so, there seemed to be a fair amount of commotion in that car, and at least one of the occupants was smoking. It also seemed they both were drinking something. They began to slip down the seat. After a while I couldn't see the couple anymore. Perhaps they were tired.

Suddenly, there was a burst of light from inside the car which caught my attention. The light grew brighter. Other people in other cars also fixated on the car with the light, as did my mom and step-dad. It was difficult to see directly inside because the light flickered, and the windows were clouded. The light grew brighter. We could hear elevated conversation, then some shouting.

My dad said, "What the . . . ?" and mom, too, was in a full stare. What was going on in there? The light became even brighter, and the voices inside became louder. Suddenly, the light flared very brightly! Just as suddenly, both back doors burst open and both people inside burst out into the night.

The prior occupants gradually became illuminated by the light—and they *both were naked!*

It was now apparent there was a fire inside their car! Gray smoke billowed out the open doors. Of course when this happened, it seemed as if every other car door in the whole drive-in theater burst open at the same time, including ours. People bailed out of their cars and ran toward the car with the fire. Doug and I followed close behind the growing crowd. Being smaller than the adults, I was blocked in a direct path but was able to worm through the crowd and winnow my way up front.

I had a great "front-row view" of what was unfolding!

The young woman who had been inside the car now screamed fairly loudly, shrieked would be a better description. Her male companion, who had bailed out of the other back door, had now run around the back of the car and tried to comfort her. Everything was a flurry of motion with flailing of arms and legs, and much jumping around.

But what fixated me was that the light coming from the fire inside the car now illuminated two grown-ups who were totally naked! Without a stitch! It was the first time in my life I had ever seen either a grown man or woman fully naked. And, even with it being nighttime, I still had a great sight of it because of the now-roaring fire inside the car. My eyes expanded, and my eyeballs worked overtime to focus and follow the motion of the couple before me.

I have to admit that I was not focused so much on watching the man, but was more entranced by watching the naked woman before me in the light. I saw her from all angles, and she moved and jiggled without restraint. She crossed her arms and tried to cover her breasts, but her actions were not fully adequate to shield my prying eyes. I was mesmerized and could not look away.

I had seen my mother's breasts before when she had nursed my sister Cindy, but here, for the first time, I was seeing all of a naked woman. I have to say that I was most impressed with the small triangular-shaped patch of furry hair I saw at the juncture of her abdomen and legs. Being shorter than the adults, and in the front row, I probably had the best straight-line view of that triangle than anybody else in the crowd! I had never seen that before, and I had no idea what it was about. What was it? Why was all of that curly dark hair there?

I noticed the naked guy had a fair amount of hair in his corresponding area too, but his didn't fascinate me as much as hers. All of my senses were on overload as I tried to capture as much of the action as I could. People now gave orders, pushed, and everything became fairly frantic.

Finally, someone thrust through the crowd with a blanket and threw it around the shoulders of the woman. Momentarily, another blanket appeared for the man, and they both drew the blankets around themselves. The car continued to burn as the fire grew, and the flames licked up the outside of the car. By now the movie had stopped and the house lights had come on. Clearly, the movie was no longer of interest. I mean, how often in your life could you ever *see* something like this?

My mom spied me in the crowd and grabbed for my arm to pull me away. I tried to avoid her hand from contacting my arm, but it was futile. She was able to get a good grip, and she pulled me with the admonishment to "get away and stay back."

I then noticed that my brother had also made it to the front of the crowd and, presumably, had also seen the same images I had. He, too, was in rapt concentration on everything that was happening. He, too, had seen "the naked lady," as she was to be called by us for many years to come.

Mom again yelled at me to get back. I slowly backed up, and then she spied my brother and made a lunge for him too. I'm sure she wished she could have erased our memories at that moment, but even she knew it was too late. Once you've seen a naked lady for the first time, you can't forget it! Where our step-dad was, none of us had a clue, but I knew he also must have seen her because we were one of the first groups of people on the scene.

The burning car eventually was totally consumed, becoming a smelly heap of ash, scorched metal, and disfigured soft parts. The plastic melted and the steering wheel had a grotesque curved shape. Clearly, this hot-rod was not going to cruise the avenue again. The naked couple disappeared from our view, and my brother and I were pushed/dragged by mom to the rear of the crowd. Eventually, she herded us back to our car and made us get inside with Cindy, who had slept though the whole event. Also, eventually, our step-dad showed up.

His first words were, "Man! That was really something!! . . . Man!!! . . . Did you see that woman???"

Now we knew for sure. The burning car was interesting. Maybe the naked guy was also fairly interesting. But clearly, the most fascinating part of the whole evening for our step-dad was the naked lady dancing around, in fine form I might add, with everything softly illuminated by the fire and with every important detail clearly visible and jiggling. It was clear he too now had "the memory," and it was equally clear that mom would have liked to also wipe his memory clean. In fact, she might have wiped it clean with a rolling pin upside his head, if she'd had one nearby at that moment. She threw a stare at him that was . . . well, shall we say "piercing?"

There was speculation for weeks by the "regulars" as to what actually happened that night, inside that car, to actually cause the fire. And all of it was, well just that . . . speculation. Most of the theories had to do with . . . uh . . . something flammable—like perhaps whisky, a starter fire in some form—like maybe a cigarette lighter, and . . . um . . . frolicking, whatever that was. How all of these combined to produce the undeniable results we all witnessed remains unknown and unclear to this day.

Nobody ever saw either of the couple again. And Doug and I (and my step-dad) would have recognized them, especially the woman! Remember, we had "the memory" of the naked lady. In fact, I can still close my eyes, decades later, and vividly recall specific details of that impressionable event in my life. I certainly remember the "triangle," and my brother does also. I know, because every once in a while we still wistfully bring it up and chuckle.

We went to the Duwamish drive-in off and on until my family eventually moved from Seattle. Even though Friday was a family movie night at the drive-in, that never prevented Doug and me from also going to the Saturday matinees at the Columbia theatre to see our heroes. Movies were in our blood, although I have to admit, we never saw a naked lady in any of the matinees.

Our Willys Jeep Wagon. Our step-dad, Doug, me, and Cindy.

7

CUB SCOUTS

Uniforms, crafts . . . and "The Duchess"

In my classes at Columbia Elementary School was a girl with whom I became friends, of all things. I first met Sally Donovan in the projects when I was eight years old. She was slightly taller than me, had long reddish hair, freckles, bluish-colored eyes, and always seemed to wear a smile. She usually pulled her hair back in a pony tail. She did everything girls did: dressed like them, played with them, laughed and giggled with them, basically fit into "girl-dom" quite well. But she never treated me like most of the girls treated boys, meaning that from their view, we boys were "contemptible." She always accepted me and my gang as other people. It was not that we were boys; in her view we just were "non-girls," and that was somehow different. She tolerated us, didn't mind talking with us, and always was nice. I liked that.

For some reason, she liked me too, because for all the time we sat near each other in all those classes I never tried to pull some boyish prank on her. We had what I guess was a *détente* between us. Without words we agreed to befriend each other and suspend the opposite sex stereotypes toward each other. I saw her after school on occasions when there wasn't something going on with the gang. She never had an interest in joining our gang, as did Jenny, and never would have been allowed in anyway, because for as much as she tolerated us boys, she definitely was not one of us. Jenny was a special case. But I still liked Sally. After a while her mom met my mom and they also liked each other. Eventually, our whole families became friends and we all occasionally spent holidays or other special times together.

We all enjoyed going to Sally's project unit because she and her family lived in the "good" projects. These were duplexes, rather than four-plexes like ours. But their most redeeming feature was they did not have coal bins in their neighborhood because they had electric furnaces. I always was impressed when I spent time at her house because it was uniformly warmer than ours.

When Sally and I were eight years old, she joined the Brownies. Once in a while I would see her wearing her Brownie uniform. I was intrigued, because at that stage of my life I always noticed uniforms. I still remembered servicemen staying in our house on weekends during the Second World War, before we moved into the projects. Their uniforms always impressed me. Similarly, during the Korean War in the late 1940s and early 1950s there also were military men around in snappy uniforms. I took notice. So when Sally began to wear her Brownie uniform I asked many questions. She told me about some of the craft-like things they did in their meetings, and it seemed like fun because I liked making things.

One day she asked me why I didn't join the "Cubs," meaning the Cub Scouts. I thought that was a great idea because if I were a Cub Scout, then I could also get a uniform—I was sure they gave them out to everybody, just like in the Army or the Navy.

When I asked mom, she said "No" even before I had completed my question, explaining that the Cub's parents had to *buy* the uniform, and we, being "dirt poor"—she always used that phrase— could in no way, ever, afford to buy a uniform for me. The subject was closed in her mind.

But I didn't take mom's "no" for an answer, being fairly tenacious for anything I wanted—a characteristic that has defined me for most of my life. One of the guys in the Pinewood Court Gang happened to be in the Cubs and I tagged along with him once to a "den meeting" just to get the scoop. I asked the den mother about joining and especially about the uniforms. She said the uniforms were purchased by the parents, as mom had said. However, there was a program for "needy" kids, whereby their uniforms could be provided by donations from people who could afford to do so.

This stimulated two thoughts in me: one was I figured I was as "needy" as anyone, since I was always in need of something I couldn't have; and second, I envisioned those donors as being rich doctors or businessmen, people who lived in palatial estates along the shores of Lake Washington. In my mind, such people had horses in the country and clearly resided in a world I would never see. They could afford to donate a uniform to a deserving Cub Scout, and that was OK with me. I wasn't proud.

Mom, however, was proud. She had what we called the "Arthur Farmer's Pride" since her maiden name was Arthur and everyone in the Arthur family seemed to share that characteristic. Her "Prairie logic" was that we may not have as much as others, but we didn't need handouts from anybody, when in truth we actually could have enjoyed handouts all of the time, in my thinking. If some rich person wanted to step up and donate a Schwinn® Phantom bicycle to me, I would take it in a heartbeat, without question, hands down! Unfortunately, that never happened, in spite of my fantasies. But eventually, mom softened, I suspect more from the realization that if I were in the Cubs, then I would not be hanging around the house whining so much about not being in.

She finally agreed to let me join and receive my uniform as a recipient under the "needy child" program. Boy, was I excited! Not only did I now have a new set of "duds," but I was in a program that would change my life, a program filled with excitement and thrilling adventure, a program where I could make things with crafts . . . a program that would put me on the same page with Sally. We would both be in uniforms, she in her little brown dress and me in my blue twill shirt and pants. We both had hats too. Hers was a little brown beanie and mine was a blue cap with a small bill in the front with yellow piping on it.

Additionally, my uniform had a bright yellow scarf around my neck, the tails of which were twisted according to the "laws of the pack" and then tied in a "square" knot. One of the primary slogans of Scouting was to "be square." This was not the connotation that the words later came to have of being dorky and socially "out of it." No, this was more in line with *be truthful and honest*. Fine! I could be as honest as the day was long, just so I could wear that bright yellow scarf. I was sure my cowboy hero, *Roy Rogers*, even with all of his scarves, never had a yellow one as nice as the one I now wore around my neck every Tuesday after school.

The other item that really set off the uniform was the brass buckle for the web belt. It had to be polished brightly every week. I loved polishing the brass, tying the scarf, and really looking spiffy. It was a practice that would come in handy for me many years later when I was in the Marine Corps.

The Cub Scouts were organized into "packs" and "dens." As you worked your way though the program by doing good deeds, attending meetings, making things of value, and generally just growing older, you achieved status levels. You were a "Wolf," a "Bear," or a "Lion." Get it, wolf cub, bear cub, or lion cub? These status levels were designated by fabric patches you earned and then sewed onto your left chest pocket, right over your heart. All together now, "... *Awww!*" There were also gradations of class where for each level of achievement you could be awarded a gold arrowhead and then two silver arrowheads. These arrowhead patches were sewn right under the wolf, bear, and lion patches.

There were two types of regular meetings. One was a "den" meeting. This was the small group, or den, to which you were assigned. Den meetings were once a week after school, for about an hour and a half. These were in the home of a grown-up who was the "den mother." I guess there could have been a "den father," but as I remember, we only had den mothers. Our den mother was Mrs. Bronson. In these den meetings we learned about the core values of being a Cub Scout, which were truth, honesty, fair play, loyalty to God and country—the same messages we also received from

Roy Rogers and the Lone Ranger, a fact which made me wonder if Roy and the Lone Ranger were ever Cub Scouts in their own youths. These principles were the keys to good living and being a good citizen.

Dens were numbered and you also received a den number patch to be sewn onto your left arm below the shoulder seam. I was in Den 5, along with nine other Cubs.

The dens were part of a larger whole, and that was the pack (get it, "pack of wolves"). Even at eight years of age I knew that lions didn't travel in packs but rather in prides. However, I was not about to throw the whole scouting movement off its axis by raising that as an issue. Lion packs it was! The pack consisted of all of the dens, and the pack meeting was held once a month in the evening, after dinner. These were usually at the field-house inside the "good" projects.

The pack was run by the scoutmaster, somebody who really liked doing this kind of thing. I know because he always told us so. He was usually assisted by dads of some of the Cub Scouts. Pack meetings were organized in a pseudo military formation so as to maintain order. I was in Pack 231 and we also received patches designating this, to also be sewn on our left arm below the den patch. Rounding out the patches were those which designated where you were from, and, of course, ours were of Seattle and Wash(ington). These were sewn at the top of the left arm, right next to the shoulder seam. The den and pack patches were sewn below them. I presumed these patches were needed because if I ever traveled to foreign lands in my Cub Scout uniform, and some local person asked me where I was from (because I was such a handsome looking specimen in my uniform), I could immediately turn my left arm to him and show my "Seattle, Wash" patches. He instantly would know I was not just a plain bumpkin from Podunk. I was from that great American city in the Pacific Northwest! He could not help but be impressed. I would not tell him, though, that I was part of a lion pack because that would shatter the image.

Once I had my uniform and was a true "card carrying" Cub Scout (well, I really don't remember if there was a membership card to carry or not), I went to Ronnie Landers' and Freddie Roberts' houses to impress them. Ronnie definitely was, and he talked his mom into letting him join too, now that I had paved the way with the needy kid's path. Freddie was not interested. Later, when the Owens kids moved into the Court, I discovered that Spike was also a Cub, and the three of us went to den and pack meetings together.

Our den mother, Mrs. Bronson, was a jovial woman who didn't have children of her own, but obviously liked two things: 1) being around young boys and, 2) doing crafts (she too always told us this). As such, she fit the perfect den mother's job description. She was a woman, but she also had a "capable" air about her. She could do anything, even if was "socially considered" to be within the male domain. Remember, this was the 1950s when women were supposed to be homemakers, without much more expected of them, or, in most cases, available to them. In many respects she was like my mom, who although being a woman clear through, with the femininity that went with her sex, nevertheless had been a welder in the shipyards during the Second World War and would not take guff from anybody—man or woman. She also had that air—almost a toughness.

Anyway, we Cubs all liked Mrs. Bronson and thought of her as "The Duchess." This came from the fact that one of our alter ego heroes of the time was *Red Ryder*®. He was on the radio for years and we all listened to him after school. Later, Red Ryder® made the leap to "serials" and we watched his exploits during the Saturday afternoon movie matinees. He was not as high up on our favorite Westerns' pecking order as the Lone Ranger or Roy Rogers, but he was definitely ahead of Gene Autry, Johnny Mack Brown, *Hopp-along Cassidy,* and *Lash LaRue*. He owned the Circle R Ranch in the Painted Valley. We never knew where the Painted Valley was, but we assumed it had to be the capital of the Old West.

Red Ryder® had two memorable characters in all of his stories. One was *Little Beaver*®, his young Indian friend. The fact that his trusted companion was an Indian boy (about our own ages) never seemed to raise an eyebrow at the time. Nobody asked, "Why does

Red travel with an Indian boy?" or "Where does Little Beaver® come from?" or "Who does he really belong to?" Everybody just accepted the fact that he was Red's constant companion and was integral to all of the stories. We boys all envied Little Beaver® and would have swapped places with him in an instant. The other character in the stories was Red Ryder®'s aunt. She managed the Circle R Ranch for Red and she was simply called *"The Duchess."* On the radio she had a gruff-sounding voice. This, plus her mannerisms, reminded us of Mrs. Bronson, so we began to think of Mrs. Bronson as The Duchess. Years later when I saw the actress Barbara Stanwyck in more mature movies, I remember thinking that with her unique, raspy voice she also could have played a great Duchess.

Mrs. Bronson, our Duchess, was terrific. We made all kinds of projects with various materials. Where the materials came from, and who paid for them, was not clear. But I didn't care because from my viewpoint they were always free, and I didn't have to whine to mom about getting these things for me.

One time, though, we were told to bring an empty Quaker® Oats carton to the next den meeting. The carton was a cylindrical cardboard container about fourteen inches high, with a big picture of a Quaker on the outside. The oats inside were eaten as hot breakfast cereal. Sometimes they also were used in baking pies and in cooking other things. We had a carton at home, but at the rate we were eating out of it, I guessed it would take another year to empty. True to mom's frugality, she said the only way I could take the carton was if it was emptied by the time of the next den meeting. Well, that prompted me to go into hot cereal forced consumption during the next week. By Tuesday morning I had not only polished off the last few morsels of the oats, but I also had no further interest in ever eating another bowl of cooked oats for breakfast in my remaining lifetime! But I did have an empty Quaker® Oats carton, which I took proudly to the den meeting.

The other Cubs had them too—I bet there was going to be a stir at the next Quaker® Oats sales meeting when they noticed that ten—count'em, ten—cartons of Quaker® Oats had been purchased within one week in south Seattle. Was this a trend? We knew they were merely replacements for another year's supply, but I bet those big executives at Quaker® Oats thought they had the beginnings of a runaway market!

Mrs. Bronson then told us we were going to make logs. Logs? We cut a square hole in the side of each carton and then coated the outsides of the cartons with Plaster of Paris, making sure that it was roughened to look like bark. When it was dry, we then painted the Plaster of Paris to look like a tree branch, with the ends showing a cross section of a branch. When the carton was laid on its side, we all had a "log" section in which to put all of our boy "junk," as she called it. She was referring to our baseballs, yo-yos, pea shooters, slingshots, Captain Midnight Secret Decoder Badges—things like that. Yes, I have to say, a fake log was something I always wanted to have. Being in the Cubs was already paying dividends!

I now had something that was indispensable to my childhood, a fake log! That it also weighed about five pounds, further added to its permanence—who would ever want to steal such a thing? Certainly none of the other gang members we knew. I remember the question Doug offered when I brought it home, "What's that thing?" His comment just reinforced its value to me.

Over the months we also made a number of other priceless items such as watch fobs, beaded belts, braided ropes, etc. There were two problems with the watch fob—first, I didn't have a watch (and I had about as much chance of getting one as I did of winning the Indy 500 in a "soapbox racer"), and second, I had never actually seen anyone use a watch fob. I later discovered it was something that was attached to a pocket watch. Never mind, though, if anyone ever wanted one—like if I was in a crowded room and someone cried out, "Darn, I wish I had a watch fob!"—I could whip one out of my pocket, on the spot, and be a hero for the moment.

"Being prepared" was another slogan of the Cub Scouts. (Or, was that the Boy Scouts? I'm not sure.) Anyway, I was true to that motto. I was prepared and always ready, waiting for the magical "watch-fob" question.

WHIRLY-GIG

There was, however, one item we made in the den meetings, that was one of the most marvelous playthings I've ever come across! This one toy alone made my whole time worthwhile as a Cub Scout. That item was what we called a "whirly-gig." It was quite simple, and basically consisted of nothing more than a flying propeller. It had a handle for us to hold in one hand, with an empty wooden thread spool on top of the handle. Eventually, sitting on top of the thread spool, was the propeller. The thread spool was used to get the propeller turning with the use of a string or cord wrapped around the spool and then jerked hard with the other hand. This caused the spool (and propeller) to rotate with fury, and the propeller to take off vertically.

Of course, all of this had to be done outdoors. The propellers would soar high into the sky, almost disappearing from our sight. We followed their flights and ran to catch them wherever they finally fell to earth.

The propeller was cut from the sides of an old flattened coffee can. The Duchess helped us make everything, and she was a master craftsman at cutting and forming the propellers. Apparently, Mrs. Bronson was a big coffee drinker because she had a number of empty cans to be recycled (not a concept much in use in the 1950s) into whirly-gig propellers.

It was remarkable how well the whirly-gig worked, especially considering the simplicity of the toy and the cost of the materials. But this little gadget stirred our imaginations, and soon we all were outside every spare moment, launching whirly-gig propellers into the sky. Once other kids saw us, they also were hooked and soon almost every kid in the projects had them. Many dads also thought they were neat toys—cheap too, which was the right price—and they all became whirly-gig makers. If this had happened in the 21st century, within two weeks a company would have been formed, designs would have been outsourced to India, production would have been outsourced to China, and within six months the company would have gone public, instantly making millionaires out of all of the brilliant young entrepreneurs. But this was the 1950s, and dads simply made these in their spare time, and then went on with their lives once the fad died. Our Uncle Johnny made one for Doug and one for me.

All of this was good clean fun, until one day the danger of the homemade whirly-gig became apparent. Cutting the propellers from metal sheets left the edges of the propeller blades very sharp, and once you jerked the thread, you now had a whirling propeller with two knife-like blades spinning at high speed and capable of slicing open anything the blades contacted—like children's skin. This happened to my brother once—after a vicious pull, the blade launched and then went sideways . . . right into his neck. The scalpel-like blade edges sliced his skin cleanly and instantly to a depth of about a quarter of an inch. He was lucky beyond belief in two ways: one, the blades struck his shirt collar first, thus slicing it through and diminishing some of the energy, and two, both blades missed his jugular vein by just a smidgen.

As it was, he bled profusely for a while, resulting in much panic, from all of us kids as well as our mom, but it was never life-threatening. Well, that incident single-handedly killed the whirly-gig movement in our neighborhood. We tried to put tape on the propellers to dull the edges, but the devices never worked the same.

When word of Doug's accident circulated, whirly-gigs became banned and confiscated contraband. Parents forbade them, and they were not allowed on the school yard anymore. Being caught with one was a sure trip to the Principal for a discussion about safety and other things. Whirly-gigs disappeared almost as quickly as they had appeared. We kids were left with great memories of wonderful fun, and a lesson in how quickly something so simple could become a life-threatening and dangerous implement.

The aforementioned imaginary 21st century company now would have over-forecasted, found itself with product quality issues, governmental regulatory problems, and excess and obsolete inventory. They would have gone belly-up, and then suffered customer and shareholder lawsuits. Only the lawyers would have made out. Boy, were these would-be entrepreneurs lucky they never began!

In the Cub Scouts with my fresh new uniform.

Wolf, Bear, and Lion cloth badges.

Red Ryder® and cast from one of the matinee serials. Betcha can guess
who's the bad guy . . . here's a clue, . . . he has only *one eye!*
Notice The Duchess—could she run the Circle R Ranch, or what?

PART TWO

MISCHIEF AT SCHOOL

8

SCHOOL DAYS

I never let my schooling interfere with my education.
—attributed to Mark Twain

America's future walks through the doors of our schools each day.
—Mary Jean LeTendre

Education was viewed as one of the core strengths of America in the 1950s. It was a time when the fabric of America was more visible in all aspects of our lives, and it was everybody's *duty* to keep America strong. For children, our "job" for America—and it really was portrayed that way—was to be serious in school, learn as much as possible, and pass on to the next grade! If we did all of those things, everything else would take care of itself, and America would remain strong. It was a simple view.

We kids from the projects were destined to go to a large and wonderfully built public school a few blocks away. Its official name was Columbia Elementary School, but we always called it our "grade" school or "grammar" school. It was built in 1922 with a designed capacity of 350 students, but the enrollment in the early 1950s was over 600 due to the "baby boom" after the War.

The administration thus prioritized admissions and there was a wait list to get in. As a result, my brother Doug and I temporarily went to a smaller school a few blocks away called Rainier Vista. This school had only four classrooms—kindergarten, first, second, and third grades. I was in the third grade and Doug was in the first. We both were there one year and then transferred to Columbia.

Columbia grade school occupied a city block and had sizable

outside playgrounds, some of which were covered because of the high probability of rain. Kids could not be sent out for recess in the rain. The teachers had successfully lobbied for the covered play areas. They insisted there be recess for us little darlings, *rain or shine*, so we could achieve our allotments of educational play. At least this was the "official" story, but I believe the main purpose of the recess truly was to give the teachers' time to fortify and strengthen themselves for another few hours with us. Yes, we were that difficult. That's what forty students per classroom, without the benefit of an aide, could do to a teacher!

Columbia had all of the elements of a quality institution: beautiful classrooms, playgrounds, a gymnasium, a cafeteria/auditorium (cafetorium?), and an administration office where the Principal, Mr. Robison, did whatever he did. All of the school's entrance steps were built with stone slabs. The hallways and classroom floors were all constructed with hand-laid hardwood, varnished until you almost could see your reflection. Clearly, our school was far more beautiful and spacious than where we lived. Home, in the projects, was where we ate and slept, but our *job* and much of our fun occurred in and on the grounds of Columbia school. Doug and I both were in heaven when we set foot on its premises.

There was a strong emphasis on the academics. They were the three "R's" (Reading, 'Riting and 'Rithmetic), as well as Language, Science, and Social Studies. Other areas of great importance, for which we also received *written grades*, were Penmanship, Spelling, and—get this—*Cleanliness and Posture.*

Clearly, America then was concerned about not raising a whole generation of dirty slouchers—people who didn't wash before meals, and who slinked around or didn't sit with both shoes squarely on the floor! I can't tell you how many times I heard the instructions from all grown-ups: "Wash your hands!" "Sit up straight!" or "Walk erect!" as though we all were knuckle-dragging Neanderthals. Our fingers were constantly examined by teachers for "fingernail cleanliness," and it seemed that anybody, not actually in school, was obsessed with a need to have good posture. Can you imagine a child of today not getting into a college because his cuticles were "dirty," or he had bad posture? School Administrator: "Yes, I know he made 1,600 on his SAT's, but he doesn't sit up straight . . . and I don't like his fingernails either!" Gasp, the horror of it!

Equally important as the academics, though, was training for the other areas of life. Our "Citizenship" was critical. There was a heavy emphasis on imparting intangibles such as *respect* for authority and institutions. People to be honored were—let's see—all grown-ups, policemen, firemen, armed-forces servicemen, bus drivers, movie ushers, basically anyone in any uniform, and anyone over the age of eighteen. Even our school "Safety-Patrol"—sixth graders who manned the crosswalks with "STOP" flags, web belts criss-crossing their chests with badges on them, and funny red hats on their heads—even they, too, were to be respected. A trip to Mr. Robison's office awaited anybody who gave sass to a twelve-year-old Safety Patroller!

Also very important for respect was that you could never address any of the above by their first name, even if you knew it and had known those people your whole life. You never, ever, called your parents by their first name. Aunts, uncles, and grandparents were OK by their first name, but you had to preface it with their relationship, e.g., Uncle Johnny, or Grandma Pearl. For Doug and me, any infraction of this general rule meant that we could expect a slap coming out of left field and landing on the side of our head about as fast as we could imagine!

School thus was about *learning*, being a *good citizen*, being *respectful*, having *good posture* and *clean hands*, and *knowing your place as a kid*. If you demonstrated all of the above, you had no problems. Respect was king, though, and everybody had to, well, *respect* it—again to make America strong. It began at home, but was reinforced, with a vengeance, at school.

In the classrooms, the desks at Columbia school were made of tables and seats fastened together in rows. All of the parts of the desks were built for longevity, meaning the material of choice was solid oak. Both the tables and the seats were heavy, really heavy! Once the rows were aligned properly (front to back) by the custodian, they couldn't be pushed out of alignment, by even a team of kids trying hard; such was the combined weight of a row of desks. We kids always marveled at the strength of the custodian and there were rumors he once worked in a circus as the Strongman!

The seats were hinged and could be raised for ease of exit and entrance. As a result, during class change the whole room was filled with a clamorous din from the clattering and dropping of the tables and the clanging of the seats being worked up and down. This excessive noise never seemed to bother us kids, but it must have grated on the (already "on the edge") nerves of the teachers who always tried to get out of the room ahead of us kids at the beginning of recess.

The tables had a horizontal section where they attached to the back of the seat in front, and in the right side of this section was a hole about an inch and a half in diameter. In this hole was an "ink well" with a hinged flap of metal on top of it as a lid. The teachers all had large jars of Scripto® ink from which they kept the ink wells topped up. During Penmanship, we kids dipped our scratchy metal pens into this ink well and then made continuous "O's," or up-and-down lines on paper trying to contain all of the scribbly marks within the large parallel lines.

These exercises went on interminably with excruciating boredom. As a result, strange things occurred with the ink in the wells, and often it found itself on things for which it never was intended, like our hands, the long hair of a girl sitting in front of a boy, pencils, or who knows what?

The fact that supposedly smart people in the educational systems of America actually conceived of and implemented an idea where boys were given a well of ink in front of them ... all day long ... with that ink well blaring out an invitation to **PLAY WITH ME** ... is remarkable to me now. What could those supposedly brilliant people who ran our schools possibly have been *thinking*?

Needless to say, more than once we boys ended up staying after school to clean chalk erasers because of either not being able to contain our ink, or worse, rattling the top of the ink well during extreme periods of boredom. I'm sure every elementary school teacher in the world was grateful when the ballpoint pen was invented. Unfortunately for them, that momentous occasion occurred after I moved on from Columbia grade school.

To continue with the desks, across the width of the desk's surface was a hinge which allowed the table to tilt down at an angle. This was our writing surface. This table could be raised up on the hinge to expose a cavity inside the desk in which we kept all of our books and legitimate supplies, such as pencils, erasers, papers, clay, etc. . . . and our other essentials such as pea shooters, slingshots, gum, and other contraband.

Did I say "gum," the absolute nemesis of schools everywhere? We were never supposed to have gum at school, ever! But, of course, every boy always carried gum, out of contrariness, if nothing else. Nothing showed daring and bravado to our fellow classmates like whipping out a stick of gum and clandestinely chewing a little *during* class. Chewing on the playground was one thing, but chewing during class was the height of bravery, or stupidity, I'm not sure which. And the punishment for being caught was capital, meaning the teacher sent a note home to our parents as a first offense, followed by having a counseling session with our parents for additional crimes. It was horrible. Can you imagine the likelihood today of a teacher having a conference with *both* parents because their child was caught chewing gum in class?

I'm sure old man Wrigley never dreamed of such things when he decided to sell Juicy Fruit, one of our favorites. Of course, the absolute "mother of all gums" was Bazooka, because not only could a kid demonstrate great daring with a good chew, but he also could emit a small bubble at precisely the moment when the teacher turned to the blackboard. He then prayed he could get it back into his mouth, and hidden, before the teacher turned around to again face the class. These were the kinds of activities that kept our attention during Arithmetic or History, and the kinds of activities that drove countless teachers home every night with tears in their eyes. It certainly did the new teachers, the ones fresh out of teaching school, those who were not sure they could make it to a second year.

Our fourth grade teacher was Miss Mary Dillon. Even being a seasoned veteran, she once broke down in class toward the end of a particularly harrowing day when the Cedarwood Court gang, on a double-dare, all began popping Bazooka bubbles before the day was over. We Alderwoods (Ronnie Landers, Freddie Roberts, and I) were impressed, even though the Cedarwoods all suffered detention (staying after school) for a week after that escapade. I still remember Miss Dillon fondly. And sadly for her, it is completely possible that she also remembered me for the remainder of her life.

I mentioned having to clean erasers. That is because we had "blackboards" and chalk. Large sections of the walls had been painted black leaving flat scratchy surfaces. We used sticks of white chalk to write on these surfaces. All of this was long before today's smooth, clean, and enameled "white boards" with writing dispensed from liquid markers.

Our "cleaning" of the erasers after school was assigned punishment, and consisted of each boy taking an eraser in each hand, outdoors, and then banging them together multiple times. A cloud of chalk dust then enveloped us, causing a choking fit from which we emerged looking like albinos. Yes, the erasers now were "clean," but most of the chalk dust had been transferred to our skin.

I was generally what might have been called a "good" student strictly on academics. I seemed to be mentally quick and learned the lessons without difficulty. Reading and Arithmetic were easy for me. My Writing was OK in terms of sentence structure, but my Penmanship, quite honestly, sucked, although that was not a descriptive term used at that time. I think Miss Dillon would have said: *"Penmanship needs improvement,"* which actually meant that in the next war I should become a coder because anything I wrote in normal English would be completely undecipherable.

But my largest issue in school was that I had the attention span of a nervous Chihuahua, combined with a devilish tendency to create *mischief* and be a general distraction. I approached the classroom as a battle ground of wills between Miss Dillon and me. Oh, I liked her, I actually liked her very much, but I also liked driving her right to the edge of tears. I do not know why. I could be "good," but that goodness only lasted while she stared at me. Once her glance moved away, and it had to occasionally because the other thirty-nine students also deserved a look once in a while, I was all energy and motion to make faces, pass notes, talk to others, or whatever. Each day was a five-hour cat-and-mouse game between Miss Dillon (bless her soul) and me. During the 1950s, teachers simply put up with my types, but today, I would be a candidate for forced doses of Ritalin.

I began the school year sitting amid the sea of faces, but within a few weeks I had been moved to the seat closest to Miss Dillon's desk in the front of the room. This was not a promotion, but rather a move which afforded her the best chance to monitor and minimize my distractions. Also, I remember many occasions when I was assigned to sit on a stool in one of the back corners of the room staring at where the walls joined. Presumably, this was the most effective scheme to isolate me and keep me from being an even greater distraction during my more legendary disruptive periods.

I still have my report card on which Miss Dillon wrote my first quarterly summary to my parents in masterful understatement: *"Jack has made a fine effort to correct his continuous talking and restless habits. He does good work and is efficient about it. Please encourage him to take more pains with his writing and to continue trying to be a good citizen."* Translation: "This kid is a snot, and if he were my own child I would brain him!"

By the second quarter's review I apparently had relaxed somewhat, though, as Miss Dillon wrote, *"Jack has improved. He talks less than he used to. Please encourage him to continue trying to be a quiet and dependable worker. He must make a greater effort to learn to listen better and not whisper, make noises with pencils and things, or turn around during an explanation."*

My third and fourth quarter's reviews were progressively more positive. Miss Dillon summed up my year by saying that, *"Jack has done well in both his studies and in improving his restless behavior."*

She then gave me high marks in almost every academic category and eventually passed me on to Mrs. Farris' fifth-grade class.

Mrs. Farris was a challenge too—her for me, and also me for her. Whereas, Miss Dillon was patient and professional when she was exasperated, Mrs. Farris on the other hand was strict and unforgiving. If you were out of line, punishment would follow. Mrs. Farris never sent anyone to Mr. Robison's office in her entire career; she always dealt with the matter herself. I cannot tell you how many times I had my knuckles rapped with a ruler by the "witch," as we Alderwoods called her. But I somehow made it through the fifth grade, with all of my fingers intact.

Mr. Cramer, in the sixth grade, was one of the most genial and funny teachers I ever had. He was my first male teacher and he understood boys. Gosh, do you think he once was one himself? He had a great sense of humor, and occasionally fun was allowed in his class. But it was a fine line that Mr. Cramer accepted and often we exceeded his limits, to his frustration. He finally nicknamed all of us "troublemakers" the "Gaylords Club."

The Gaylords had the distinction of holding "club" meetings on a regular basis after school, attendance required. Many times I did not get out of the club meetings until after 4:00 PM and every eraser in the school had been cleaned. I never understood why it never occurred to my mother to question why I often came home in the evening looking like *Casper the Friendly Ghost*.

There was one other minor issue on my first quarter's report card from Miss Dillon. Little did I appreciate the significance of it at the moment. Mom always knew the dates of the report cards. We always wondered about that clairvoyance, and it wasn't until a few years later that I learned the PTA had alerted all moms to "Report Card Days." They were thus on mom's calendar. She asked for my card as soon as I entered the front door, even before I had time to remove my jacket and discard it somewhere in my bedroom with a random toss.

She slowly scanned all the grades. I waited, proudly. We were awarded either an "L," "M," or "H," for "**L**ow quarter," "**M**iddle half," or "**H**igh quarter" placement. I had received mostly "H's" with a couple of "M's." But then mom scrunched up her nose. I knew she saw the "L" for Penmanship. But this was not a surprise. Even she knew my writing was practically illegible.

"What's this 'L'?" she blurted.

I waited, unsure.

"What 'L'? The Penmanship?"

"No. This other 'L,' for *Posture!* You got an 'L' for Posture?" She looked at me with obvious disappointment. "Why can't you sit properly? Why do you hafta always be squirmin' around like you got ants in your pants? Huh?" Her last word was raised a few decibels.

"I . . . uh . . . er . . . " I fumbled. I had no answer. To me, posture was the last thing on my mind. I felt like saying, "You try sitting straight . . . with no talking for a whole five minutes! You try that!! No one can do it!!! It's impossible!!!!" But I knew better, because now it clearly was on mom's "hit parade." A clever evasive maneuver was required.

"What about my Arithmetic and Science? Aren't they good?" I blurted.

Mom paused, but she didn't fully bite for the diversion.

"Yeah, they're good . . . but this slouchin' stuff *isn't* good mister! You better sit up straight from now on . . . do you understand? Do you? Otherwise I might hafta rethink your allowance. Get me?"

Now this was a threat I did understand because the receipt of my weekly allowance had become one of my most precious moments every week. Pay day! My allowance of forty cents made so much possible in my life.

After a few more moments of threat and punishment on mom's side and pleadings and promises on my side, we finished the discussion. I had received mom's message: I could laze around any way I wished once I grew up and left home. But as long as I lived with her, she required that I "sit up straight" and behave properly in school. A tentative truce was declared.

I damaged this truce when I came home with another "L" in Posture at the end of the second quarter. But thereafter I suggested an agreement with Miss Dillon: If she would give me an "M" in Posture, I would try with all my might to write better and talk less. If it happened that I couldn't ever sit straight, at least I would try to write straight. She never acknowledged our "agreement," but she did give me "M's" in Posture for both of the last two quarters. I did try to contain my talking in class, and I worked hard on making straight up-and-down scratches with my pen, and everybody was happy. Another of life's lessons was: **Success sometimes requires "give and take."**

One other thing schools (and society in general) were big on then, and Columbia Elementary was no exception, was Civil Defense. It was soon enough after the "Big War" that occurrences like air-raids and atomic bombs were still fresh in everybody's mind. These actually were perceived as *possible* threats, although in the early 1950s it wasn't clear to any of us which country might suddenly mount a strafing run on Seattle's populace. But the image of Pearl Harbor lived in our country's collective paranoia for years. By the latter half of the 1950s, the "Cold War" with the "Communist Empire" had become fully entrenched, and the threat of enemy fighter aircraft had been replaced with the threat of enemy nuclear-armed missiles overhead—at any moment. Civil Defense was a huge concern for everybody for a long time, certainly through all of the decade of the '50s.

At Columbia school, the result of this "**CD**" (as it was called) was the *"Duck-and-Cover"* drills. It was determined that if an atomic bomb should suddenly fall out of the sky, aimed right for Columbia grade school, the safest place for us kids would be under our desks! Hmmm. You got it! Those heavy oak desks would be our salvation and protection. Right! And so, we endlessly practiced Duck-and-Cover drills. When the school siren went off, we all (in an orderly fashion and with no talking) were to get under our desks, preferably under the seat, put our hands over our heads, and stay there quietly in that position until an "all clear" second siren sounded. This Duck-and-Cover maneuver would prevent us from being incinerated somehow, don't ask—just trust that it would.

Actually before the Duck-and-Cover became popular, we practiced the "Shield-Your-Eyes-Prone" trick. This required all of us kids (again in an orderly fashion) to march over to a classroom wall which had windows, lay down on the floor below the windows, with our heads next to the wall, and cover our eyes with our hands. This was to protect our eyes from the flash of the atomic blast, which was rumored to be very bright. Of course, we boys knew that we all would *peek* at the last moment to get a good look at just how *bright* that sucker was, and we would do it *so fast* that no teacher could stop us! Nobody in authority had told us that following the flash there would be a shock wave of unimaginable destruction, which certainly would obliterate that wall with the windows, and would be of far greater concern than how bright the flash had been.

Such was the way it was with Civil Defense lessons. We also were instructed in something called "ConelraD," but about all we knew of it was that if "The Bomb" was dropped, we should then get to a radio and tune 640 or 1240 to receive instructions on where to go and how to get there. Presumably, radio transmitters were impervious to atomic bombs and they all would be fully intact and functional. *Trust authority*, remember.

It never occurred to us to ask why the teachers never participated in any of the drills. They never laid down on the floor, covered their eyes, or scurried under their desks. They must have possessed some miraculous protection against A-blasts, which wasn't taught to grade-schoolers.

For all that was taught in school, though, it is interesting to also note what was *not* mentioned or even present. One of these was racial diversity. We were a school, and a neighborhood, of poor people, but almost all of us were white people. There was a very small number of black kids in school, who then were called "Negroes," even by themselves, but again, very few. There were Negro areas in Seattle for sure, but they were far from where we lived. Our family, however, drove through those areas on Sundays when we sometimes went to our Grandma Pearl's house. We traversed "Dark Town," as it was known. But we grew up surrounded by other white kids. The diversity that did exist in our life came not from race, but instead from cultural and ethnic heritage. That diversity was from those who were Irish, Italian, Scandinavian, and German, or others.

Also, there was no religious diversity. Everybody was some sort of Christian, and God was a part of society. Our national flag also was God's flag, we knew it. Even those who weren't religious still were assumed to be Christian. To be American then, meant to be Christian, and perhaps Jewish which was OK too. But if there were Jewish people in our neighborhood, they must have kept a low profile because we never knew any.

That was our school environment. It was very homogeneous. Yet it was also quite focused in content, and was especially centered on issues of community and nation, much more so than today. Our best friends in the projects were also our best friends in school. For all of us kids, school was our home away from home.

A desk similar to those at Columbia Elementary School.

9

"BIG BAND" BROTHERS

There is nothing remarkable about it.
All one has to do is hit the right keys at the right time,
and the instrument plays itself.
—Johann Sebastian Bach

Being a member of the Cub Scouts was one of the most fun and rewarding activities of my childhood, but it was not the only "group" that I joined during my school days at Columbia Elementary. A few days after I began the fourth grade, I was given a handful of papers to ferry home to mom, some requiring her signature, some merely informational. I didn't look at them, I just carried them. I was a young, but trusted, courier. Like scattered seeds, the administration probably assumed some papers would never make it home, and less would make it back. With our kid's devotion to play after school, it was highly likely their assumptions were correct; there was ample opportunity for distraction. But this first collection miraculously *did* arrive home in my lunchbox. And there was one notice that caught mom's attention. The school band was forming, and musicians were needed. In fact, as a lure for joining the band, music lessons also were provided . . . for a small fee, of course.

This caught mom's attention. In the 1940s and 1950s, bands were "big," I mean really big! They were one of the great social entertainments, and "Big Band" leaders were huge stars of the day. The music the bands played was called "Swing," and most people my mom's age became addicted to it during the War. *"Swing was King,"* as was the saying. It was very rhythmic and catchy. It was impossible to listen to Swing without wanting to move, which led to wanting to dance. Dancing was a very inexpensive way to purge the troubles of the day. Mom loved to dance and, of course, she loved big bands.

When she read that announcement it must have stimulated her imagination in the extreme. She very quickly determined that my brother Doug and I were future Big Band leaders and that all we needed was some opportunity. No one on mom's side of our family had ever demonstrated any musical talent, but in her thinking the magical musical genes had simply skipped a few generations and without doubt had now reappeared in Doug and me. They were simply dormant, waiting to be turned on with the proper encouragement.

Music lessons at school were a "Divine gift" for us, so that we could become the future stars she imagined us to be. As time went by, it became more than an invitation, it become a mandate without choice. Mom's mind was made up. We would be musicians. Mom would find the two dollars a month for the lessons, and the half-dollar a month to rent an instrument, even if she had to "wash dishes" as she often said. Since Doug and I were the dishwashers in our house, by decree, that was perfectly OK with us—except that Doug and I did not have the money to pay mom so she could afford the lessons we never wanted to take. Somehow she found it elsewhere, and set aside the required five dollars a month for the two of us. We were in the band, like it or not!

What were our instruments to be? Mom had three favorite bands and bandleaders: Glenn Miller, Benny Goodman, and Harry James. The instruments those gentlemen played, respectively, were the trombone, the clarinet, and the trumpet. Those were our choices! Hmmm. I chose first. I couldn't see lugging around a trombone, and I knew the clarinet came apart in sections and could be carried in a small case. Plus, I had tried a trumpet once, and didn't like the way my lips tingled blowing until I was almost blue in the face. I chose the clarinet. The trumpet was Doug's; he didn't mind the tingle.

Mom signed the forms and went to rent our instruments. By now Doug and I both had dreams of becoming accomplished musicians, leading our own bands with perfect musical refrains filling the air. In our imaginations, we occasionally would solo on our instruments to demonstrate our skill and to let everyone know we were *the men*! I would be Benny Goodman, eliciting sweet notes from my "licorice stick," as the clarinet was called. And Doug would be Harry James, hitting "hot licks" on his majestic looking golden trumpet, pointed upwards as he strained to reach the upper ranges. We were ready!

Then mom came home with our instruments. Mine was not the beautiful black creation with the shiny silver keys of my fantasy. No, it was a straight one-piece metal clarinet. It did not come apart to fit into a tiny velvet-lined case. Instead, it fit into a long beat-up case, which made me think I was carrying around a toilet plunger. Doug's trumpet also was tarnished silver—not golden—*dirty silver*, and it looked like it had been used to hammer wooden walls together. It had dents all over, and the horn part was misshapen into an oval instead of a circle. It looked like an elephant had sat on it. Even the pearl top on one of the valves was missing. Two of the valves stuck in the down position, and slowly rose at their own speed, much as an arthritic old man rose out of a chair.

We were crushed. We stared at mom with that silent "*why*?" She understood immediately, and said the black clarinets and the golden trumpets were much more expensive to rent. These were all we could afford. But we shouldn't be concerned, because we could still make beautiful music with them. In her logic, the music was inside of us and all we had to do was push it out through these "practice" instruments. The instruments of our dreams were out there for us, somewhere in our future—as soon as we learned to play the ones now in our hands.

It was one of the first great lessons for us, that **dreams are wonderful, but they are not *always* achievable.**

We began band lessons. The assembled band practiced every Tuesday morning for an hour, and we were excused from our regular classes. The fact that I now missed class allowed my teacher Miss Dillon to appreciate band time as an answer to her prayers. Additionally, we each had private fifteen minute lessons with our band leader, Mr. Barton. My lesson was after school on Tuesdays and Doug's was on Wednesdays.

Mr. Barton was a short and excitable man. He had a crew haircut, just like us, and he wore glasses with round lenses and black frames. The frames slid down his nose, especially when he was emotionally into our "music," which was quite often. He always wore large bow ties which never aligned properly on his neck, one side always flopped downward. He also wore a sports jacket over a sweater. His sweaters all had diamond patterns of bright colors knitted into them. His pants were dark and the cuffs were short so his socks were exposed. They always were argyles, again with diamond patterns—the man loved bright colors and diamond patterns. But the topper was his shoes, which were cordovan lace-ups with squishy crepe-rubber soles. Mom met Mr. Barton one day, and later that night, when she described him to dad, said his shoes were "brothel creepers." Neither Doug nor I understood that. When I asked mom, she realized she had spoken something she regretted. She instructed us to never repeat that phrase, which made it even more intriguing in our memories.

There was something about Mr. Barton that was different to Doug and me. His voice was a little higher than the other male teachers, and he moved his arms and hands with a unique flourish. When pointing at the sheet music during our lessons, his fingers bent in ways we had never seen from other men. And, when exasperated or excited, he would put his hands up in the air as though he were a waiter carrying an invisible tray.

But he was kind and we liked him, although he had an intensity for music, which even we latent and gifted geniuses couldn't match. He was big on practice. We were less so. We knew the music would come in its own time—we knew someday we simply would begin to play the music of our destiny, and wondered why we had to spend so much time laboriously blowing squeaky notes from these instruments of torture. He never accepted our arguments, and always answered, "Practice, practice, practice, Master Jack. Practice makes perfect, and you're far from perfect, little man." I thought, Master? What's with this "Master" stuff?

After a while it became apparent during our weekly private "lessons" that Mr. Barton was having some of the same issues with me as Miss Dillon. He was having a difficult time understanding life from my viewpoint. He often would throw his hands in the air, palms upward, and say things like, "Oh, my . . . no!" Sometimes to emphasize this, he'd shake his head sideways and spit out, "Lordy!!"

I had two difficulties. First, as much I willed beautiful melodious notes to come from my clarinet, instead various squeaks and strained bleeps filled the air. Why couldn't this silly metal "woodwind" do what my mind wanted? Second, the concept of rhythm and timing, as components of music, were completely foreign to me. "You mean there has to be a beat? Why can't I play the notes as they come along, and why can't I keep playing a note until I get it right?" It seemed perfectly logical to me. My approach was if I made a mistake, I repeated the note until I played it correctly. Only then could I move forward. This "technique" slowly drove Mr. Barton crazy. Finally, we had the big talk.

"Um . . . Jack, . . . you're having difficulty, I can tell. . . . You're not practicing, are you?"

"Yes I am! I practice all the time!" I lied.

"Well. Hmmm. You need to practice at least thirty minutes every day. Are you doing that much?"

"Sure! Sometimes more than that." I lied again. The truth was that I hated practice and found it to be the lowest on my priorities. It was hard work and no fun. I rarely practiced; some days not at all. Doug mirrored me, although if the truth be told, he needed less practice than I. Our lack of practice was a problem for mom too, and she always nagged us. Her issue was not that we were not learning, but that she had paid for the time and was determined to get her money's worth—with our practice time.

"Then, this is even more serious," Mr. Barton said with a scrunched-up face and with his hands on his hips. "My . . . this is a sad state! What are we to do?"

"Dunno," I said. "I'm practicin'." Hmmm.

He sighed, bent back his head, and looked to the ceiling. He sighed again. "OK. That's enough for today," he conceded. "I want you to keep working on 'Smoke Gets in Your Eyes.' Alright?"

"Smoke Gets in Your Eyes" was one of my least favorite songs. It was even worse than *"Stardust."* My favorite was *"In the Mood,"* which I especially liked because it had about three notes in the whole song and I could really get into a groove on those notes. *"Smoke Gets in Your Eyes"* was much harder—it had as many as eight or nine notes, and often they had to be held for different lengths of time. Talk about difficult! I was convinced even Benny Goodman would have a hard time with *"Smoke Gets in Your Eyes."* Doug had an easier time on his trumpet. He could play ten or twelve notes and I thought he was a "natural."

The weeks labored on and I continued to make every effort to practice. Notice I didn't say practice—I said *make every effort* to practice. However, in mid-December there was an assembly for the school in the auditorium. The band was to play the songs we had been learning. The band consisted of six trombones, seven clarinets, four saxophones, and eight trumpets. Doug and I were ready.

I took my position sitting in the front row at the end of the clarinet section. All of the other clarinets were the real black "licorice sticks." I was the only one with the metal "practice" clarinet. Doug stood in the back row with all of the trumpets. His trumpet in the "play" position was slightly above my head. Mr. Barton came to the center of the stage and lifted a baton. He waived it like his wrist was rubber. Instruments up . . . downbeat! We launched into *"In the Mood."* Man, we were swinging! I was in the groove with my three notes—right on pitch, right on time! I felt moved by my *virtuoso* performance. Even Mr. Barton smiled as though someone was giving him a backrub right at that moment. We ended to applause—even the first, second, and third graders liked it. Next came *"Stardust."* We performed that one fairly well too, with only a minimum of squeaks.

Now for the grande finale: *"Smoke Gets in Your Eyes."* Down came the baton and we were off. I tapped my feet and focused hard on the notes dancing across my sheet music. The trumpets blared in my ear and the trombone slides jabbed the air. The saxophones swayed side to side. We were hot! Suddenly my clarinet squeaked— I missed a note. It was awful. Well, I better do it right. I played the same note again . . . and I squeaked again, loudly. Now I really was determined! I played it again, and this time I made it right—perseverance ruled. Except, now, everyone else was ahead of me.

I had to catch up! I played my string of notes faster. In my haste, I squeaked again. Once more I played the note over, losing further time. More determinedly than ever, I raced ahead. Others, hearing my notes and my squeaks out of synch with their beat, began to lose their own timing. Squeaks and botched notes became obvious from other instruments. Quickly the whole band disintegrated into an inharmonious din of squeaks and discordant notes, with no sense of melody, timing, or organization. It was awful.

Mr. Barton waved his baton furiously and pointed at certain people for emphasis. I caught his glare once when I looked up from my sheet music. He had a look on his face as if someone had just stepped on his recently shined "creepers." Finally, he waved his baton sideways in submission. We were beyond any reasonable point of recovery. It was a mess. What began with such hope from the two previous "masterpieces" had now become an embarrassment. We were not ready for Carnegie Hall. We all laid down our instruments to the relaxed position, and there was silence in the auditorium. There were a few scattered claps from some of the teachers, then tepid applause from most others. The Principal, Mr. Robison, jumped up and said, "The band!" with his arm outstretched. "Thanks everybody, for your fine performance." He milked the last bit of mercy applause out of the audience. We slinked off the stage.

That was my last effort with the clarinet, or any musical instrument. Doug continued to play the trumpet for another month, but then he gave it up too. Playing in the woods after school was far more fun and rewarding than practicing music. Mom resigned herself to never having Big Band sounds from anyone in our family. The one who most regretted the debacle was probably Miss Dillon. She once again had me back in her classroom all day. Her "sanity" break was over.

10

SHOTS DAY

Good friends are good for your health.
—Irwin Sarason

The other memorable use of the Columbia school auditorium was for "Public Health" days. In the early 1950s there were aggressive diseases of all kinds at war with society. These included typhoid fever, smallpox, whooping cough, diphtheria, scarlet fever, mumps, various influenzas, anthrax, tetanus, and polio to name a few. Who knows, bubonic plague, black death, and jungle rot might also have been just around the corner. How anyone ever survived beyond the age of sixteen was a mystery!

Anyway, it was determined that all children had to be vaccinated against these diseases, if possible. The public health organizations decided the easiest way to make sure this happened was to attack the children where they congregated. After much planning and study, these same organizations discovered that most children were in school every day. Amazing! They would be easy pickings for an assault, aha! Notices were sent out and PTA meetings were held to inform parents that on "Public Health Day," with the parents' permission, children could be inoculated against these health scourges. Twice a year was "shots day" as we kids called it.

To parents this was a godsend. They did not have to take their children to a doctor's office, and the immunizations were free. The governments assumed the responsibility and cost, and the schools were their accomplices. Parents had to indicate which inoculations their children were to receive, up to a choice of two (one in each arm). Also, a smallpox vaccination could be given by scraping the arm with something to break the skin, then applying a serum intended to cause a reaction. If the dosage "took," your arm could form a painful scab, which would leave a scar that looked like a moon crater. I had numerous smallpox vaccinations over the years, except my arms never formed the scab/scar. Every year my mom argued with the public health people that I already was protected even though I never carried the telltale crater-scar.

Preparations for the "shots attacks" were feverish. Rows of tables with instruments and medications were set up. Long rows of syringes were prepared and laid out containing various inoculants. Some efforts were made to shield the viewing from the hallways with hanging curtains, but without great success. Nurses scurried in and out of the auditorium as though they were robots, each time throwing the curtains to the side and offering any kid an instant glimpse of staged syringes. Then, to no surprise, every kid's imagination was ignited.

All of the nurses were dressed solely in white—head to toe, even with white stockings, as though they were walking snow-ladies. Their starched uniforms and folded hats looked like they had escaped from the laundry a few hours before. "Shots days" were to be dreaded, and it's amazing how many kids called in "sick" those mornings and never made it to school. It's also amazing how many parents fell for the "sick" trick.

The second "shots day" of my fourth grade year was in late April. The shots began in the morning after first recess. There was much trepidation during recess and every kid's imagination ran without limits. Groups huddled on the playground and talked, fueling each other's worries even more. I stood with Ronnie Landers and Freddie Roberts discussing how maybe we could make a break for it, much as we had seen prisoners do once in a movie. Sally Donovan walked up. Normally, a girl's presence would have killed any "guy conversation," but today was not any day. These were extenuating circumstances, and girls had a right to be apprehensive too.

"Darn . . . darn!!!" Freddy said. "I wish . . . I wish I could stay out here! I don't wanna go in there!! I remember last fall. It hurt. Man, it hurt a lot! I'm telling ya, my arm was sore for a month!!! I hate needles!"

I had my own worries. Who didn't? It wasn't like I wanted to take on Freddie's fears on top of my own, but I vaguely remembered last autumn.

"Last fall?" I asked. "Freddie, didn't you have a smallpox?"

"Uh . . . yeah . . . I had one of them. And . . . well, it wasn't good!"

"But," I said, "that wasn't a needle. It wasn't bad, Freddie; it was just a scrape on the arm. I don't get it."

"Oh yeah, well it was too!!!" Freddie spat back. "It made my arm swell up for a month." He began to roll up his sleeve as if to prove with his crater-scar that the pain was still there.

"Aw, Freddie," said Ronnie. "Don't do that. We've all got 'em. . . . But what about me, huh? I had one of them shots, and she shot me forever! I thought my arm was gonna balloon up, she pumped so much into me! I was squirming around, kicking my feet and everything, trying to get free, and still she kept shooting in me!!! Huh! What about that?"

I couldn't tell if Ronnie actually believed his words or if he was just fooling Freddie, because he had a completely straight face. But it didn't matter what Ronnie meant because Freddie bought it all, every word! Freddie's eyes grew large and his anxiety rose like a thermometer in the direct sun. He almost perspired now.

"Yeah . . . well," he sputtered, "I don't want to get one of them. Besides, I have an allergy. I'm allergic to needles! Needles make me break out all over!"

"What!" Sally said, beating Ronnie and me to the question. "Are you stupid? You can't have an allergy to needles?" Even to a girl this logic simply wouldn't fly. Ronnie and I looked at Sally with more admiration, and then we both swiveled to Freddie. He now had a perplexed look on his face as if he realized he had been caught in the middle of a hyper-exaggeration that even a girl could debunk. We waited. He thought.

"Well . . . maybe it's just my mom's sewing needles. Maybe that's it." He backpedaled trying to salvage any self-respect. "It coulda been!!" he declared.

"What about you?" I asked Sally.

She thought for a moment and said, "I dunno. I have to get something, but what's the difference? It's not like they're trying to hurt us. . . ."

"Oh, yes they are," Freddie interjected. "I know they are. Those nurses like doing it to us!"

We all looked at him like he was over the top again.

Sally continued, ignoring the interruption, "I'm gonna get some kinda shot, but I just don't think about it. If it hurts, well, I tell myself it'll be over quickly, and that's all. What about you?" she directed the question back to me.

I wasn't at her level of self-control yet. I knew I had to get two shots, and I wasn't looking forward to them at all. I was trying not to worry too much, but "before" was always worse than "after."

"Um . . . I dunno. I wish it was tomorrow," was all I could mumble.

The bell rang.

We tried to return to our studies, but our minds were like those of death row inmates waiting for the call. Finally, it came! A robot (nurse) came to the door and said it was time for our classroom. We looked at each other with dread. Miss Dillon instructed us to file out of the room in a single line. The walk up the hallway, as we hugged the wall, was somber. I heard a sniffle. I turned my head to see who, and it was one of the biggest Cedarwood Court gang guys. I couldn't believe it! This guy was twenty pounds bigger than me and he was sniffling . . . already! Then another was heard from somebody else. Soon there were more sniffles.

We reached the auditorium and stopped, and waited. We looked at each other to see who was cracking and who was still together. Freddie looked like he could cry any minute. Sally looked good. Ronnie was apprehensive, but he held together. I was not feeling well. I hated needles. I hated shots! I wished I could have been anywhere else in the whole world at this moment. But, I thought, if Sally can do it . . . well, it would look pretty stupid if I cracked and she didn't. So I kept a straight face.

They began to call kids out in alphabetical order. I wished I could instantly change my name to Zymo Zywenski. Once called, a kid schlepped up to the curtain, where a robot waited to take their hand. They then disappeared behind the curtain. We all listened intently for any sound. Sometimes, we heard nothing and then the kid emerged out of the other curtained door down the hall a few steps. Usually, these kids acted like nothing had happened. We hated those smug snots! Sometimes, as soon as a kid disappeared behind the curtain, we heard a big bawl. That stoked our fears and more sniffles appeared. Freddie began to sob slightly.

Sally was called! I stood next to her. She gave me a look of assurance and stepped forward. She disappeared behind the curtains. I listened with all my might . . . and heard nothing. A few moments later she emerged from the other curtain and looked for me. We caught each other's glance. Her look was calm as she stared at me purposefully. We couldn't speak, but we couldn't stop looking at each other either. It was as if she wanted me to know it was OK—that I shouldn't worry about it. That helped. She passed me without saying a thing, so as not to let on to anybody else about our "secret" communication. Then she walked back to the classroom. I took a deep breath and waited.

Ronnie was called, and again I held my breath, listening for any sign of agony. He emerged from the second curtain a few moments later and wiped his brow as if to signal, "whew." More waiting.

"John Osborne."

I heard my name. Oh no! This was it. This was the moment of my dread. Please God, help me, I thought. My stomach fluttered. I was *tense, tense, tense!* I stepped forward and slowly shuffled through the curtain. I had a slight tremble. The nurse took my hand and led me between tables on either side of me. I didn't want to look, but I couldn't help myself. Syringes were laid out waiting for victims. Another nurse reached for my left arm, rolled up my shirt sleeve, and rubbed a cold wet cotton swab on it. Then a third nurse suddenly pulled out a syringe from behind her back, as if she were the Lone

Ranger quickly drawing his six-guns on a bad guy. It looked to be a foot long and the needle seemed to be large, long, bent, and dripping! Up it came. My eyes followed. I thought I detected an evil sneer on her face! My head was ready to spin. I couldn't look! I shut my eyes, scrunched up my face, held my breath, and expected a searing, burning, tortuous pain in my arm. I wanted to cry, but I remembered Sally's look. All of this flashed though my mind in an instant.

I felt just the slightest nip at my skin. Before I could open my eyes and look, it was over. The nurse placed the dispensed syringe back onto the table. I was amazed. She said, "Good boy," to me as if she were talking to a five-year-old. Before I could relax though, another nurse grabbed my right arm and the same sequence was under way. I watched as her partner jabbed me softly with the needle, squeezed the plunger, and withdrew. Again, just a nip. It was nothing! As she deposited the spent syringe back onto her table, I recognized it as a small and simple instrument with a short needle. In fact, both syringes were the same. What a few seconds ago had looked like a large torture tool now appeared completely harmless. I was elated as I straightened my sleeves and moved toward the second curtain. I was so relieved that I smiled broadly. The tension and tightness in my neck drained immediately.

But quickly I wiped the smile from my face and hid my relief. In fact, I acted scared and almost cried as I exited the curtain. I walked down the line of "Ps" through "Zs," trying to make eye contact. I looked for Freddie. I saw him.

"It was awful, Freddie! It hurt awful!!" I said as I approached him with my lip in a fake quiver. I reached to rub my arm, and feigned pain. His face drained. He looked for any hope, but I wouldn't give it to him. I walked past rubbing my arms, almost now walking with a limp. When I was a few steps beyond Freddie, he broke into a sob, but I kept walking. I smiled and never looked around. Oh, I was a devil, I knew it. I knew I probably would rot in hell someday for this, but not today. This day, I had played a big practical joke when the opportunity presented itself. I knew Freddie was in terror at this moment, but I also knew that sometime later, when he was over his anger, we all would laugh about it. I also knew from this moment on, he would begin plotting a "get even."

But I couldn't worry about that now. All I wanted was to savor this moment. And, I was happy with myself.

I was also happy with my bravery. It was helped by Sally to be sure, but still I hadn't crumbled. I had faced my trepidation and met the challenge. I was brave through it all. I had learned something of value from the group and from this experience: **Fear is contagious, but bravery stands alone.**

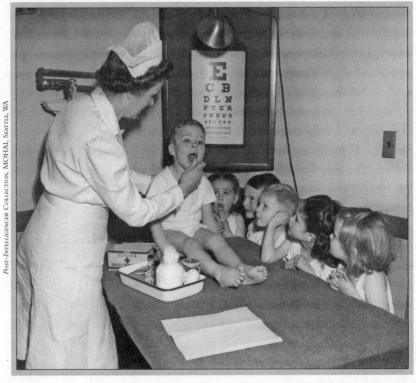

"Snow-lady" attending to kindergarteners at a Seattle elementary school on a Public Health Day, before turning into a "robot" nurse. . . . Just wait 'til she gets out the shots!

11

GRADUATION

I just graduated and already I'm way behind.

—Unknown

As the days lengthened and spring advanced into late May, every kid's countdown began for the end of the school year in mid-June. We knew exactly how many days were left, as though we ceremoniously ripped pages off an imaginary calendar each afternoon when we left the school grounds. Another day gone! Our concerns turned to grades and "passing." We weren't focused on grades as much as our parents, but we were attentive to passing into the next grade level.

For some reason, even the class "geniuses" had a fixation on whether they would "pass," as we called it. If someone didn't pass, the term we used was not "failed," it was "flunked." To us, you either passed or flunked, there was no in-between. Flunking carried a great stigma with it. Heaven help you, and your social standing on the playground, and even in the larger community, if for some reason—not always made public—you flunked a grade. You and your whole family might as well pick up and move, so as to be able to begin fresh in another school, in another city, maybe even in another state, it was that bad! It was known that sometimes families did just that, when a flunk occurred with one of their children.

By the first week of June, I yearned for any possible indication from Miss Dillon as to my "passability." My greatest hope was that one morning when I entered the classroom, our glances would meet and she would silently flash a big "thumbs-up," toward me, complete with a wink that only I could see. This would set my mind at ease and I would then know I was a shoo-in for fifth grade. But this never happened; she was stoic, and I never could get a read on my status.

On Wednesday afternoon of the last week, Ronnie Landers and I rode our bikes to the "good" projects for a big baseball game, with more players than normal. As was typical when he and I were going to a ball game, we were always in great spirits and we teased and talked the whole way. This day, however, Ronnie was quiet. He had something on his mind. Finally, I was dying inside. He had a secret and I had to know. I pestered.

"Um . . . I'm not sure I should tell you," he said, as we walked to the field.

Oh, now this was serious, I thought. I was worried.

"You hafta," I pleaded. "I never keep anything from you!"

He kicked one of his feet in the dirt for a moment, then said, "Freddie told me a huge secret, and I told him I wouldn't tell you. But I'm gonna anyway, 'cause you need to know."

I waited.

"Remember Freddie had to stay after class Monday . . . huh?" Ronnie said slowly.

I nodded, now in rapt attention.

"Well, he told me he was erasing the blackboards for Miss Dillon. She had to go out of the room for a minute. When she did, Freddie saw a list on her desk . . . of passes and flunks. And . . . your name was on the flunk list!"

This news was as if a thunderbolt had struck me right between the eyes! I was stunned. I couldn't even comprehend it for a few seconds. How could this be?

"Naw . . ." I pleaded. "You're lyin', I can tell." But I could tell he *wasn't* lying. He had a pained look on his face consistent with the worst possible news he had just delivered to me.

"I'm sorry. I didn't want to tell you," was all he could say.

Well, this news destroyed me that night. I couldn't eat and then

I couldn't sleep, and I was even sick to my stomach from the crushing thought of flunking fourth grade. What had I done to deserve this? My grades were OK—better than OK. I knew my math tables, I was good at reading, I studied hard at history. I could only think of two things: maybe the school was mad at me for the way the band played *"Smoke Gets in Your Eyes."* Or maybe Miss Dillon was finally getting even with me for the way I talked and disrupted her classroom. But I was getting better—even she had said so on my last report card! Maybe it was my penmanship. But I dismissed that as I had never heard that anyone had flunked due to bad penmanship. What was the problem? I wasn't sure, but I was in the deepest anxiety. I had to confirm this with Freddie. I was at his doorstep first thing the next morning, knocking to see if he was ready to go to school.

"Um . . . hi," he said as he came out. He could tell something was up because I rarely met him at his house on the way to school.

"What's this about me flunkin'?" I asked before he even took a breath.

He was evasive. "Uhh. You heard from Ronnie right? He wasn't supposed to tell you that."

"Yeah, well he did! And, I want to know what you know . . . Huh!!" I pressured.

He then told me the same story as Ronnie. He was as upset about it as I was. Clearly, this was a big issue for me, but also for all of us in the gang, because when word would get out that one of the Alderwoods had flunked fourth grade, the whole gang, by association, would take a step down in respectability! This matter had consequences.

"Let's not say anything to anybody about this yet," Freddie said.

I thought that was a good idea and agreed. For now, this would be just between Freddie, Ronnie, and me. We further confirmed it with Ronnie when we arrived at school.

That whole day was difficult for me. That second to the last day of school everybody else was upbeat, even Miss Dillon was perky. I wondered how she could be so happy when she knew she was flunking me. Even Sally asked me what was wrong, at one of the recesses. I said nothing, but I was dying inside. That night was the same; I couldn't eat and couldn't sleep. I didn't even tell my brother Doug what was bothering me, and I told him almost everything. I was worried what my whole family would think. How would my mom handle this news? What about Uncle Johnny? The more I thought and worried, the more petrified I became.

The next morning was Friday, the last day of school. It was a half-day. I somehow went through the morning routine and rode my bike to school. I should have been as happy as any other kid, but I already knew my destiny. Whereas the other kids merely wondered, I *knew* I had flunked. Every minute that morning was dreadful. Ronnie told me at recess that I should cheer up—I would always be his friend, even though I had flunked. That made me feel only slightly better.

Finally, the moment of truth arrived—just before noon and dismissal. Miss Dillon said something about how she had enjoyed all of us the whole year, in spite of some occasional traumas. I couldn't even look at her. I stared at my ink well downheartedly. She called out our names alphabetically to give us our report cards, and then we could leave. I slinked by her when my name was called and accepted the brown envelope, without making eye contact.

"Bye Jack," she said. "You have a great summer. I'll see you next year."

Oh, no, I thought. That was the last confirmation! I would be in her class again!

I trudged outside and stood at the corner of the building, almost crying, afraid to open my envelope. Ronnie came out and looked for me, then Freddie. We all huddled together. Other kids ran by and yelled joyously, celebrating the end of the school year, and I felt like my life was coming to an end.

I'd better take my medicine, I thought. With dread, I lifted the flap on the manila envelope and pulled out my report card. On the back was the section for the assignment to next year's class. I didn't want to turn it over, but finally, with my hands trembling I did. I read: *"Assignment for registration in September to Grade 5."* It was signed, "Mary Dillon."

GRADE 5!!! I was shocked! I passed!! I passed after all!!! How could this happen? I looked up and Ronnie was also surprised. He was as confused as I was. Freddie began to laugh.

"I got you!" he said. "Oh, I got you good, buddy." Then I realized I had been tricked.

"Remember shots day . . . huh? Remember what you did to me? Well, I got even—boy did I!" He was beside himself with glee.

I was furious. I jumped on him and dragged him down on the playground. I tried to pummel him good. Freddie covered himself up, and laughed as we rolled around. I felt Ronnie holding my arms so I couldn't get a good whack into Freddie. Finally, Ronnie pulled me off and kept himself positioned between us as a peacemaker.

"I'm mad at you too, Ronnie," I said. "You tricked me too!"

Before Ronnie could answer Freddie said, "Naw. It was all me. Ronnie didn't know." Ronnie and I listened. "I wanted to get even, and then I thought up this flunk trick. But, I knew if I told you, you'd 'a thought it was a trick, so I told Ronnie. I told him not to tell you, but I knew he would. It was all me, Jack. I did it. I know you're really mad at me, but now we're even, right? I still want to be your friend. We're all still in the gang, right?" He was almost pleading. Ronnie joined him in pleading with me for forgiveness. Slowly, my anger was displaced by their pleas for friendship, by the realization that I really hadn't flunked after all, and finally by the awareness that we now had a full three months of uninterrupted play ahead of us, during the best months of the year in Seattle. What could be better?

The more we three talked about all of that as we stood there, I also began to see what a good trick it was. Yes, I had been duped, but I had to admire Freddie's planning and trickery. This was a good one for sure. Freddie showed me something. Typically, his behavior was dictated more by emotions than reason, which was why it was so easy for us to trick him or tease him. We knew he had quick reactions, usually based on what he felt rather than thought. But that day I learned two great lessons in life. The first was: **You should never underestimate anyone, especially when they are strongly motivated.** If something was meaningful enough to someone, and they had the time to think about it, they could be fairly crafty. The second lesson was: **If you act with mischief toward someone, sooner or later, somehow, it will be returned to you, when you least expect it.** Or, more simply stated: **Always treat others the same way you want to be treated.** I respected Freddie more after that incident.

I picked up my report card, and we all ran for our bikes.

I had to ride home and show mom I had passed!

Somehow I managed to get through Columbia grade school with a good education, in spite of my antics. I'm sure I left an impression, even if it was not always positive. I hereby publicly apologize to my brother and sister, who had to follow me and bear the stigma of being even remotely related to me. But I know you both are tougher for the experiences you went through as a result of my trailblazing.

ASSIGNMENT

Assigned for registration in September to Grade.....*5*.........,

Room.....*11*..........

June 13., 19*52*

Teacher

Pupils who move to another school during the summer months should register before the first day of school.

Additional information relative to assignment:.................

E-25—1951

PART THREE

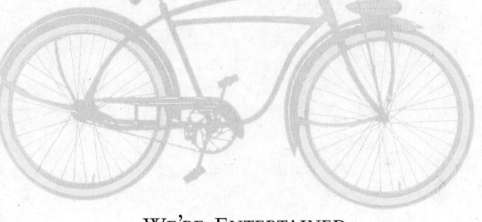

WE'RE ENTERTAINED

12

NIGHTLY RADIO

Of all the dramatic media, radio is the most visual.
—John Reeves

During the 1940s and 1950s, America was entertained with essentially three mediums: radio, films (the movies), and, eventually, television. All three dished up a steady diet of food for the soul, which appealed to the wide range of human emotions: love, lust, fear, suspense, terror, comedy, and serious drama. There were productions for every market, and the sub-teen, "baby-boomer" kids definitely comprised a huge market worth targeting. As such, when we kids were not riding our bikes, playing sports, or inventing mayhem in some form, we were glued to the delivery systems of our daily reality escapes, especially in the evenings after school. We craved adventure, fantasy, and comedy, and all three mediums delivered, especially radio.

Every house had a radio; it was our link to the civilized world. The radio generally occupied a prized spot in the living rooms of America, and evenings were spent with most family members in the same room at the same time, doing something as a family. What a concept! The facilitator of this was, of course, a little audio box that generally resembled a major piece of furniture.

Mom brought her knitting and parked in our rocking chair. Our step-dad lounged across the sofa, and my brother, sister, and

I played on the floor. I had an Erector® Set, which I worked to death in front of that talking box. We kids also had kittens, which we chased around the room. But the main task was to catch all of the laughs, drama, or suspense miraculously dispensed into our home every evening.

The great thing about radio was that it allowed, and relied upon, an active imagination of the listener in order to create within his or her mind the images that were supplied solely by the ear. I believe the mental images produced by radio were far more vivid than anything the movies and television have engendered, because in the latter media we could see the zippers on the monster's costume, or the bad makeup, or that the crashing airplanes were actually models. But in radio, everything was left to our imaginations—and they worked in hyper-drive! The sound effects of crypts opening and footsteps echoing in the night were far more real coming from the radio than what was presented onscreen in the movies. Watching the movies we didn't have to look at the screen if we didn't want to, we could always cover our eyes for relief. But when listening to the radio, it was impossible to cover our ears sufficiently to block out all the *imagined* images the sounds evoked.

Radio at that time was not specific talk and music as it is today. We listened to half-hour entertainment programs, just like today's "sit-coms" on television. For me as a kid, after school there was baseball and after baseball—at least until age nine—there was radio. I rushed home after the ball game and left a debris field of discarded clothing strewn across the floor as I positioned myself next to the talking piece of furniture, straining to hear every word about my favorite radio heroes. Those after school heroes were the *Green Hornet, Dick Tracy,* and Red Ryder®.

My favorite evening show after dinner was *Dragnet* with Jack Webb . . . He was only looking for the facts. I loved that! My mom and step-dad's favorite evening shows were *The Shadow, The Aldrich Family,* and *Inner Sanctum.* Another big comedy hit was *Fibber Magee and Molly.* This show was sort of an early version of television's *Ozzie and Harriet,* which was sort of an earlier version of *Leave It to Beaver,* which was sort of an earlier version of

The Simpsons. You get the idea. It was wacky family pap with a new dilemma each week, neatly packaged and solved within about a twenty-four minute window of time. Each show was complete with laugh tracks, in case you the listener/watcher were dumb as a turnip and had no clue about when to laugh.

Inner Sanctum was probably the most famous suspenseful show in the history of radio. It began with the sound of a creaking door sloooowly opening to the voice of the ghoulish announcer dripping words of greeting.

It then went on to deliver stories of the macabre, filled with tension, terror, and horror—sort of *Jason* meets *Freddie Krueger,* with a little *Chucky* thrown in for good measure. Everything was made more real by the great sound effects which tantalized the listener's mind. It was completely creepy, but the show's producers were on to something long before *The Twilight Zone* captivated television viewers: people like to be frightened, especially if they are in the relative safety of their own living room. I tried to listen to Inner Sanctum alone on occasion and found that it disagreed with my sleep.

Getting to sleep was difficult enough because of all the monsters that hid under my brother's and my bunk beds. I slept on the bottom to protect Doug because we both knew the monsters were only *under* the bed, and when they came out after dark, they would get me first. I was bigger and stronger (in my mind) and perhaps I could fight them off long enough for him to escape. The logic of how he was to do this from the top bunk was not apparent, but at the time it sounded like a workable plan. Also, we had shoved the bed against the corner walls to minimize the paths the monsters could take. Thus they could only come up from my feet or my left side, so I always went to sleep lying on my left side, staring at the edge of the mattress, in order to give me a better chance to see them. I hoped I could get at least one good scream out before being eaten. What a *thought!*

In the daytime I knew our fears were all nonsense and there was no reason to worry. But in bed, when the lights went out—especially after a half-hour with Inner Sanctum—it was real enough as to scare the bejabbers out of me. Sometimes I poked the springs on my brother's bunk above me and made ghost sounds. He was not amused and more than once broke into a cry.

We always went to sleep with the bedroom door shut and the room black as a coal mine. One night, when I was about eight years old, after an Inner Sanctum show, I was lying petrified, on my left side, staring into the blackness as usual, keeping guard. What I didn't know was that one of our cats had inadvertently been shut up in our bedroom, which was unusual because they always slept in the living room. Anyway, since the cat had the advantage of partial sight in total darkness, he must have decided he would rather sleep on my feet than on the cold floor. So, with no advanced warning, he leaped onto my feet.

All I sensed was that suddenly there was a creature grabbing at my feet! My gosh, I almost came apart from the fright!!! I knew the monsters had finally attacked and I was going to be eaten within a second. I screamed my lungs out and kicked my legs furiously, which made my brother equally scared. Our mom ran in and we both were screaming and shaking so hard we almost peed in our pajamas. It was the single worst scary moment of my life up to that point. I thought I was a goner for sure. Such was what the vivid reality of radio could do to eight- to ten-year-old minds, after the sun went down.

A radio of the 1940s.

Our cats as kittens.
One of these became the monster after dark.

13

TELEVISION COMES TO OUR HOME

I love Saturday morning cartoons, what classic humor. This is what entertainment is all about . . . idiots, explosives and falling anvils.
—From comic strip *Calvin and Hobbes* by Bill Watterson

In the summer of 1952, my parents bought our first television. It was a cause for celebration beyond any other event in my life up to that time, except for when the Second World War ended. We thought we finally had achieved some level of nobility, because it was not just a television, but its large console cabinet also contained a radio and a record player (78 rpm)! It was made by Radio Corporation of America (RCA) and was a beautiful large piece of furniture. But the television itself was a small, rectangular tube about nine inches high by about twelve inches wide. It was supposed to display "black and white" images but ours happened to display strange tints of green, as though the faces on the screen had an Art Deco pastel wash. The pictures were fuzzy, and occasionally broke up and swayed sideways before magically snapping back to some semblance of reality. Yes, early television had its problems, but it nevertheless was something remarkable to behold.

Most programming was local to Seattle and there was only enough content to fill certain hours of the day. We sometimes turned on the television in advance of a scheduled program and stared at a "test pattern" until our show finally appeared. We had no understanding of what the test pattern meant, but my brother Doug and I liked the picture of an "Indian" that appeared. Of course, nobody consulted us but we both were convinced the pattern also needed a picture of a "cowboy" to make it complete.★

By the following summer, Seattle had begun to receive more national and world programming. I remember that the first show we watched with a subject beyond our own borders was the coronation of Queen Elizabeth II of England in June of 1953. None of us understood how St. Paul's Cathedral in London was transmitted into our living room. But I remember we all sat in absolute awe at being privileged to witness a great moment in history, which was happening halfway around the world. Radio never had the same impact on our household after that.

Television for us kids soon became "subdivided" into two categories: the programs that were shown on Saturday mornings and the shows during the week after school.

SATURDAY MORNING TELEVISION

Saturday mornings began with cartoons, and there typically were eight to ten of them in a row. To us they were hilarious, even though as the years went by we had seen all of them at least forty-six times. They still made us laugh.

Our dear friends were *Bugs Bunny, Elmer Fudd, Daffy Duck, Porky Pig, Yosemite Sam, Sylvester the Cat,* and *Tweety Bird.* They were all characters from "Looney Tunes" Productions, and they could be paired in various combinations for any one cartoon. We also enjoyed *Tom and Jerry* and *Mighty Mouse* from another cartoon studio. Tom was a cat, and Jerry was a mouse who always seemed to outwit Tom. Mighty Mouse was sort of a *Superman,* but instead he was a "Supermouse." You had to see it, I guess.

Our favorite pair of all time was the *Road Runner* and *Wile E.*

★ This most famous of TV test patterns was originated by RCA in 1939. It was referred to within the television industry as the "Indian Head." Efforts to secure permission from RCA for its reprinting here were unsuccessful, but the interested reader can go to www.videouniversity.com/tvtestpa.htm and see a wonderful display of the image.

Coyote. These two were hilarious, even though there never was any dialogue, other than when the Road Runner occasionally uttered his signature line, *"Meep, Meep"* whenever he passed old Wile with his blazing speed. Doug and I always had arguments as to whether he said "Meep" or "Beep," but it really didn't matter because in either case it was funny. All of the humor came from "sight gags," and they were excellent, well written and well drawn. We kids knew what would happen every single time Wile constructed some special trap with materials acquired from "Acme Corp.," but that did not make the consequences any less uproarious.

Looking back on them, the interesting thing about the Road Runner cartoons was that the Road Runner was never the aggressor against Wile. Wile always was the schemer, and all of the situations were the result of what happened when his scheming backfired—figuratively, and often literally. Gravity was always his enemy, with things continually falling on him, or him falling off some tall cliff. Again, it was a simple stock formula, but that formula worked, every time. For some reason, life in the early 1950s was much simpler for everybody, except Wile E. Coyote.

After the cartoons, we were suitably primed for the *Buster Brown* show. Kids today, and few adults for that matter, have any concept of just how funny *Froggy the Gremlin* was! Froggy was a hand-puppet character who apparently had a "twanger," whatever that was. Froggy would magically appear in a cloud of smoke when the announcer asked him to plunk it. And . . . poof, suddenly, there was Froggy! He announced his presence by saying hi to all of us kids in a low, raspy, and devilish voice. The studio audience went crazy screaming for Froggy in delirious anticipation of what came next when the old *Sea Captain* showed up seconds later.

Man, could Froggy ever fool the Sea Captain! The amazing thing to me was that Doug and I could see through all of Froggy's tricks, and we already had figured out in advance what was about to happen to the Captain. We wondered why he also couldn't see it coming. We would jump around the room, screaming at the television for the Captain to "watch out." But he always had feathers dumped on his head, or papers glued to his hands by Froggy, or some equally silly thing like that. The kids in the studio audience were just as smart as we were because they, too, would all be screaming warnings. But, still, the Captain was always the last one to figure out what had happened to him—*ex post facto.* What a boob, we thought every time, but we faithfully watched the program every week.

It was the same thing on the *Howdy Doody* show which came on next. *Clarabell,* a mute clown, always played tricks on *Buffalo Bob Smith,* the show's host, or on the other human talisman of good, *Princess Summerfall Winterspring.* Clarabell would sneak up and squirt Buffalo Bob or the Princess with a seltzer bottle, and why couldn't they get it? In my entire life, I have never seen a real person use a seltzer bottle. But, according to Clarabell, they were standard appliances in every home. The kids in the studio audience—called the "Peanut Gallery"—would go crazy before and after! It was not until a few years later that I figured out there was a method to the madness: it was all part of the *schtick,* and both the Sea Captain and Buffalo Bob probably laughed all the way to the bank, every week.

Howdy Doody himself was a small cowboy marionette, although his visible strings never bothered us. We wanted so much to believe in him that we accepted that he was animated. He was a very cute little boy, with red hair and freckles over most of his face. Other marionettes on his show were *Inspector Fadoozle,* who was more simply referred to as "The Inspector," *Dilly-Dally,* his dog *Fiddle-Faddle,* and *Mr. Phineas T. Bluster.*

Mr. Bluster was the originating "schemer" of most shenanigans. His partners in crime were always Clarabell and *Chief Thundercloud.* "The Chief," as we called him, was always dressed like a Hollywood caricature of an Indian chief, complete with full feather head-dress hanging down his back to mid-thigh. He wore a Tonto-like buckskin outfit, except the fringes on his costume were much shorter than Tonto's. We suspected the fringes, nee the whole costume, was not real leather, but some cloth-like substitute. The Chief's Indian duds looked more like a uni-jumpsuit, which decades later would appear for a brief period as accepted leisure fashion before fading quickly into oblivion. His costume reminded us of a Sears & Roebuck auto mechanic's outfit with fringes.

Chief Thundercloud was never one of our favorites because we could not see him as a real Indian, let alone as a chief. To us he looked more Italian than Indian. The Chief, however, did have one memorable contribution to our everyday life—the "signature line" he spoke within the last two minutes of every show, when the nefarious scheme of the day was uncovered and he and the other perpetrators were exposed. He always uttered, *"Kowabunga!"* as an epithet to convey his shock and indignation. That word, needless to say, was picked up by all of us in Columbia grade school, and probably by countless other kids everywhere, when we also were exposed or surprised in our lives. We used it as though it was the verbal equivalent of a Monopoly® game's "Get-Out-of-Jail-Free" card to make everything right and proper.

The Howdy Doody show always began with a special opening. Buffalo Bob shouted to the Peanut Gallery the famous question, *"Hey kids! What time is it?"* The Gallery, comprised of about forty or more four- to ten-year-olds, both girls and boys, suitably cued, shouted back in high volume and in unison, *"It's Howdy Doody time!!!"* We all then were off and rolling for thirty minutes of fun and hi-jinx!

The Howdy Doody show went off the air about 1955, long after I had stopped watching it, but it reappeared a few years later to again appeal to a whole new generation of youth. When the show first left the airwaves in 1955, the man who played Clarabell-the-Clown, Bob Keeshan, then found other work as *Captain Kangaroo.* He made a living as that character and made millions of kids happy every week for almost thirty additional years. Talk about longevity on television!

One other tie-in to Howdy Doody happened to me many years later as an adult when I was in a meeting of the Board of Directors for a start-up company. I found myself surprised by financial data being presented, and I suddenly muttered, *"Kowabunga!"* I instantly thought to myself, *Kowabunga???* How did that travel across four-plus decades in my mind?

Apparently, I said it loud enough for those near me to hear, because a fellow board member, who also happened to be approximately my age, looked at me with complete understanding and said, "Exactly!"

Two other board members sitting near us, both of whom were at least fifteen years younger than we two "old fogies," looked at us quizzically as if to say, "We don't get it!"

My companion and I just smiled knowingly and never attempted to explain.

Kowabunga indeed!

The next show on the Saturday morning roller coaster ride of comedy and fun was the *Captain Midnight* show. This was sponsored by some dry chocolaty crystals which were intended to be mixed with milk. The "hook" for the *Captain Midnight* character was that he had a "Secret Squadron" comprised of all of his loyal listeners. Every boy in Columbia grade school was a member of the Secret Squadron, or so I am convinced. To get into the Secret Squadron you had to mail in part of the label of a chocolaty crystal package (advertisers of the program), along with twenty-five cents, to the "special address." After a few weeks you received a certificate in the mail identifying your secret membership, along with the most coveted prize of all—the *"Captain Midnight Secret Decoder Badge."* The Germans had the "Enigma" secret code machine in the Second World War to create and send messages, but looking back on it, I don't think it could top the Captain Midnight Secret Decoder Badge. This piece of metal was priceless! With it, you could help Captain Midnight solve every week's "secret saying."

At the end of the show, Captain Midnight gave out the secret cipher, and we kids diligently wrote it down, shielding our scribbling so no one else could see it. Then we retreated to a private location to work through the cipher with the decoder badge. The code was always some simple letter transition scheme, which said something like: "Buy more _____ (chocolaty crystals)," or "Watch Captain Midnight next Saturday morning."

Just once, I wanted my cipher to read, "The buried treasure is located in the northeast corner of the woods under the large pine tree . . . but don't tell anybody!!!" or "Let Jenny bat cleanup in the next baseball game." But, alas, I never received either of those messages. However, Doug and I were never disappointed because with our decoder badges we knew we had become brilliant undercover operatives who could solve complex puzzles to help Captain Midnight keep the world safe from evil.

All we needed was to receive the proper instructions, which could happen any given Saturday. We were part of the "Secret Squadron" and were always on watch. I can look back at that time and appreciate what a great marketing scheme the Secret Decoder Badge was.

Other Saturday shows, which rounded out the morning were *Kukla, Fran, and Ollie, Crusader Rabbit,* and *Beany and Cecil the Seasick Sea Serpent.*

Fran (of K, F, & O) was a sweet woman who talked with two hand puppets. *Kukla* was a very serious clown (I know, it does not compute), whereas *Ollie* was a one-toothed dragon, with a droll sense of humor. These characters were more soothing than funny, but still we watched. This was long before *Sesame Street* entertained my own children decades later, but the theme was somewhat the same: to make the world understandable to kids.

Crusader Rabbit was an animated cartoon, which held only our passing interest, and Beeny and Cecil I believe was a local Seattle hand puppet show that was a takeoff on K, F, & O.

After sitting through about three hours of all of the above, we were ready for lunch, and, after that, the Saturday afternoon movie matinees!

Overall, between television in the morning and the movie matinee in the afternoon, Saturday was a day for us to completely refill the tanks of our imaginations with heroes, adventures, mystery, and comedy, as well as refill our stomachs with sugar . . . we can't forget the sugar!

By Saturday evening Doug and I were sated and wired. We knew that if we could just make it through another boring Sunday afternoon—spent on a family drive, or a predictable picnic in the park—that Monday would be here, and after school we could begin all over again and watch another week of our action heroes on television (after baseball, of course).

What a wonderful cycle it was!

Buffalo Bob and Howdy Doody,
our favorite imaginary boy.

Kukla, Fran, and Ollie.

The Captain Midnight
Secret Decoder Badge.

The Enigma
code machine.

When we received this picture from Captain Midnight personally, we became true and dedicated members of his Secret Squadron. The picture also came with a letter addressed to our parents reminding them of the nourishing value of the chocolaty crystals. Hmmm.

14

AFTER SCHOOL TELEVISION

Clark Kent was super! . . . man.

Hey Seeeessscooooooooo . . .

O ne of the shows my brother Doug and I watched every week after school was *Superman*, starring George Reeves. Even at our ages, we had difficulty accepting George Reeves as Superman. He did not have a chiseled muscle in his body, and every time he leaped to take flight, we mentally pictured the mattresses he must have fallen upon after the camera panned away. And the pictures on television of him flying with his outstretched arms never were convincing.

We had a View-Master® (didn't every kid?), which was a device for viewing color pictures through a viewer/holder. The pictures were on a flat reel which was inserted into the holder, and then indexed with a finger lever. The charm of the View-Master® was that the single picture you saw in the viewer was composed from two pictures on the reel, taken of the same subject but from slightly different angles. Thus, when combined in the viewer, you saw a picture in three dimensions, meaning the picture had *depth*. This was supposed to add realism because everything your eyes saw in normal life also was in "3-D."

One of the reels we had was of George Reeves as Superman. Even on that reel, the shots of Superman supposedly flying through the sky, with his arms outstretched and his fists clenched, seemed hokey to us. Nothing about the show worked for us. We kids figured that everybody in the cast must have been as stupid as a cucumber, because supposedly Superman was disguised as *Clark Kent,* a newspaper reporter. Except the only thing distinguishing Superman from Clark Kent was a pair of dark horn-rimed glasses which Clark wore. We doubted if they even had lenses in them.

Supposedly, Clark transformed into a man of steel by suddenly ripping off his glasses and his Clark Kent clothes to reveal his Superman costume. He apparently wore this *under* his reporter's suit—complete with a cape to his knees. Right! Even we could not understand how this was possible. . . . Let's see . . . a guy wears glasses, but he rips them off—and his clothes—and then people instantly recognize him as Superman. Duh!!! The truth was that Clark Kent looked *exactly* like Superman, with or without glasses, or whatever he wore, because *they both were* George Reeves. This was easily discernable by even a one-year-old baby. As a result, Superman, the show . . . well, just did not "fly" for us.

It was not only that Superman and Clark Kent were the same person, anybody could see that. It was not even the dramatically under budget costumes and stage props. We could have forgiven any of that. This is what it was: simply because we accepted all of the imaginary heroes in our lives did not mean we were naïve. We knew they were not real people. But each of the heroes we did accept offered a very basic premise: that he *could be* plausible and believable, if we stretched our imaginations. We wanted to believe that what happened was *possible!* We wanted to be able to say, "Coulda' happened!" It was that simple: we only asked of the character that he give us the opportunity to believe. George Reeves and the television Superman never passed that test. But still we watched, with the remote hope that someday, somehow, we would finally see one episode that really *did* capture our *imaginations*.

However, the Superman shows had one essential item that every successful movie, serial, or television show needed in order to capture our attention, and that was a great "lead-in." Even though the story lines of those old Superman episodes are now long forgotten, the lead-in, or introduction, is still remembered almost verbatim by all

kids from that era. The show always began with the now famous
words about speeding bullets, (leaping) tall buildings, birds and planes
in the sky, . . . Superman!

I challenge you . . . find any person who was a kid during that
time—the early 1950s—and say the words above. There is a high
likelihood they will recite the whole introduction from memory!
Absolutely!!!

As exciting as the show's introduction was, Superman only made
us yearn more for our truly favorite shows, the television Westerns.
The Westerns became one of the great staples to lure kids about
my age into a lifetime addiction to that small screen.

TELEVISION WESTERNS

One of my favorite Western programs was the *Range Rider.*
Langendorf Bread will always have a soft spot in my heart for
being the sponsor of that great after-school reality escape. I knew I
was destined to grow up and become another *Dick West,* the "All
American Boy," who was the Range Rider's trusty sidekick. The
actor who played Dick West was Dickie Jones, and that "Dickie"
thing was not appealing to us kids, though. It was OK for us to
have names that ended in "ie," and many of us did, but it was
something we expected to shed by the time we could shave. To see
a reasonably grown-up guy still calling himself Dickie produced a
conflict of emotions within us. We loved his character, but were not
sure about him as the actor.

We had the same reaction to the Range Rider. His real name
was Jock Mahoney. At first we all thought it was a misprint in the
credits. However, when we realized his name actually was Jock,
that always brought hoots of laughter because being above the age
of five, we were fairly well into potty talk and we knew a jock
was an unpleasant thing we guys would one day wear in gym
classes. To hear someone calling himself "Jock" tickled us every time.
Nevertheless, we were able to separate real-life Jock and Dickie from

their frontier characters, and we loved those guys on the tube. It all came down to the fact that we believed, and the Range Rider and Dick West were still wonderful heroes to us all.

We also watched Gene Autry, the "Singin' Cowboy." He was OK, but he always seemed a little too prissy for Doug and me. There was something about him that didn't convey ruggedness to us. It was as if his main tactic to catch the "baddies" was to serenade them into submission. We wanted action—not ballads. He did have a good voice, but that appreciation didn't come to us until much later in life. In real life, Gene Autry also was a great businessman and he became one of the richest men in America. But that was not apparent to us in the 1950s. He was just another crooning cowboy with a fancy hat and plaid bandana.

On the other hand, I very much enjoyed *The Cisco Kid*. *Cisco* was the svelte and sophisticated member of a Mexican crime-fighting Western duo. He was the thinker and planner, who dressed as though he had come from a mariachi party where he was the lead guitarist. Seriously, he dressed in an all black costume with silver stitching on the pants and shirt. *Pancho* was his slightly rotund, less-refined *compadre*, who simply tagged along and always was good for laughs. Pancho was underdressed, compared to Cisco, but he did have the big floppy sombrero. Cisco had a sombrero too, but his usually matched his mariachi uniform with silver threads on it. Pancho's sombrero, on the other hand, looked like he picked it up at the Mexican Army surplus store.

Cisco was played by an actor named Duncan Reynaldo. Pancho was played by Leo Carrillo, which always seemed to be more of a real Mexican name.

The show had a distinctive opening and closing. In the opening, the announcer teased dramatically with descriptive words promising "adventure" . . . "romance" . . . and "excitement," and then concluded with—*the Cisco Kiiiiiid!*

The words rolled out of his mouth, each building upon the

other, until the word "Kid" finally was spoken, long and drawn out. By then, we all were suitably primed for everything and anything—even though at our age, we could have cared less about the "romance" part of it. Cisco was a different kind of Western hero in that he actually did put some "charm" on all the ladies. Very early on, we kids all figured that Mexican cowboys were just different from American cowboys. Cisco tried to spin the lady's heads with his rugged good looks and smooth sophistication, whereas Pancho employed loveable cuteness and "hug-ability"—he was a big teddy bear with a mustache. Pancho seemed to have little success, though, whereas it always was implied that the ladies, all in their off-the-shoulder fiesta dresses, wanted Cisco to return later for a midnight "tango lesson."

The closing every week for every episode was also very memorable. I can still hear Pancho's "signature line" as they rode off into the desert at the end of each episode: *"Hey Seeeessscoooooooo!!!"* Then Cisco answered with: *"Hey Paannchoooo!"* Man, dialogue like that brought tears to our eyes.

One other distinguishing fact about The Cisco Kid was that it was the very first television show to be broadcast in *color!* Yes, I know it is stunning to comprehend this now, but there actually was a time when television was broadcast only in black-and-white. The Cisco Kid broke that barrier.

"Hey Seeeessscooooooooo!" . . . what a way to go!

Television had a huge impact, not only on *our* lives, but also on all of America. Yes, nightly radio was special and it stimulated our imaginations, so much so that often it ruined our sleep. But for all the wonderment radio offered, it lacked one thing, one extremely important ingredient, which the movies and television had: action. You could hear *and see* the story. This sometimes left less to our *imagination*, but that was more than overshadowed by the intensity and timing of the action.

Our heroes were all about action. We were not interested in

lengthy or complex plot development. We wanted blazing six-guns, galloping horses, knock-'em-down-punch-'em-out fistfights (where our heroes always prevailed), daring leaps off cliffs, smoking rocket ships, tumbling avalanches, etc. We wanted all of that and more, and we wanted to see it, as well as hear it! Television did that . . . plus, it went two steps better—it was all in our living rooms, and it was free! What could be better that that? Escapism and adventure were there, in our house, at our beck and call, every day after school, and every Saturday morning. It was wonderful!

It was the first intrusion of significant technology into our lives, and once invited in, it "pulled up a chair" and stayed (forever), like an old, comfortable relative.

Superman—
He smiles because he
thinks he has us fooled.

Clark Kent. Waaaiiitt a minute. . . ?
Doesn't he look like Superman? Take off those glasses and. . . ."

The Range Rider and Dick West.

The Cisco Kid and Pancho.

15

SATURDAY AFTERNOONS AT THE MOVIES

Heroes, villains, posses . . . and sugar!

My brother Doug and I escaped from the reality of life in the projects and entered a world of adventure and glorious fun every Saturday afternoon. The vehicle by which this was accomplished was the movie matinee. And, we were not alone, as most other kids in our age range, say about six to maybe twelve, also looked forward to the weekly diet of fantasy, group mayhem, and sugar overload.

In our time and our neighborhood, the Saturday matinee was a rite of passage from the period when our moms began to trust our safety away from the house for a few hours, to when we became aware there were other creatures of some general interest, namely girls. But prior to the secretion of hormones, the matinees held all of our attention. And they generally were guy domains; very few girls ever went to the matinees. Girls generally were not interested in being in a closed, dark space filled with young boys running amok and behaving without any level of decency and decorum. To us boys, every Saturday matinee was a release of inhibitions, as if we had any in the first place.

In the early days (before we received an allowance) mom gave us thirty cents apiece for the movie afternoon. Twenty cents was for admission, and the remaining ten cents was spent on a veritable smorgasbord of sugar. Almost everything was a nickel, whether it was a candy bar, a box of candies, a soda pop, or popcorn. The only treat that was a dime was a box of *Cracker Jack*®, which was caramel-coated popcorn with a few peanuts thrown in. The lure of Cracker Jack® was that each box contained a toy surprise—usually a plastic something-or-other that held our attention for about ten seconds. Both Doug and I went for the candy, foregoing the popcorn or the Cracker Jack®. If we bought popcorn, then we also had to buy a soda to wash it down. But if we did that, then there was nothing left for candy. And if we bought Cracker Jack®, we had used our whole budget. Ah, those were the meaningful dilemmas of life at that time. How often I yearned to have just one more nickel, or in my wildest dream, to have another whole dime—then I could have everything I wanted, including popcorn.

The great advantage of popcorn (and Cracker Jack®) was that it was an ideal missile. You see, only a fraction of the popcorn sold in matinees was eaten. The balance ended up on the floor, either because it was spilled, or more likely, thrown. The launching could occur during any appropriate time of suspense or displeasure in the plot on the screen, or more likely when the mood "called." Someone suddenly decided it was time for a preemptive strike, and the popcorn flew. Of course, this was followed by a retaliatory barrage from the victims. There were times when it seemed as if popcorn snowed from the ceiling, and, of course, when the popcorn was airborne it was always accompanied by much screaming.

I was a creature of habit and I determined over the years that my most satisfying selections for my remaining ten cents were a *Big Hunk*® candy bar and a box of *Holloway Milk Duds*®. The Big Hunk® was about the size of a 12″ ruler and was about one-quarter inch in thickness. It was wrapped in purplish-brown waxed paper with white block letters. Inside was a solid slab of white nougat with peanut halves cemented randomly here and there, on which you could break a tooth if you were not careful. Getting a chunk to chew meant working the bar back and forth between your teeth until a piece finally snapped off, or it stretched into a flexible mass approximating non-vulcanized rubber. I discovered the best way to deal with it was to immediately snap the whole bar against any hard object a few times—the restroom sink worked fine. This shattered the bar inside its wrapping. Half the fun of the Big Hunk® was that it was a good half-hour's entertainment just to get it broken and then consumed. It was a special challenge for kids our ages because we seemed always to be in some state of tooth rotation—"baby" teeth out, "adult" teeth in. A Big Hunk® bar was either an insidious torture tool, or was the best piece of sweet and crunchy glop any kid could imagine.

My other choice was Milk Duds®, which were drops of caramel covered with chocolate. Man, were they good! I could throw two or three of those droplets in my mouth at once, and risk completely locking up my jaw forever. But eventually, with effort, I could finally get it broken down enough so that my teeth moved freely and the saliva streamed. Of course, this usually coincided with a hilarious cartoon scene where the "Road Runner's" proverbial antagonist, "Wile E. Coyote," was about to get hit with a falling anvil because another of his schemes had gone south, literally! Also, my attempts to laugh, shout a warning to Wile, breathe normally, and swallow all at the same moment were usually met with a river of chocolate-colored juice escaping down my chin, to be wiped away by my bare hands. Within twenty minutes of the show's beginning, every boy's hands, bare arms, and chins were sticky landscapes of sugary skin. It was wonderful!

Other favorite candies were *Junior® Mints, Dots®, Crows®, Necco Wafers®*, and *Jujubes*. My least favorite, but one Doug seemed to like, was *Good & Plenty®*. They were excellent for throwing and were the most fulfilling because they were the hardest. If you heard an "ouch" emanate somewhere in the dark after you had let loose a handful of Good & Plenty®s, you knew you had scored!

The filling of the theater was an adventure in itself. Kids ran around trying to find acceptable seats, with much yelling and "rough-housing" right up until the lights dimmed. This was not a night at the opera; rather it was disorganized mayhem. But somehow everybody finally settled in.

When the lights dimmed, we all cheered. We were on our *journey* now! First on the screen were the previews of "coming attractions."

These were about three-minute snippets of future movies to be shown at the matinees. They were meant to tease and tantalize us about specific movies, but their only real benefit was to give us more time to get our candy and get settled. We never paid much attention to the previews because, hey, we were coming anyway, every week. The previews were just the "warm-up acts."

Next up were the cartoons. Sometimes these were the same cartoons we had seen on television earlier in the morning, but it never was a problem for us to see them again. We knew every scene and humorous predicament of the characters, but still we laughed.

SERIALS

Following the cartoons were the serials. These were continuing stories of action heroes, always risking peril and fighting to save the girl, the city, the statues of gold, the rocket ship, etc., or the ultimate—Planet Earth. A complete serial ran between ten to sixteen episodes, but most averaged about thirteen, or three months of excitement. Each episode was about fifteen to twenty minutes long and began by first extracting the hero(es) from the certain death and destruction they were facing at the end of the previous episode. There would then be about ten minutes of plot, setting up the ending, which again left the hero(es) on the very brink of the worst fate imaginable.

The predicaments each week were designed to leave us so tortured inside with concern for our hero(es) that we couldn't possibly see how they could escape, yet we knew that somehow they would. After all, there were another six episodes remaining. Each episode's ending left us craving for more, and we had to come back next week to find out how they survived, or at least how they had averted disaster for another fifteen minutes. The episodes to us were powerful dramas of mystery, mystique, danger, adventure, and salvation. And, "Good" always, every single time, triumphed over "Evil." We tolerated nothing less.

Since the serials were continuous installments of the same story, it should be evident that they needed to run in sequence. Well, one week the worst thing imaginable happened. *Dick Tracy*® was left in an unbelievable situation, where certain death was apparent. Dick was tied up in his car as it was speeding toward a cliff, with a timed bomb ticking in the back seat. Without a miracle, he would go over the cliff and simultaneously be blown to bits. That's where it ended, with the accompanying groans and disappointment of the packed theater.

Next week we couldn't wait to discover how Dick had survived. When the serial came on, to great cheering and anticipation, we discovered the episode on the screen was not the next one in the sequence. We now had *no idea* what miracle had occurred, and further we were now watching a new direction to the story that was not related to last week's "cliffhanger." We were furious and immediately expressed our feelings with much screaming accompanied by volleys of Jujubes, Good & Plenty®s, and Dots®. Many were directed at the narrow slit in the projector room from which the flickering light emanated.

Suddenly, a whole cup of soda flew up against the projector room window. Then, the unexpected happened. The movie stopped and the theater lights came on! Our eyes squinted from the sudden brilliance. The bright light freeze-framed kids in various acts of running in the aisles, climbing over seats, wrestling, and throwing things. It was a major uprising. Everyone quickly slinked to silence and froze in positions hopefully offering the most camouflage.

A stubby, slightly rotund man walked through the curtain connecting the theater to the lobby. It was obvious from his expression and the flushed color of his skin that he was not there to join our party. He walked to the center of the aisle, looked around to calm himself, and then shouted into the already hushed auditorium.

"Awl rat ya little hoodlums! SHUT UP!!! Shut yo' mouths!"

He paused, not so much for dramatic effect as much as to let his brain catch up with his anger. From his speech it was obvious he was raised south of Seattle.

"Ah'm the man'ger o' this hyar movie, and ah'm sick an' tarred o' ya-awl's behavior! Ah'm tarred o' havin' to clean up after ya-awl ever week! Just look at yer selves, ya-awl otta be 'shamed!"

Again, there was a verrryy long silence. Nobody moved except for eyeballs clicking in their sockets. Doug quietly tried to drop the Good & Plenty®s in his hand onto the floor, as if he was expecting to be strip-searched any minute. Out of the corner of my eye I looked at Freddie Roberts in the row in front of me. He was in "suspended animation" with a naked Big Hunk® in one fist and a hand full of Crows® in the other. The look of fear on his face was as if he had been caught mid-stride in a prison break by the searchlight. I slowly glanced to my left and saw Ronnie Landers in the seat next to me. My glance met his. Neither of us said a word.

"Now, ah'm half a mind to shut down this hyar pitcher and send ya-awl home!" Again a very long pause, while the pressure slowly escaped.

"Now, ya-awl hear me good. When ah turn the lights off again, ah don't wanna hear no mo' screamin' from ya-awl! And, if ah see any ya-awl throwin' so much as one piece-a popcorn, ah'm gonna break ya-awl's arm off. Ya hyar!!! Wahl, do ya?"

There was instantly about one hundred and fifty heads nodding in unison. Yes sir! We all would be real good. There was safety in numbers and none of us at that moment wanted to stand out in the least bit.

The man turned and slowly walked toward the curtain, pausing one last time to indiscriminately throw a scowl around the room for emphasis. Then he passed through the curtain and jerked it closed behind him. There was a slight murmur from all of us heretofore frozen ruffians. I slowly began to chew again and breathe easier.

Doug looked at me and uttered, "Wow, that was scary! I thought he was going to take our names and call mom. She wouldn't let us come anymore."

That was a thought more scary than if the manager had actually beaten us on the spot without mom finding out. Given the choice, we would have taken our medicine gladly so long as doing so did not risk our future at the matinees. The Saturday movies were in our blood.

The light again dimmed, then extinguished, and in a few moments the dancing images were once again displayed on the screen. Dick Tracy® was alive, as were we, and life went on. We never found out how he survived the cliff or the bomb in his car, but within ten minutes he was in another equally serious predicament leaving us gasping as the episode came to a close. We never again sat in our seats so quietly, and yet with so much anxiety restrained within us.

All of the serials had various heroes in various venues. There were Westerns with Hoppalong Cassidy, Johnny Mac Brown, Red Ryder®, and the Lone Ranger, among others. There also were the super heroes such as *Captain Marvel, The Phantom,* and *Batman.* Then there were the spacemen: *Buck Rogers* and *Flash Gordon.* At that time, the term "astronauts" had not yet been invented. There also was a unique, bigger-than-life serial character, a man of the jungle named *Tarzan* (the "Ape Man"). He, too, was a very important and well-liked hero by all of us kids.

THE MAIN FEATURE

After the serial, came the main feature, the movie of the day. The movies shown in the matinees were about 60–70 minutes in length, shorter than today's standard film. That length was about the maximum attention span we could hold, especially after all of the previous emotion-draining first features. Also, midway through the main feature, our candy, drinks, and popcorn either had been consumed, spilled on our seats, or magically through gravity had found their way onto the floor and under our feet. By then, the theater floor took on the tackiness of fly-paper. Even we kids were repulsed by the general "gooeyness" of our surroundings.

The crunchy noises from kids trying to navigate their way to the restrooms were sufficient enough to disrupt our ability to hear the dialogue. By the end of the movie, we were anxious to get out of the place and clean the bottom of our shoes by scraping them on the sidewalk.

A mystery to me was how they cleaned the theater after the matinees. I suspected that behind the screen there was a secret large drain in the floor, and as soon as we kids were out, firemen came in and hosed out the whole place. How everything was then dried and made ready for the evening shows was beyond me.

The most popular matinee movies were Westerns, and a whole genre of these "B" grade films, as they were called, were cranked out by Republic, RKO, Universal, and a few other Hollywood studios during the period of, say, 1932–1955. Hundreds of them! In the trade they were referred to as "horse operas" and "oaters" (horses eat oats). They had similar formulas as the serials and the same general appeal. The formula involved good guys, the heroes, who typically were fair-skinned, clean, honest, and able to walk upright with good posture. The good guys always had a partner or trusty sidekick in a subservient position, sort of a *Sherlock Holmes* and *Dr. Watson* relationship.

Then there were their counterparts, the bad guys, and I do mean "guys" because there were not many female villains. Women always seemed to either play passive roles, or line up on the "good" side of the ledger.

The bad guys were generally darker skinned, sometimes with a "five-o'clock shadow," less intelligent, shifty-eyed, hunched, and often too slick for their own good. They were usually liars, cheats, and scoundrels, and they had a monopoly on those characteristics. The bad guys seldom acted alone and often had a gang of helpers. Sometimes Indians were involved as foils between good and bad, but not always. The bad guys tried to unfairly exploit people who couldn't protect themselves, and the heroes were there to restore decency, uphold the law, and right all wrongs. "Good" always triumphed over "Bad," but not without some crazy twists and turns along the way.

The other matinee genre was comedy. We loved *Abbott and Costello* and they always played to packed houses. Also big were *Laurel and Hardy*, even though they were generally older and were outdated by this time. However, they were still hilarious. *Dean Martin and Jerry Lewis* movies were fairly new and a little more grown up for our taste than the oaters.

When the movie finally ended, and the lights came up again, we filed outside fully sated and satisfied that the world was good. Our heroes had again outsmarted the bad guys and had escaped any present danger. It gave us hope that we, too, could make it through another week, before we could return for another date with afternoon mayhem.

My favorite movie treat . . . I still enjoy them today.

PART FOUR

SPECIAL HEROES

16

TARZAN

Habutu bamba! Um-gowa!!!
—Natives' movie dialogue translated
(we think) as "Man! Can that guy swim!!!"

Tarzan was a favorite hero to all of us kids. He was a good-looking white guy (a natural requirement for any action hero at the time) who ran around the jungle wearing only a loincloth. He lived in the trees and swung through the jungle on hanging vines, which always happened to be conveniently placed an arm's length away, and, of course, always supported his full weight without breaking. We always wondered about that. He had a knife tucked into his loincloth and with it he could fend off any danger. Danger always came from the bad hunters (also white guys) who were poaching ivory or stealing gold from the (black) natives' burial grounds, or something equally no good.

Danger also came from the bad natives, who often were indistinguishable from the good natives, being that they all looked like black guys carrying spears and speaking in native "mumbo-jumbo." Each sentence seemed to always end with the words, "Um-gowa!" Tarzan was also called "Buwanna" by all the locals. We thought it meant "King of the Jungle," but who could be sure? It might have meant "naked white guy."

Tarzan had a mate, named *Jane,* although the relationship was never fully explained. She wore an outfit that conveniently covered only the main essentials, and as the serial episodes increased in number her outfits seemed to get increasingly skimpy, which we

number her outfits seemed to get increasingly skimpy, which we
boys liked very much. Eventually, both Tarzan and Jane wore thongs
that left their whole thighs and sides completely open for viewing!
These thongs were magically held in place with a single leather tie
that went around their waist. Talk about exciting—the bare skin
for us in the audience, and for Tarzan and Jane the prospect of
instantly being fully exposed if that single string should have . . .
say, a "wardrobe malfunction." ·

Tarzan and Jane eventually had a son, whom they named *Boy*.
Even we kids knew that if they later had a daughter, her name
would be . . . perhaps . . . "Girl"? The family was completed with
their chimpanzee, whose name was *Cheetah*—go figure. I always
thought there must also be a cheetah roaming around the jungle
with the name "Chimpanzee." How would he explain that to his
fellow Cheetah friends? Their son Boy we understood, but Cheetah
was a puzzle for us; we couldn't understand if he was a pet or an
adopted "son," because he certainly had a greater role than just as pet.

There were times when Cheetah seemed to have an IQ of 180
because Tarzan and Cheetah talked often, much more than Tarzan
and Boy. The magic of this "communication" was explained because
Tarzan had been raised by the apes, and he understood their "language." Jane went along with whatever occupied Tarzan; she was
the perfect subservient heroine, always looking darned good in her
outfit. There were always hoots and hollers, and popcorn in the
air, when Jane came on screen, especially when we could get a
side view.

There was one very distinguishing detail about Tarzan—his
"jungle cry." He could call bull elephants at will, or get the attention
of native tribes in the next county, by simply putting his hand up
to his mouth and emitting a bellowing call. It sounded like a cross
between a Pavarotti-like yodel and the cry of a Howler monkey. It
was inspiring, and alarming, at the same time—the ultimate jungle
telegram.

The story of Tarzan was ageless, and the character was portrayed
by many different actors through the years. The most famous Tarzan
of all was the one we were privileged to watch—Johnny Weismuller.

To us kids in the early 1950s he *was* Tarzan, and not just an actor playing Tarzan. We believed.

In real life and prior to becoming an actor, Johnny Weismuller had been an Olympic swimming champion, and was probably the best swimmer in the world up to that time. Becoming Tarzan was a "natural" because, other than jungle vine swinging, Tarzan's main mode of transportation was swimming. There was always a river handy, even in the middle of the jungle, and Tarzan dove in and swam as though he had an outboard motor connected to his side. There never was a single alligator that could catch him; the man was mythical. The impression was that he could put Jane, Cheetah, and Boy on his back, and still go like a Chris-Craft®. All the rivers had falls, and we suspected that Tarzan could also swim *up* the falls if necessary.

Since we identified Johnny Weismuller the man so closely with Tarzan the character, it was a great shock to all of us when, during the same period, another collection of serials and movies were created about a character named *Jungle Jim*. And the person playing Jungle Jim was . . . Johnny Weismuller. Talk about an identity crisis!

We went to the matinees and saw a Tarzan movie one week, followed by a Jungle Jim movie the next week, and both characters were played by Johnny Weismuller. We were beside ourselves with confusion. It was as if we were being forced to choose, and we all knew our votes were with Tarzan. He was my favorite vine swinger, until *Spiderman* came along many decades later. Our worst fear at the time was that we would see a Tarzan movie and Jungle Jim would be a character in the story, and then both characters would be played by Johnny Weismuller. Our minds were in overload mode. It was too much to think about. But we came back faithfully every Saturday.

Jane, and Johnny Weismuller
as Tarzan. Notice the
open sides of their loincloths.

Johnny Weismuller as Jungle Jim.
The young boy is thinking, "Wow!
You look a lot like Tarzan!"

17

FLASH GORDON

We've got to save planet Earth . . . and get home alive!!!

The king, absolutely *the King*, of all Saturday matinee serials was "Flash Gordon." Flash was the first interplanetary space traveler I remember. And his mission was . . . right . . . to fight evil and save Planet Earth! Flash was not only your typical handsome white guy, but he also had a handsome head of very blond wavy locks. A strange thing about his hair was that it seemed to get blonder as the episodes wore on; either he was prematurely aging or space was filled with ethereal oxidizing agents.

Here is a short summary of the entire thirteen episodes. To watch these all at one time would have taken about four-and-a-half hours. To read this summary will take considerably less time, but unfortunately will not convey the true depth of drama and emotions experienced by us kids while drooling over every gripping scene with a Big Hunk® in our mouths.

Flash is an All-American idol because he happens to be a Yale graduate and world famous polo player, something the average American probably had trouble relating to in 1936 when the serial was made. He is flying in a small plane with his girlfriend *Dale*

Arden, who is a smashing beauty, also with wavy blonde hair. She often says things like, "Oh, my," and she always has a shocked expression on her face to convey suspense and impending danger. She also faints quite often for emphasis. But she loves Flash, and that counts more than anything.

Suddenly, they encounter terrible air turbulence. It's so bad they decide to bail out. Two parachutes are behind their seats. Flash and Dale come down in the backyard of *Dr. Alexi Zarkov.* He is a brilliant scientist, who looks like one of the Smith Brothers® cough drop guys, with full beard. Dr. Zarkov is building a spaceship in his backyard. I swear! The reason is that he has discovered there is a wandering planet named "Mongo," approaching Earth with death and destruction in its plan. Mongo is the force behind all of the turbulent air, earthquakes, and erupting volcanoes now plaguing Earth.

Dr. Zarkov talks Flash and Dale into going with him to Mongo, to try to divert it from destroying Earth. The spaceship resembles a large silver pickle with fins. On its front is an appendage that looks like *Pinocchio's* nose after about an hour of lying. The spaceship emits sparks and smoke from its tail. Additionally, it travels on a clearly visible wire, wobbling from side to side. Even we kids recognized it as one of the phoniest models ever made. Every scene where the model, excuse me, "space ship," was sliding down or up the wire was met with jeers, boos, and waves of thrown popcorn, candies, etc. We wanted to believe, and we were willing to accept almost anything except this bit of trickery. We were gullible, but not stupid. We took bets during the show that the entire model, sparks and smoke included, probably cost the studio no more than the price of our admission.

But on with the story! The threesome land on Mongo and are immediately captured and taken to the Emperor of Mongo, "Ming the Merciless!" Ming is one of the most evil baddies in the history of filmdom up to that time. He is bald with a sinister very dark Fu Manchu moustache, and wears a cape, with an outlandishly large collar framing his head. And he really *is* nasty! He has never been known to smile, and you get the feeling that if he ever does, his face will instantly shatter. Ming is the cause of all of Earth's problems and his mission is to destroy Earth by crashing Mongo into it. Why this will not also damage the planet Mongo is not explained. Ming immediately hates our fearsome trio because their overall goodness is a threat to his imperial evil.

But Ming softens regarding Dr. Zarkov, whom he recognizes as a fellow genius of science. He sends Zarkov to his own special laboratory where they both can later work calculus problems together. While waiting for Ming, Zarkov single-handedly finds a way to redirect Mongo, and Earth is saved.

Ming has a daughter, *Princess Aura,* who commands our attention from the very first scene she enters. We know something special has happened because every mouth in the theatre goes silent the second Princess Aura appears. She is tall, with dark almost black, wonderfully curly hair, and has black arching eyebrows on a remarkably attractive face. Above the waist she wears something similar to a sports bra, but with decorative piping sewn around the straps and edges. Most of her shoulders and all of her arms and midriff are bare, displaying beautiful creamy white skin.

All of the bare skin focuses your attention on the bra . . . and its contents! The bra envelops two wondrous mounds of what can only be described as bountiful pulchritude. You could easily say that Princess Aura's cups runneth over, so to speak. And . . . each cup seems to move freely without the restriction of an underlying support.

The immediate effect was to cause every mouth to drop open (and chocolate drool to again appear). Even though we all were young boys, we still took notice, and I remember thinking, Whoa . . . if this is what evil looks like, I could get used to it!

Once you moved past the bra, you then noticed that below the waist she wore an ankle-length skirt. You never saw her legs, but who cared? She glided when she walked, but each step still produced a mesmerizing jiggle in both sides of the bra. Princess Aura, alone, was enough to make us want to see the whole thirteen episodes. No women's costume created more visual impact until Linda Carter appeared many years later as *Wonder Woman.*

Two romantic attractions are instantly kindled when the heroic threesome are ushered into Ming's court. Princess Aura immediately develops the "hots" for our hero, and as such she figuratively drips venom toward Dale, her competition. She wants Flash, but makes it clear that she will kill both Flash and Dale if she can't have him. Flash is ambivalent toward Aura, true to his purity. The second, equally dastardly attraction, is by Ming . . . for Dale. He lusts and makes plans for her to become his future wife, to which, Dale flashes one of her shocked expressions and says, "Oh, my."

Ming effectively drugs Dale with his "dehumanizer" ray—the fiend!—and she is taken away to be prepared for the wedding. When she next appears, and for the balance of the serial, she also has been transformed into the "harem girl" look. Now, she, too, is wearing a costume with open midriff and a long veil skirt that nevertheless fits tightly across her butt. Her breasts also seem to be more prominent. Her hair, previously pinned, is now free and flowing, and even more blonde. She's still virginal and pure, compared to Princess Aura, who is more forceful and uninhibited.

With Earth now saved from destruction, the focus of the plot shifts to the struggles for Dale's virtue, Aura's desire for Flash, Ming's sovereignty, and Flash's need to solve all issues and make everything work out in the end. Along the way he is forced to fight a vast array of creatures and beasts among whom are the fanged men, the hawk men, the shark men, the lion men, the monkey men, a large simian creature called the *Orangapoid* (a monkey with a rhinoceros horn in the middle of his forehead), a tentacled creature called the *Octosak*, the *Gocko*—a fire-breathing dragon with huge claw-arms of a lobster, and on and on. . . . Each time he is near defeat and death, but miraculously survives at the beginning of the next episode. All of these struggles take place in venues such as the "Arena of Death," the "Tunnel of Terror," the "Underground River," the "Atom Furnace," the "Execution Room," the "Static Room," and so on. . . . On more than one occasion Flash is saved by Aura, to reaffirm her love (lust). For example, she kills the Orangapoid with a simple spear.

This struggle brings us kids to a crescendo of screaming excitement because not only is a very present danger extinguished, but Aura's chest is also jiggling and heaving like there is no tomorrow. Whew!

Dr. Zarkov assists Flash by developing rays in his spare time in the lab. He magically creates a ray for whatever application is needed. Some examples are rays to disintegrate matter, rays to cause memory loss, rays to restore memory, rays to make matter invisible, rays to make matter visible, melting rays, gravity defying rays, etc. And, to counter any ray, there is also a very special "resisto-force," which is handy to have in most situations but, as you might suspect, is often in very short supply. Dr. Zarkov is always working on making more. Ming never catches on, despite his awareness of everything else.

The serial ends when Ming, finally on the run, escapes to the Sacred Palace of the Great God Tao. The High Priest announces Ming's death, and Flash and Aura believe it completely. Princess Aura is now ruler of Mongo and in her benevolence allows Flash, Dale, and Dr. Zarkov to return to Earth.

They board the spaceship and, amid much sparks and smoky outpouring, the ship wobbles up the wire. But . . . a bomb has been planted onboard. Not to worry! Once in outer space, Flash finds it, opens the door, and tosses it outside just in time. Whew, another close one! They land in New York amid a ticker-tape celebration. Flash kisses Dale, and Earth is safe again. Everybody can exhale.

It should have been apparent through the above synopsis that Flash Gordon actually was produced with a much larger audience in mind than sub-thirteen-year-olds at matinees. In fact, the whole serial also became a staple of evening movies, to pull in the adults with its overt sexuality and time-worn clichés. There was something for everybody, not only Princess Aura and Dale for the guys, but also many scenes of Flash, his beefy chest naked as he fought one peril after another in the "Tournaments of Death." Also, he always wore very tight short shorts that appeared to have been sprayed on.

Even as young boys we often let our imaginations run wild as to what Princess Aura looked like with nothing on. We were drawn to her jiggle and we fantasized about her, even if Flash Gordon didn't because he was too pure. Neither my brother Doug nor I suffered from that affliction.

The original Flash Gordon serial was so successful that it was followed with two sequels that were equally as good, "Flash Gordon's Trip to Mars" and "Flash Gordon Conquers the Universe."

POSTSCRIPT ONE

One of the true testaments of our ability as kids to separate fantasy from reality came with Flash Gordon's real life name. We knew Flash was a mythical character, but we still were consumed totally by him as our hero. He became my alter ego on most important things I understood about life then, as an eight- to twelve-year-old. At that time he was *Han Solo, James Bond,* and *Indiana Jones* all rolled into one. He captured all of our dreams and imagination, and he lived with us all during the week while we waited for each Saturday injection of excitement that came from seeing another serial episode at the matinee. But every time the credits came on at the beginning of the episodes, we all were reminded that Flash Gordon, our fictional superhero, was played by a real live man whose name was Buster Crabbe. Buster Crabbe! You've got to be kidding!!!

Those two names never fit for us. I only knew of one other Buster and that was "Buster Brown" on the Saturday morning television show. He was a mythical spokesman (spokeskid?) for children's shoes with the same name.

Crabbe! It conjured up such negative images. Why "Buster Crabbe"? Why couldn't his real name be Rock Steele, or James Hero, or something similar? But Buster Crabbe—never! John Wayne—now that was a real name that we all loved.

POSTSCRIPT TWO

The part of Princess Aura was played by a very attractive starlet named Priscilla Lawson. She made twenty movies, mostly all "B" grade, before joining the armed services during the Second World

War. Unfortunately, while in service, she lost one of her legs in a jeep accident. She never returned to Hollywood, and died in August 1958 at age forty-four.

Flash and Dale before their journey to Planet Mongo.

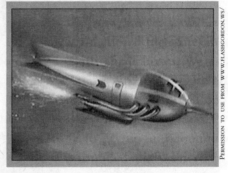

Flash's space ship, a "silver pickle" with fins.

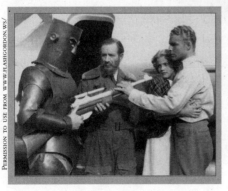

Dr. Zarkov, Dale, and Flash captured on Mongo by a Mechanical Man. We kids knew we could build the Mechanical Man's suit with scrap metal and buckets found in our own neighborhood. Only Dale is convinced this guy is a real threat.

Ming the Merciless, Emperor of Mongo—the most sinister villian in the Saturday matinees. His robe with imperial collar, mustache, beard, arching eyebrows, and menacing stare all conveyed evil.

Flash and Princess Aura in Ming's castle.
Notice the Disintegrator Ray.
We boys were captivated by Princess Aura, and despite the danger, would have traded places with Flash in an instant! She was a temptress—turned heroine—and we wanted her by *our* sides.

Dale is drugged and prepared to wed Ming.

The "new" Dale and her "harem girl" look.

Dale, Princess Aura, and Flash in an anxious moment.

The Gocko in the "Tunnel of Terror."

Oh, the terror!
I sense a faint coming on.

Princess Aura and
Flash spend a few last
moments together.

Princess Aura says "goodbye" to Flash.
She tells him to buy a cape with a smaller collar
upon his return to Earth. He listens intently.

18

"HI-YO SILVER, AWAY. . . . "

Who was that masked man?
—from *The Lone Ranger*

My all-time favorite television show—the one show I could not wait to see each week was the "Lone Ranger." There was something special about him, as well as his partner, Tonto. The Lone Ranger always dressed as if he was going to a Saturday night square dance, wearing a pullover Western shirt with large collars. The shirt front was laced with a thick black string from below the sternum up to the open neck. A scarf was tied around his neck, the ends flying out in the wind. His pants were tight fitting and were of similar looking material as the shirt, almost Spandex-like, without a single wrinkle. It was as if his outfit had been designed in a wind tunnel. The shirt and pants were all the same color, light gray, which looked silvery on television.

The shirt and the pants were bisected with a thick dark-leather belt, capped with a silver tip inserted through a silver buckle. Hanging below the pants belt was another silver encrusted thick belt, with an even larger silver buckle and studded with very shiny bullets. Hanging off this belt was a silver-decorated holster on both hips, each filled with a sparkling "six-gun," as they were called. These were not the everyday working kind of pistols with wooden handles that later "real" cowboys would tote in the so-called "adult" Westerns. No, these were glorious works of art, with silvery shining barrels and brilliant pearl handles that reflected the sun when the Lone Ranger walked. These were pistols that would have made General George Patton launch another desert campaign. If you were a bad guy, you were already intimidated at seeing the Lone Ranger's guns sparkle when he rode into town.

Sitting on his head was a classy Western hat, also appearing to be silver in color. It had a wide brim and a flattened top with a slight peak in the front. He looked veeerrryy masculine, as if single-handedly he had captured a monopoly on all of the best male genes in mankind's pool. He would have made Darwin proud. And he walked with a swagger that conveyed he was a man of action seeking justice, much like John Wayne, but with less of that side-ways sway that was Wayne's characteristic. I always was impressed. Someday, I definitely wanted to get an outfit like his and saunter around as though I owned the world.

He was the Western "messiah" to the everyday townspeople; in case there happened to be any evil around, he was there to deal with it. He looked like what today would be called a "cool dude," although, strangely enough, at that time the word "dude" would not have been complimentary.

The Lone Ranger wore a mask, which was against the trend, because in every other Western, only the bad guys wore masks. That was how you knew right away that they were the bad guys. The Lone Ranger's mask was a dark band that covered his eyebrows to about half of his nose. It was drawn back above his ears, and tied in the back of his head. It had two large holes for eyes, but not like the little openings that were typically seen in Halloween masks.

You could see all of the Lone Ranger's eyes and sockets, and this made the purpose of the mask a mystery because it left very little to the imagination as to what his complete face looked like. However, it was his defining garment and it stood out. And it always prompted the mental question: "What is he hiding? Dandruff? Pre-mature gray temples? A massive uni-brow?" It was not clear, and I cannot recall that it was ever explained. It was just the way it was, period! The Lone Ranger was a masked (good) guy.

The last wardrobe oddity about the Lone Ranger was that he

always wore tight-fitting leather gloves. It could be 118 degrees in the shade and he still wore his gloves, even when walking around in the saloon looking for scurrilous characters of no good, or inside the church talking with the town mothers. We also wondered about this. We could understand it when he rode his horse hard, because his horse was a high-spirited steed, which could rear up at a moment's notice.

Maybe the Lone Ranger was afraid of dangerous rope burns from grasping the reins. But even the Lone Ranger had to have "time off"—those moments when he was just sitting around working a crossword puzzle, or drinking an Oly. Surely his gloves were not needed for those times. We suspected he even slept with them on, and also wore them when he took a bath. Why did he always wear the gloves? Maybe he had a skin rash—psoriasis of the hands—and was embarrassed beyond belief.

By the way, as kids, we always heard about "the heartbreak of psoriasis," but not a single one of us had ever seen anybody with psoriasis, or even knew what it was! But, whatever it was, we suspected that the Lone Ranger was secretly afflicted. Or maybe he really was a Walt Disney actor, and we knew all Walt Disney characters only had four fingers on each hand. Maybe he was hiding this from us. Maybe some day someone would accidentally rip off one of his gloves and we would discover that the Lone Ranger had only four fingers! Wouldn't we be surprised? But, gloves or no gloves, he was still one of our main television role models.

Even though he never dressed like a cow-punching working cowboy, but rather more like a "Sunday-go-to-meeting" cowboy, when called upon he could still fight the bad guys forever—rolling around in the dirt, smacking the other guys through break-away fences and saloon doors galore. It was just that he never became dirty or had a hair out of place. In fact, as I recall, his hat never came off. It was as if it was virtually Velcro®-ed to his scalp, although that was a material that came into being many years after the Lone Ranger's last roundup.

The Lone Ranger was rich too. We knew that because he owned his very own silver mine, the location of which was a secret. We always hoped we would be able to find it with one of our secret decoder badges, but I don't believe any kid was ever so lucky. Why did he need a silver mine, you ask? Because he was the only cowboy in history who shot silver bullets! And he never missed! Being poor ourselves, we all assumed that the reason he never missed was because his bullets were so expensive and that it had nothing to do with him being the world's most accurate pistol shooter, or because of the show's script for that matter.

Those, also poor, bad guys, with cheap wooden-handled pistols and cheap lead bullets could shoot all day and never hit anything. We knew that one of the reasons was because their bullets were not made of silver. Another reason was because they all fired their pistols with a snapping action of their wrist, as if they were trying to throw the bullet out of the gun's muzzle. That was the way we kids played imaginary "shoot 'em-up" with our cap pistols, but even we knew that you couldn't shoot a real gun like that and expect to hit anything, except maybe your own hat, or your foot accidentally. At least the Lone Ranger held his glimmering "irons" steady when he squeezed off a shot.

We were convinced he owed his success to the silver bullets. In fact, the Lone Ranger liked silver so much he named his horse . . . "Silver!" And what color was his horse? Of course! Silver!!! There was a pattern here. And, as another trivial factoid, the real name of the Indian actor who played Tonto was Jay Silverheels. Get it, *Silver* . . . heels. The man just had a thing for silver.

The show was also distinctive in its format. It opened with one of the greatest "attention getters" in the history of television, even to this day.

The scene: the Lone Ranger riding Silver hard, the horse flying across the prairie at about ninety miles an hour with his mane and gorgeous tail trailing straight out behind, and flinching in a slight shake with every gliding stride as if to display every single beautiful silver hair. Silver probably had been galloping at this pace for forty-five miles, but of course had nary a drop of sweat. Where they were going was never explained, but they sure were in a big hurry.

Playing in the background was one of the most stirring and recognizable scores in the history of music: the *William Tell Overture.* It was not until years later that I discovered this was the title of the piece. We kids all knew it as "the Lone Ranger's song." At any moment if you broke into: *"Dum, diddle-dum, diddle-dum, dum, dum . . ."* every kid—even girls—knew it was the Lone Ranger's song. It just sounded like riding music! To this day, whenever anybody who was a kid during the 1950s hears the *William Tell Overture,* they have to think of the Lone Ranger. *Have* to!

Then, with the French horns blaring, the horseman and steed rode high up into the rocks, and the gallant stallion reared high up on his two hind legs, with his two front legs majestically pawing the air. Atop him, the Lone Ranger was stuck in place as though epoxied to his saddle, and the music *crescendoed.*

Overriding all of this was the deep-toned narrative from Thad Thunderthroat, the announcer—it still rings out, blazed into my memory:

> *. . . A fiery horse, with a speed of light, a cloud of dust, and a hearty . . . Hi-Yo . . . Silverrrrr. . . . Return with us now to those thrilling days of yesteryear. . . . The Lone Ranger rides again!*

The mounted pair then thundered down out of the rocks and disappeared in a mighty cloud of dust while the music faded. Wow! After all of that exciting preamble we were ready for action! Bring it on!

True to form, the Lone Ranger also had a trusty sidekick. Were there ever any non-trusty sidekicks? I doubt it. But the Lone Ranger's was Tonto, an Indian.

Tonto was a serious looking Indian, and handsome in his own right. He wore suede buckskins, pants and tops, with long fringes on the arms and across the front of his tunic. This was a similar look later perpetrated by Kit Carson, Wild Bill Hickok, Davy Crockett, and even *Shane*, in the big-screen adult Western of this period. I guess this look was common at Central Costuming: "You don't want the dress up square-dance shirt? Hmmm. . . . Try these buckskins, they make you look rugged."

To further the look, Tonto had long hair, which today is common but not then. The only man with long hair then was Jesus, and now

Tonto. And Tonto kept it under control. Everything about Tonto conveyed "control," including a headband, a leather thong across his forehead, which was tied in back. I do not recall that he had a feather in it, although the old shoestrings we kids tied around our heads to play Tonto always had at least one feather sticking up in the back. My Uncle Johnny used to tie his own flies for fishing and Doug and I would each steal one of his long feathers for our Tonto headbands. They probably were plucked from pigeons, but to us they definitely came from Bald Eagles.

Tonto was unique. He had an answer for everything, and a manner that, with almost no words, seemed to get the point across that, "Hey, everything is going to be OK." Tonto tended to speak in very minimally structured sentences, often with only nouns and verbs. In every episode he also had a number of lines where he very gruffly said, "Ummmm," which conveyed, "Tonto understands and is much smarter than you think."

He was very effective in conveying confidence. His common line was, *"Me go to town."* Tonto always went to town "to get the information." A well-known comedian did a routine about Tonto always going to town "to get the information," and it just cracked me up because he finally asked the *same question* all of us loyal kids had been asking of Tonto for years—namely, why does *he* always go to town to get the information? Because every time Tonto went to town, he had the living stuffing beaten out of him by the local baddies.

It was the formula: Tonto goes to town, Tonto gets beaten up, Tonto nevertheless comes back with the information; the Lone Ranger gets mad because Tonto was beaten up, the Lone Ranger vows vengeance, and gets even. That seemed to be the story line for every episode.

We used to yell at the television set: "No, Tonto, don't go to town!!! Tell the Lone Ranger to go to town himself; let him get beaten up. At least you know his shirt won't get dirty." We were adamant about it, but Tonto never took our advice. Every single time he went to town and was beaten within an inch of his life. But he never seemed to be angry about it. Just doing his duty, I guess. Maybe he was hanging around to get a piece of the silver mine and knew all of his beatings would one day be rewarded. At least that was the only justification we kids could rationalize.

Also, Tonto had an "endearment" he used for the Lone Ranger. He always called him *"kemo sabe"* (pronounced *"key-mow-saw-bay"*). That was never translated, and we often speculated, that every time Tonto was beaten within a heartbeat of needing trauma-room care, it really meant "dumb-ass," as in the next time the Lone Ranger asked him to go to town, we wanted Tonto to reply, "Tonto *no* go to town. *You* go this time, kemo sabe. Me wait in rocks. Me keep Iodine and Band-Aid®s ready for kemo sabe's return." All of us kids seemed to have our own appropriate translations for kemo sabe.

We all loved Tonto, though, and secretly wished that some day in our lives, we too could enjoy the luxury of having a similar Tonto as our trusty sidekick. Life would be so much easier with a friend like him.

The Lone Ranger and Tonto apparently were never interested in romance. Even in the other Westerns, the heroes sometimes had a kind and special word or two for the town ladies or the ranch matriarch, such as, "Evenin' ma'am. Mighty nice gingham dress you have on there." But the Lone Ranger was all business. He was ferreting out evil both night and day, and was single-minded in that cause. But we could easily imagine that any female in one of the Lone Ranger episodes above the age of sixteen, married or not, must have immediately had the "hots" for him, because he looked so good. He oozed raw testosterone from every pore, even though none of us kids then had a single clue as to what testosterone was. We just knew that he had "a man's man" written all over him, and we all wanted to be just like him.

Even though Tonto's opportunities with the fair sex must have been more limited, since he was a light-year away from the reservation, he still never expressed any warmth, or even a casual look, toward any women. But no, he was only thinking about either the last beating, or the one he knew was coming some day soon the next time he went to town.

There was a also a "signature line" at the end of the show, after the Lone Ranger had caught all of the baddies and he and Tonto had ridden out of town, at high speed.

One of the townspeople always said: *"Who was that masked man?"*

I kid you not! The Lone Ranger and Tonto had been in town for over a week rounding up all of the cattle rustlers, bank robbers and general vermin of no good, and had turned them over to the local (obviously ineffectual) sheriff. Yet, suddenly, this guy in the background says, like *Dopey*: "Duh . . . say, who was that masked man?"

Then somebody else always answered: *"Why, he's* . . . [pause] . . . *the Lone Ranger!"*

The enormous dust cloud from the two horses—galloping like fury—was the last thing you saw as the scene faded to credits. It was thrilling, and every kid slumped back into their sofas—content for another week that the frontier had been scourged of evil and was again safe for Sunday school ma'ams to stroll the streets.

We didn't know if there was a God, but when I was ten years old the Lone Ranger was the next best thing.

POSTSCRIPT

The Lone Ranger had a creed, which were his words for all "good citizens" to live by. We kids never knew them by heart, but we read them on occasion, and we believed whole-heartedly that if the Lone Ranger lived by them, then we should do no less. The "Lone Ranger's Creed" was:

I believe . . .

- That to have a friend, a man must be one.
- That all men are created equal and everyone has within himself the power to make this a better world.
- That God put the firewood there, but every man must gather and light it himself.

- In being prepared physically, mentally, and morally to fight when necessary for that which is right.
- That a man should make the most of what equipment he has.
- That "this government, of the people, by the people and for the people" shall live always.
- That men should live by the rule of what is best for the greatest number.
- That sooner or later . . . somewhere . . . somehow . . . we must settle with the world and make payment for what we have taken.
- That all things change but truth, and that truth alone, lives on forever.
- In my Creator, my country, and my fellow man.

The Lone Ranger and Tonto.

19

ROY ROGERS AND DALE EVANS

Woll . . . thar's galler slurish bon fargor burnum!!!
—attributed to Gabby Hayes
(At least that's what we thought he said.)

My favorite Saturday matinee movie hero, and later my favorite television hero, was, without question, Roy Rogers! Roy was the "King of the Cowboys," and for a unique twist, he paired with his wife Dale Evans, the "Queen of the West." What a combination they were—the only husband and wife Western team! And Dale (Evans) was much more than just another subservient heroine. Compared to the other Dale (Arden), Flash Gordon's companion, Roy's Dale actually had a functioning mind.

She also participated in the action. She helped Roy concoct some of the traps to catch the bad guys, and he validated her ideas as good and of value. Roy always affirmed that Dale was his equal. She also drew *and shot* her six-guns to stop the bad guys in their tracks. The fact that she, a woman, wore six guns was rare in Westerns; the fact that she *used* them as more than a fashion accessory was a breakthrough. She did everything Roy did except engage in fisticuffs with the crooks, but she made up for that by always helping to outsmart them. Yes, Dale Evans was one great woman to have on your side.

This was all new to us boys—a female heroine who had authority and capability. She helped draw in a whole new segment of adoring fans—young girls and women. As a result, Roy and Dale's popularity among the afternoon television and Saturday matinee crowds soared. And it didn't stop there. They became hugely popular to all demographic groups. They both were so downright whole-some and wonderful that all of America loved them, not just us kids. Roy and Dale were ubiquitous: they appeared on radio, in the movies, on television, in the magazines, in every "Rose Parade," you name it. You expected to go to the grocery store and perhaps run into them at the meat counter.

They were so successfully marketed as good and pure "larger than life" heroes that they had an enormous effect on the behavior of all of us kids—boys and girls—their loving fans. Roy had his own "Roy Rogers Rider's Club Rules" for good living, and unlike the "Lone Ranger's Creed," we kids all knew the club rules by heart. They were as close to being an effective "code of conduct" as we ever had at that age. These were far in advance of Robert Fulghum's book, *All I Really Need to Know, I Learned in Kindergarten,* but they were just as effective in influencing our daily lives in the 1950s.

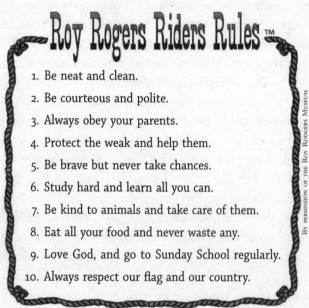

Roy Rogers Riders Rules ™

1. Be neat and clean.
2. Be courteous and polite.
3. Always obey your parents.
4. Protect the weak and help them.
5. Be brave but never take chances.
6. Study hard and learn all you can.
7. Be kind to animals and take care of them.
8. Eat all your food and never waste any.
9. Love God, and go to Sunday School regularly.
10. Always respect our flag and our country.

By permission of the Roy Rodgers Museum

Many Happy Trails
Roy, Dale & Trigger

Roy broke into the entertainment business as a singer, eventually joining with a group called the "Sons of the Pioneers." He had a reasonably good, smooth voice, but his distinction was yodeling. Probably the last time you heard a yodel was in *The Sound of Music* with Julie Andrews, but believe it or not, there was some call for it in the 1930s, 1940s, and even 1950s. I don't know why, but some singing cowboys thought yodeling was a path to stardom, and Roy Rogers was the best cowboy yodeler there was. It offered him an entry into the movies when Republic Studios needed a backup to possibly replace Gene Autry (the original singin' cowboy) in case Gene walked away from his contract. Roy Rogers was thus cast in his first Western in 1937, and the rest is history, as they say.

Dale Evans had a very nice singing voice too, and she and Roy often sang duets together. Their theme song, "Happy Trails," which Dale wrote, became one of the most recognizable songs in America. It was always sung at the close of every Roy Rogers television show. "Happy Trails to you . . . until . . . we meet . . . again. . . ."

You had to have heard it.

Roy Rogers distinguished himself from other lead cowboys of the genre not only by his yodeling, charisma, honesty, and American goodness, but also by his dress. He became one mighty fine dressed up showy cowboy. Whereas some of the cowboy heroes wore buckskins, then even dressier buckskins, then square dance costumes with bandanas, to eventually the sleek, tight, and mono-color very dressy look of the Lone Ranger, Roy Rogers stepped out of that mold, and wore colors galore! Dale eventually followed.

It was a while before I realized this because many of the movies were in black-and-white, and the television shows were also in black-and-white. From these, all that we could see was that he wore many plaids and decorations on his shirts, bandanas, and boots. But one day I finally saw a movie studio promotional picture of Roy and Dale in color. WOW! Both of my retinas instantly went into seizure from sensory overload; too much color! Roy and Dale looked like two rainbows standing side by side. Even their boots were adorned with inlaid leathers of various tints and hues. I could not believe anyone would dress so garishly: it was like peacocks on parade!

From that moment on, they definitely seemed out of place riding into some dusty town dressed like that. They were even overdressed for the "Rose Parade!" But, what the heck, somehow they made it work, and none of the other cast members ever remotely implied there was anything unusual about them. At least the Lone Ranger always heard the "Who was that masked man?" comment, but nothing was ever said toward or about Roy's or Dale's attire.

Their trusty sidekick was George "Gabby" Hayes. Over the years, many great caricatures have been done of Gabby, but he was the "original." Gabby was an older gentleman who looked exactly like the "Old Prospector" stereotype. He had a full-grown, gray and grizzled beard. On his head was the typical prospector's hat that was occasionally flattened in front and folded back. He often wore what looked like long red underwear or plaid shirts. He was very animated and when he talked he flailed his arms around, bobbed his head, and occasionally stamped one of his feet for emphasis. He burned up so much energy in excessive body movements that you suspected he probably napped often.

He obviously felt strongly about anything he had to say. The only problem was that nobody we knew could *understand* a word he said! You see, he had no teeth and all of his words slurred and mushed together. It was as if he had a mouthful of marbles, or Milk Duds, every time he talked. He said the most outlandish things such as, "Migawsh, thars hepps an genixl in th' roks!!!" And his arms would windmill for emphasis like he was about to elevate right off the ground. He would continue: ". . . annn, gettin sormer in the clangger thannng!!!" When done, he would extend his jaw, tilt his head slightly, squint, and maybe stamp his right foot, to convey the importance and urgency of his words. We kids always looked at each other as if to say, "What'd he say? I didn't get it!" But Roy and Dale *always* understood every single word, and instantly responded with alarm and action.

Roy and Dale also had a couple of other sidekicks in their career.

One was Andy Devine, a great old oater character actor. He was a tall, somewhat rotund man with the most distinguishing soprano, screechy voice. Andy meant very well and he was always good for laughs. He could somehow always stumble into the bad guy's lair, or overhear a major clue at the saloon. He, too, went to town often. Andy also later became a trusty sidekick of Guy Madison on another popular television show, *Wild Bill Hickok*. He played a lovable old character named *Jingles*.

Another sidekick for a while, especially on the television series every Sunday night, was Pat Brady. Pat was unique in that he did not ride a horse. Rather, he drove around in a jeep, which he had named "Nellybelle." Obviously, Roy Rogers and Dale Evans had made a leap forward in time from the "Old West" to the "New West," now requiring not only oats for power, but also gasoline. For me, the Nellybelle era never seemed to work as well.

Roy's horse was a majestic looking golden Palomino stallion named "Trigger." He was the smartest horse in the world. In fact, Trigger acquired his name because supposedly when Roy first saw him, Roy thought he was "quick on the trigger." And, Trigger was *multilingual!* He could understand Horse, English, and "Hayesian," which was the language spoken by Gabby Hayes. If Roy told Trigger to move left, Trigger moved left. If Roy told Trigger to move backward, Trigger moved backward. If Roy told Trigger to move left, then right, then cha-cha-cha, you suspected Trigger would do it. It was easy to assume that Trigger worked Rubik cubes in his spare time.

Trigger paired with Roy Rogers for his whole career of eighty-seven movies and over six years of television. In fact, when Trigger finally died, Roy had a taxidermist mount the horse full-size and placed in Roy's living room. Rumor had it that when Dale Evans saw that, she worried that if she were to die before Roy, she would end up in their living room also on display.

The pair also had a German Shepherd named "Bullet." He was referred to as the "Wonder Dog." Bullet not only was a Mensa partner with Trigger, but he could run faster than any dog on earth, and farther too. Roy could say, "Bullet, go get the jail keys in Abilene," and off Bullet would go at about sixty miles an hour.

It didn't matter that his starting point was Denver! Sometimes Pat Brady would be driving Nellybelle and Bullet would be running alongside or behind. Bullet would be running like fury, with his tongue hanging down to his front knees, and we always thought, How strange? Why doesn't Bullet ride *in* the jeep? It made us question just how smart Bullet actually was. "Rin-Tin-Tin" was the most famous German Shepherd in history prior to Bullet, but he became a has-been after Roy Rogers and crew took over the matinees.

Of all our heroes—the spacemen, the cowboys, the Indians, the jungle characters, you name it—our favorites, without question, were Roy Rogers and Dale Evans. And why was that? We never consciously understood it at the time, but the reason was because they were *real* people. Roy Rogers and Dale Evans were not actors playing characters, much like the Lone Ranger, Tonto, Tarzan, Flash Gordon, and all of the others. No, they *were* Roy Rogers and Dale Evans in real life, they just happened to *juxtapose* themselves back into the Old West.

Logically, it made no sense. But we, and the rest of America, never cared. They appealed to us as people—wonderful, wholesome people. And if they wanted to play themselves for our fantasies, in a made-up story, somewhere in a prior time, we could accept it. They were the only action heroes who tried and succeeded in that transition. In fact, they were so uniquely loved they were the only ones who could have pulled it off.

And it wasn't just them, it was the whole cast. They were all lovable and believable. Yes, we couldn't understand a thing Gabby said, but he still was funny, and he said whatever he said with such convincing emotion that we just had to accept it. Yes, Andy Devine was not a typical side-kick. He was large, overweight, slow, bumbling, and his high-pitched screechy voice grated on us. Listening to Andy talk was like listening to a eunuch on helium. But still he was lovable, in a way that Tonto wasn't. For as much as we loved Tonto for his trustworthiness, he was difficult to connect with emotionally as a real person—he was an Indian *actor, playing* an Indian. Andy was Andy, though. It was the same for Pat Brady. He was both Pat Brady in real life and Pat Brady in the Roy Rogers shows. We knew it and we accepted it.

Lastly, Trigger and Bullet were not just Hollywood animal actors! No, they were Roy's and Dale's real live pets, who lived with them daily, went out to shopping centers with them, and rode with them in the "Rose Parade." They, too, were special, and most importantly, they were part of the believability that worked so well.

The ultimate compliment for Roy and Dale was that they became our ideals. They were everything good about life, and adults, and parents, and America. For us kids, if we could have had our choice of who we wanted to live with, it would have been Roy Rogers and Dale Evans. Everything about them conveyed honesty, goodness, Godliness, family values, love, charity, warmth—whatever adjectives you describe. They were the perfect ambassadors of American ideals in the 1950s. We never had better role models, for us children, or for our country.

POSTSCRIPT

We shared our lives with Roy Rogers and Dale Evans weekly, into the mid-1950s. But my mom had a special affinity with Dale. In real life, Roy and Dale had a daughter who died a couple of years after birth from complications of Down's Syndrome. Dale then wrote a bestselling book about the experience, "*Angel Unaware: A Touching Story of Love and Loss.*" While we were living in the projects, mom gave birth to her fourth child, my half-sister. She died less than three days after birth from a heart defect. One of the few things that helped mom through that tragedy was the many times she read Dale Evans' book.

Roy Rogers and
Dale Evans.

Gabby Hayes.

Trigger and Roy Rogers.

20

ANOTHER MAGICAL AFTERNOON:
SOME HEROES ARE REAL

When I was a small boy growing up in Kansas, a friend of mine and I went fishing and as we sat there in the warmth of a summer afternoon on a riverbank we talked about what we wanted to do when we grew up. I told him that I wanted to be a major-league baseball player. My friend said that he'd like to be President of the United States. Neither of us got our wish.
— Dwight D. Eisenhower

Whether the heroes we discovered and enjoyed throughout our childhood came to us from the Friday night drive-in movies, radio, television, or from the Saturday afternoon movie matinees, each and every one of them stoked our imaginations. Most heroes were fictional, we knew that, but still we pretended. But then . . . once in a while . . . rarely . . . we found a hero who *was real,* and who allowed us *to catch a dream,* and make that dream real. I discovered this for myself, very unexpectedly, one sunny afternoon, and I have carried that reality with me my entire life.

My mother let me ride the Seattle metropolitan bus system alone when I was eight-and-a-half years old. I became very good at it. I had a bus schedule and I could look up any line in the whole system. I could also figure out how to get where I wanted to go, and how to get home again. I learned about transfers and tokens and how to play the system. I learned that for a little amount of money (and that was exactly how much I had) I could plan an excursion and go. It gave me a great deal of freedom, much as kids today have when they finally get their driver's license.

An issue to disrupt my plans was whether the buses actually ran on time. But that was something beyond my control. I learned that **if you miss a bus, another will come along soon,** one more of life's great lessons.

I ventured out slowly, taking short trips, but after a couple of months I had it all down pat. Heck, if old people with most of their possessions in shopping bags, with drool running down their chins, and with invisible people engaging them in animated conversations, could ride and master the Seattle bus system, I could too. After all, I was in the third grade and I could do the multiplication tables up to nine!

Having learned this transportation skill, I now wished to employ it on my passion for baseball. In the early 1950s there was no major-league baseball on the West Coast of the United States. The small numbers of teams at the major-league level were all on the East Coast. Out West, we also had adult baseball but it was minor-league. This Pacific Coast League played the equivalent of what today would be called AAA, or "triple-A" ball. Seattle had a team in this PCL, the Seattle Rainiers.

I loved my Seattle Rainiers! Radio carried only some of the games, so the majority of my news about the Rainiers occurred when I could find a discarded newspaper and locate the sports section. Sometimes the news I read was three or four days old, but it didn't matter to me.

I came to have a great appreciation of the skills of all the players in the league. I read the box scores and the statistics and knew who was doing well, and who was in a slump. In 1951, the Rainiers had the best player in the league. His name was Jimmy Rivera. From my reading I knew when he had hit an important home run or had picked somebody off base with a great throw at a key juncture of a game. He was my idol. Just reading about his accomplishments and listening to an occasional game on the radio had my imagination fully engaged. Jimmy Rivera to me was the embodiment of everything that was good about baseball, and the fact that he was the leader of our own team, was . . . well . . . almost heaven sent.

I desperately wanted to go to a game, but my step-dad never went where there were crowds. His idea of a great time was for all of us to get in the car on a Sunday afternoon and go for a drive, cruising through the arboretum or somewhere similar. They were dreadfully boring times, and both my brother Doug and I came to appreciate the family drives as much as a dental appointment.

I, on the other hand, loved the energy of crowds! I liked to be where there were people interacting and having a good time. I loved the movies. I loved riding my bike to the main street of Columbia. I especially liked riding the bus to downtown Seattle and wandering among the large buildings where real shopping was done.

I imagined that the one place where I could be part of a good crowd, and also enjoy my favorite sport, was the baseball park. I had talked myself into a journey to see the Rainiers play. One day I brought it up with mom and asked if I could go to a baseball game on a Saturday afternoon. I showed her the bus schedule and talked her through my afternoon's plan on how to get there, how to get into the game, and how to get home. Everything!

Mom asked, "How much will it cost?" I expected that question, since it always was her first question on any proposal. I detailed my answer.

"To ride the bus is a dime, twenty cents round trip. To get into the game is a quarter. To buy a program is a dime, and then I need another dime for two pieces of candy," I said.

She was no fool about money and said, "Sounds like it's about twice the cost of the movies."

"Yeah but . . . that's only because I have to take the bus, and I want to get a program and some candies."

Kids always had "yeah, buts." Even my own children, a few decades later, would throw a "yeah but" into an argument. Children are universal.

I wanted the game's program because it had pictures of the players and it had reams of statistics: tables on batting averages, hits, homers, runs batted in, earned run averages, and on and on—stuff I could dwell on for weeks and memorize as well as any CIA spy memorized his secret codes. This was critically important minutia and was worth far more than a dime! There was no response from mom.

"What if I didn't get the program?" I asked. Still nothing.

"What if I didn't get the candy?" I asked, although that thought struck me as a major sacrifice. "Then the only extra is the cost of the bus rides. Could I do it then? Could you give me the money for just the bus and the price to get in? Could ya, mom . . . huh . . . could ya?" I pleaded. It was obvious I was desperate and running out of negotiating chips. "If dad could take me down, then I wouldn't have to ride the bus to get there and we could save another dime."

Mom thought for a few minutes while she went about her cooking. I trailed, waiting for her to say something. Finally, she stopped and waved a spatula at me.

"I'll tell you what," she said. "You're going on nine years old now and you should be able to make some of your own decisions. I'll start giving you a weekly allowance of forty cents instead of the thirty cents I give you now for the movies. You can do whatever you want with the allowance. If you want to use some of it for the movies, you can do that. If you want to use it to go to the ballpark, you can do that. If you want to save any of it, you can do that too. It's your money. What do you think of that? Do you understand how that works?"

Wow did I! I wasn't brilliant, but I wasn't stupid either. An allowance! What a great idea! It was like I had landed my first job, only I didn't have to do anything for it, other than "be good." I had some regular money now—*and this is the best part*—I could make my own decisions about how to spend it! What independence! It was wonderful! I sat at the kitchen table and figured. After a few minutes of simple addition and subtraction, I realized that I couldn't do everything I wanted, but, **as long as you don't overspend, you can do most of what you want.** What a great lesson in life that was! I was elated.

I said, "Thanks mom. But, what about Doug? Will he get an allowance too? Can he go to the baseball games with me?"

Mom said, "I guess he should get an allowance too, but he can't ride the bus with you. He's six and he's still too young. We'll make his allowance thirty cents, just like I give him for the movies."

"But that's no different than now," I countered.

"Yes it is," she said, "he doesn't have to go to the movies and he still gets it. It's his decision to spend it or not!" Aha, now I understood. It was a done deal, and both Doug and I began to get a weekly allowance from our mom. I began to plan for a day at the ballpark.

The Rainiers played at Sick's Stadium. We had occasionally gone by it when out for our Sunday drives so I knew where it was and how to get there on the bus. It was built by Emil Sick, who owned the Rainier Brewery, which produced the other popular local beer besides Olympia. It was one of the first minor-league stadiums built of steel and concrete, similar to those built for major-league ball on the East Coast. The seating capacity was nearly 12,000, and the Rainiers in the early 1950s had the largest seasonal attendance in America for any minor-league team. The stadium looked huge from the outside. It had a large concrete-arced edifice with its name spelled out across the top front of the walls in giant upper-case black letters against a white background. I couldn't wait to see it from the inside!

The day finally came in late May when all of the stars in the universe aligned for my first real baseball game. The weather was sunny with a beautiful blue sky, and the temperature was balmy. There was no wind; it was a beautiful day. I had planned all of the details for two weeks in advance. Mom packed me a lunch and I stuffed it inside my jacket pocket. I wore my Rainiers baseball hat that my Uncle Johnny had given me a year earlier. I couldn't get any of the other Alderwood Court gang members to go with me. Their parents either wouldn't let them, or they didn't have the money.

The Rainiers were playing the San Francisco Seals, and I was ready. After all of the games I had played on the school playgrounds and the open fields near the projects, I was finally going to see a real baseball field! I was so excited that morning I could barely eat my breakfast.

I said goodbye to Doug and my mom and walked over to Empire Way to the bus stop. When the bus came, I climbed on, dropped a dime in the coin hopper, and announced to the driver, "I'm going to Sick's Stadium."

"Going to take in some baassee ball?" he said, dragging it out with a big smile on his face, probably secretly wishing he could be doing the same instead of driving his bus around all day.

"Yep!" I said. "We're gonna play the Seals. I hope we get a win!"

I sat down in a front seat and watched the cross streets go by. Finally, the park loomed ahead and grew larger as we approached. I stood up and waited for the bus to roll to a complete stop. When the doors accordioned open, I jumped down and both feet hit the surface of an enormous parking lot. Half the bus emptied behind me.

"Have a great time, sonny," said the driver. "Eat a hot dog for me."

I looked back grinning at him and thought, I just might do that. I've got sixty-five cents in my pocket and I'm going to have a great time!

My heart raced. I finally was at the park! I felt I had crossed an imaginary threshold to bigger and better things in my life; I was going to see a real baseball game, live, played by professionals! I walked with others toward the stadium and saw four ticket booths in front. I stepped in line and waited behind a man with his two sons. They all were happy and were also enjoying the anticipation of a wonderful afternoon at the ballpark. One of the kids was about my age and the other I assumed was his older brother. Both wore baseball gloves.

Then it occurred to me, darn, I should have brought my mitt! I knew baseballs flew into the crowds from foul balls. And, if you could get the ball, you didn't have to throw it back! They played the whole game with more than *one* ball; think of it! We in the projects could play two whole years with the same ball! But I hadn't made the mental connection that I could bring my mitt to the game. I thought, Well, I'll just do it the next time I come. And, in my mind, there definitely were going to be many next times. The father stepped up to the ticket kiosk and ordered three box seats. Box seats, I thought, Wow, I bet they are going to have a great view of everything!

They left the line and it was now my turn. The counter top came to about my eye level. The man inside looked down and asked,

"What'll it be son? You want to see a game today?"

I replied in a my most self-assured voice, as if I had been attending ball games all my life, "Yeah! I want a bleacher seat!"

He smiled and said, "O . . . kay, one more for the 'knot-hole' gang."

I was not sure what that meant, but later found out it was what they called people who sat in the bleachers. Fine with me, as long as I get in.

He said, "You got a quarter?"

Did I? It had been burning a hole in my hand ever since I stepped off the bus. I placed my quarter on the counter and as quickly as it was swiped away, a bleacher ticket appeared in its place all in the same motion of his hand. I picked the ticket off the counter and held onto it as though it was my Captain Midnight Secret Decoder Badge. My excitement took another notch upward.

I followed others to an open door near the base of the stadium wall and gave the man my ticket. He said that entrance was for grandstand and box seats only. The entrances for the bleachers were down the lengths of the stadium depending upon whether you wanted to sit in the left field bleachers or the right field bleachers. Hmmm. Big decision. I stepped back out of the way of others and thought for a few minutes. Let's see . . . left field . . . right field . . . left field . . . right field? Hmmm. Since I was naturally right-handed, since most things I did favored my right side, and since my lucky rabbit's foot was in my right pocket . . . I decided to sit in the right field bleachers. I walked down the right side of the stadium and came to another entrance. I stepped up and gave that man my ticket. He tore it in half and gave part of it back to me with a nod of his head. I was finally in!

I stepped into the bowels of the stadium and ran up a sloped ramp, emerging into a walkway that was slightly above field level. Upon reaching the walkway, for the first time in my life I saw the field. My jaw dropped open as I stood there in a gaping stare at the vision before me. Here was the most *beautiful* expanse of perfectly manicured lawn I had ever seen. It was lush, and it defined a plane that was absolutely flat without a ripple or indentation anywhere. There were no weeds like we kids played on. It was wondrous!

I scanned around and saw the infield. It also was impressive. Screened dirt defined an equally flat surface. There were three stunningly white bases anchored into the proper locations. Inside the infield was another patch of manicured grass. I saw the pitcher's mound and home plate, a distinctive white rubber polygon anchored into the dirt near the batter's boxes. I stared at the awesome beauty in front of me. A whistle escaped my lips and I thought, Wow, this is really something! It's far grander than I ever imagined.

On the field there was a flurry of activities with groundskeepers preparing the field for play. I was totally surprised by the players in the outfield throwing baseballs and doing stretching exercises. They were wearing clean uniforms that were "glare-in-your-eye" white! I had never seen baseball uniforms up close before and these were more impressive than even I had imagined. And the players inside the uniforms were *men*, who could play baseball the way it was meant to be played. They were paid for doing it too! At that moment I would have sold my entire life to the devil if only he would have assured me that I would grow up to become a baseball player. Flash Gordon and Tarzan were suddenly just "average Joe's" compared to the uniformed men in front of me. And, the balls they were tossing around . . . they were white! White! That meant they were *new* balls. The only time I had seen a new baseball was when we went to the sporting goods store and I lustfully saw a pile of them, each wrapped in cellophane.

I had never in my life played with a new baseball. Our balls were dirty and scuffed; some even had rips in the covers. But even so, we knew they were good for at least another whole season. In total, I was overwhelmed with the panorama stretching out before my eyes. Coming to the stadium was *already* more than I had possibly hoped for, and the game had not even begun!

I walked down the aisle-way toward the bleachers with my head swiveling around to the field and then the grandstand and then back to the field again. My eyes were constantly in motion, absorbing everything. Near the end of the fair/foul line I entered the bleachers area. There were not many other people in the bleachers, just a number of kids like me and some single men here and there. All bleachers seating was "open," so I climbed up the rows. I finally chose a seat which I thought fulfilled my destiny. But it really didn't matter, since I could move around to other seats any time I wished.

The next half-hour passed quickly while both teams and the grounds crew finished their preparations. The umpires (dressed in black) took their positions and the *"National Anthem"* was played. The stadium was slightly over half full, even where I sat. The hawkers of every conceivable delight roamed up and down the steps shouting their wares. I could not have been any more excited and ready. The first Seals batter stepped into the batting box, the home plate umpire hunkered down behind the catcher, the Rainiers pitcher took his wind-up, and the first pitch was thrown. The game was underway. My very first professional baseball game was unfolding before my eyes! I already had some candy to chew on, and I cheered at everything and anything. I was in heaven!

I was awestruck with the size of the players and their speed and strength. They could throw the ball anywhere with both power and accuracy. They could pick up "hot grounders" perfectly in the webbing of their mitts. They never had to throw off their gloves and shake their hands to soothe the sting, like we kids did whenever we caught the ball on our palm instead of in the webbing. The pitchers had to be throwing strikes at about a hundred miles an hour, judging by the blur of the ball and the noise it made when it snapped into the catcher's mitt. I couldn't imagine standing in the batter's box trying to hit those pitches. Every player out there was now another of my heroes. I wanted more than anything to grow up and be one of them!

The game progressed at its own pace, and almost before I realized, it was the bottom of the seventh inning. The score was tied four-all, and Jimmy Rivera was coming to bat for the Rainiers. A buzz formed in the crowd: tight game, late innings, our best player coming to bat. I stood and clapped with each pitch, cheering Jimmy to get on base and make something happen! On his fourth throw, the pitcher delivered a hard fastball slightly below Jimmy's waist and toward the outside of the home plate, right in Jimmy's "power alley."

Jimmy was on that ball like a wolf on a lamb chop. His bat was a blur as it left his shoulder and arced through the strike zone with power. It smashed into the ball with a resonating crack.

The ball exploded off Jimmy's bat, into the sky . . . high . . . and . . . deep, rising to an apex and then slowly arcing into a descent. But its trajectory also had a curve toward the right fair/foul line. Would it remain a fair ball? Finally, it became obvious it would fall out of play . . . *and* . . . it probably would fall into the right field bleachers! I watched in awe, as it became apparent it would land near me!

With that thought, I scrambled toward the spot where I thought the ball would drop into the stands. About thirty other kids and grownups had the same thought and were equally in motion. It reminded me of when I once saw chum thrown into the ponds at the trout hatchery. First there was anticipation by the fish, and then turbulent competitive motion to try to snatch a morsel. In my excitement I moved as fast as I could, but I had to keep looking at the ball, and also at the seat benches I stepped over. My head swiveled. My legs and arms were challenged by the arcing ball, the obstacle course underfoot, and the elbows and arms I took in my sides from others intent on grabbing the same prize.

I stumbled and smacked my left shin on the edge of a bench. The crowd moved ahead of me with dozens of arms reaching higher and higher for the white sphere dropping from the sky. The ball struck a mass of hands and caromed off in another direction. The humanity moved amorphously in that direction with arms, legs, and torsos flailing to gain an advantage. I watched the ball's movement as I picked myself up from my fall, and felt an overwhelming urge to rub my pained shin, but resisted. The pack was now about ten yards from me, but I stared intently as the ball struck the stands below a bench and then ricocheted in an oblique direction. But now, miraculously, it was heading for me!!! I reached out with one hand and made contact, knocking it down below my feet.

The chase was on as it rattled between bench stanchions and footways. I saw it clearly and made a dive. My right hand wrapped around it and grasped it tightly. It was *mine! Yes! Yes!! Yes!!!* I tried to rise to my feet but my left leg was not fully cooperating.

Nevertheless, I raised the ball high in the air and jumped excitedly as much as I could with my right leg. I screamed with excitement. The crowd of wannabes near me, who wanted as desperately as me to grab it but didn't, initially groaned. But then, just as quickly, they joined everybody else in the stadium in a cheer seeing that the ball had finally been grabbed and held high. They all joined in my excitement—the thrill of it all. I felt like a gladiator in the Roman Coliseum raising his victorious sword high in the air. What a great moment. I was so exhilarated.

Most of the mass of people who had missed the ball came over and wanted to see it, as I would have done, to verify its reality. An old man rubbed the top of my cap in that back-and-forth sideways cranking motion like he was squeezing the juice from half an orange.

"Nice goin' sonny," he complimented.

My shin could take no more and cried for attention. I rubbed it with my free hand until the pain eased, but I never once let go of that clean, white, brand-new baseball.

I have the best souvenir possible to forever remember this day, I thought. I have a ball hit by my hero, Jimmy Rivera.

With the next pitch Jimmy laced a double into center field. He was then driven home by the next batter, scoring the go-ahead run. I was not attentive though, as I was in dreamland from the shiny new baseball held in my hand.

That's how the game ended: Rainiers five, Seals four—a victory for the home team.

As I filed out of the stadium I retraced the path I had taken to get to the bleachers. When I came to the exit near the first base, I saw all of the players had left the field through their dugouts, but there still were some Rainiers coaches standing near their first baseline dugout. A thought struck me: this is my one chance. I put my feet in motion and ran down the aisle through the box seats toward the dugout. A security guard saw me and jogged after me, yelling, "Hey kid, you can't go there!"

But I continued running, and when I approached the first row of box seats I yelled to the coaches, "Hey mister! Can I get Jimmy

Rivera's autograph?" Hearing my yell, they interrupted their chat and one of them turned to look in my direction.

"Fat chance kid," he said.

"Please," I pleaded, almost in a whine.

The guard finally caught up to me and between huffing and puffing said, "Sonny, you can't be here. . . . You've gotta leave. . . . You can't be botherin' the coaches."

"But I caught a ball Jimmy hit!" I said excitedly. I then held it up for all to see. "Couldn't he sign my ball? He's my *hero!*"

Now there was silence and a pause from all. The guard said to one of the coaches, "What do you think Fred? Can you ask Jimmy to come out and sign the kid's ball? That would be sorta special, don't ya think?"

Fred paused for a few seconds and said, "OK, I'll ask him." My heart jumped in anticipation. "But don't get your hopes up!"

Too late for that, I thought.

He disappeared into the dugout. After a couple minutes of waiting, which seemed like five hours, the coach emerged from the dugout . . . *and following behind him was Jimmy Rivera,* in the flesh, up close! He had removed his uniform top, and was now wearing only a T-shirt. He was without his hat, so I could see his head of dark wavy hair. As he walked over toward me, he seemed even bigger than he had looked while standing in the batter's box, and he certainly was more real. My heart pounded again.

Jimmy looked up at me standing behind the waist-high barrier and said, "Hey kid, how' ya doin'? How'd ya get that ball? How'd ya come up with it? Did ya have to fight the other kids for it?"

Here was a stream of friendly questions from a real, full-of-life hero standing right in front of me, and I could not find my tongue to speak a single word. I just smiled and looked into his face. My heart now was ready to burst from my chest. He came closer.

"Let me see it," he said. "I wanna see if it's got a flat spot on it!"

I slowly reached out my arm and handed him the ball. He took it and turned it over in his hands, examining it well.

"Nope, this one's still round. You can use it for your own ball games, it's still good. . . . Sometimes when I hit 'em they get a big dent on one side, and they're no good after that. They won't roll anymore with that big flat spot on 'em."

A smile came out of the corner of his mouth, and he looked over at Fred and gave Fred a wink. He looked back at me and said with a smile on his face, "You believe that, kid?"

Some words came from my mouth as I sputtered, "Anything you say, Jimmy."

Then Jimmy said, "Fred here says you want me to sign your ball. Do ya?"

My head bobbed up and down affirmatively. "Yeah, Jimmy, would you, please? That would be great!"

Jimmy looked at Fred again and said, "Yeah, sure. Fred you got a pen?"

Fred felt his jacket pockets, then his pants, and said, "Nope. Dang, I don't got no pen."

My face fell.

The guard said, "I got one," and he took a pen out of his shirt pocket and handed it to Jimmy. Jimmy took the pen and said, "What's your name, kid?"

"Jack," I said, "my name's Jack."

Jimmy scribbled on the ball, turning it slightly as he wrote. Then he said, "Here you go."

He handed it back to me and gave the pen back to the guard. I looked at the ball and he had written, *"To my friend Jack. Jim Rivera."*

I beamed inside and thought my chest would split open. Jimmy turned and jogged toward the dugout. After a few steps, he looked back, gave a wave of his arm and said, "'Bye, Jack. You get some hits of your own with that ball, OK?"

"Sure. Thanks, Jimmy! Thanks a lot!" I said. "Win the batting crown, Jimmy!" He disappeared in the dugout with Fred jogging behind.

I looked up at the guard and said, "Thanks, mister. That was neat!"

The guard said, "Sure kid, now you better run along."

I turned and ran up the stairs and outside the stadium. I pushed the ball with my hand around it deep into my jacket pocket and didn't take it out again.

When I arrived home, with the ball still in my jacket pocket,

I told the story to Doug, my mom, and my step-dad about meeting and *talking* with Jimmy Rivera at the end of the game. I didn't mention the ball, though. Doug followed every word, mesmerized, because we always talked together about Jimmy Rivera. My mom and step-dad gave me that look which communicated they were happy I had a great time, but this was another tall story. Mom said I should get ready for dinner.

Finally, Doug blurted out, "Liar, liar, liar!"

That's just what I was waiting for! I pulled my hand out of my jacket pocket and produced the incontrovertible evidence, much like *Perry Mason* would do on countless occasions in later times. I held out in front of me a shiny white baseball with writing on it.

"See!" I said. "Look at this! I caught a ball he hit . . . and . . . I even got his autograph!!! I'm not making this up!"

Mom glanced at my step-dad with an inquisitive look and took the ball from my hand. She read it, passed it to my step-dad, and then said, "Well, I'll be. . . . That's great, Jack. You really should be proud of that." Of course I was.

Doug now had gained control of the legendary ball and turned it around, feeling it as if some of the magic would rub off onto his own hands. He had a huge smile on his face and said, "I can't wait to be eight, so I can go to the park and get my own ball, and my own autograph!"

I thought, Yeah, like it happens every day . . . but, instead I said, "Sure! Why not? . . . And, I'll take you, 'cause I know the way."

For all of the imaginary play that our media heroes delivered into our lives, it was transitory, requiring constant renewal and continual investment by us. Reality, though, always returned, if only for a few hours, when we left the woods or the playgrounds and went home for dinner.

But once in a while, often unexpectedly, a real hero emerged or a real event occurred which surpassed even our wildest dreams.

Such an event showed us that real life *could* sometimes deliver aston-
ishing results directly into our souls and our hearts. And, when it
happened, *that* reality never left. Those memories and feelings were
testimonials that if you imagine, *really imagine,* sometimes dreams
really can come true . . . and that single realization alone was worth
more than all of our imaginary piles of buried treasure.

Such was the importance for me of catching that fly ball from
Jimmy Rivera and then getting his signature. It confirmed to me, in
a magical afternoon, that heroes really do exist and some time, any
time—*you never know when*—they might answer your prayers, fulfill
your dreams, and enrich your life in ways you *never* dreamed possible.
When that happened, it was proof that *anything* was possible.

You can catch your dreams!

**If you are properly positioned, and can grab a little luck,
anything can happen—**another of life's great lessons.

POSTSCRIPT ONE

I walked on air after I came home with that autographed ball
and was the talk of the schoolyard. Every kid wanted to see "The
Ball," as it came to be known. I told the Jimmy Rivera story so
many times that even I finally tired of it. But the story and that day
of wonderment and dreams fulfilled have never left my heart.

I kept "The Ball" in one of my dresser drawers as one of my
most prized possessions. Contrary to Jimmy's command to get some
hits of my own with it, I never let it see any further action. I
never played catch with it, or ever let it touch the ground. It was
a souvenir for me of a great moment in my early life, until, during
one of our many family moves in my early teens, it was lost forever.
How it was lost and where it went was always a mystery. But the
memories remain.

That year (1951) the Seattle Rainiers won the Pacific Coast
League championship. Jimmy Rivera also was selected the Most

Valuable Player (MVP) in the league, and he won the batting crown with the highest batting average. That was the last year Jimmy Rivera played for the Seattle Rainiers. The next season he was promoted to the major leagues and fulfilled most of his baseball career playing for the Chicago White Sox of the American League. In the majors he became "Jim" Rivera, but we Seattle kids from the early 1950s always remember him as "Jimmy."

He played with a fervor and excitement that was rare, even for major-leaguers, almost kid-like. He became known as a "character" for the sometimes outlandish things he did and said, all in the spirit of fun. On Opening Day in 1961, Jimmy asked President John F. Kennedy for *his* autograph, much as I had done of Jimmy a decade earlier. When the President gave it to him, he looked it over and then commented, "What's this? This is just a scribble! I can hardly make it out! You'll have to do better than this, John!"

He was a man who could tease presidents, or ignite the passion inside a young boy's heart, simply by engaging them with his "boyish" enthusiasm. I always looked at him as one of our better "local boys made good."

POSTSCRIPT TWO

I have enjoyed the game of baseball all of my life, playing it and watching it. Unfortunately, the game on television does not capture much of my interest, unless it happens to be the World Series. Appreciation of baseball does not come from television. It comes from experiencing it in the flesh, in the open air, in front of you. It has a cadence that is unique and different in every game. No two games or situations are ever the same, and for that reason it always has interest. Oh sure, some games drag on interminably to the point of boredom, but just when you become complacent, you will suddenly see a play, a feat of chance and athleticism that will create wonder in your soul. Something will happen that will stir your imagination and your envy, and for that for one moment, just once in your lifetime, you wish *you* could have done that.

I cannot tell you how many times I have dreamed of hitting the bejabbers out of Sandy Koufax's curveball in the bottom of the ninth inning, of the seventh game of the World Series, to win the championship. Such is what childhood dreams are about. *And, to confess, grown men have the same dreams; they just don't talk about them as much as children do.*

Along the years I have had the great fortune to see, firsthand and live, some of the greatest baseball players in history doing what they did best on the diamond. They include Stan Musial, Roberto Clemente, Johnny Bench, Reggie Jackson, Don Drysdale, Willie McCovey, Juan Marichal, "say hey" Willie Mays, and Barry Bonds.

I have never seen a curveball like those thrown by Sandy Koufax. Anybody who has never seen a game in person and who argues that a thrown baseball never really curves—that it is all an optical illusion—never saw Sandy Koufax pitch. His curve would break three feet sideways and downward, all within the last fifteen feet of approaching home plate. He called it his "roll off the table curveball!"

I once saw, Roberto Clemente throw a runner out at home plate from right-center field, a strike thrown "on a wire" from about 330 feet away! What an incredible arm he had!

I was fortunate to see Barry Bonds' record home run number seventy-three in the year 2001. I remember he hit a knuckle ball pitched no more than fifty-five miles an hour, almost floating up to the plate, but dancing and darting the whole distance. Barry hit under it and it looked like a huge pop-up entering the gray sky overhead. But it went up for what seemed like a quarter mile, and gracefully fell back to earth 420 feet from home plate into the right-center-field grandstand.

Baseball has always been a joy to me. It is a sport that appeals to children of all ages and stimulates the imagination of what has been, or what could be.

Our beloved Seattle baseball stadium as it looked in the 1950s.

Watching a game in Sick's Stadium.

JIM RIVERA
OUTFIELDER—CHICAGO WHITE SOX

PART FIVE

COMING OF AGE

21

SLIPPIN' AND SLIDIN'

Breathless, we flung ourselves on the windy hill,
laughed in the sun and kissed the lovely grass.
—Rupert Brooke

Summer in the projects was both a challenge and a joy. There was no summer school in those days, at least not in our neighborhood. About mid-June, Columbia grade school shut down for good until after Labor Day. It was not until later in life that I could look back and imagine that the school building, assuming it had a personality, was also counting the days to mid-June just as much as every one of us kids. Surely it needed rest and recovery for a few months before it would be refreshed enough to welcome another nine months of ruffians with boundless energy running through its hallways and tearing up its playgrounds.

In early June we kids had almost breathless anticipation for the actual moment when we could run off the premises—completely free to pursue life's whims for three whole months. Despite the weather, we played baseball, soccer, dodge ball, and kick-the-can, along with countless expeditions of serious play in the "woods" amid the blackberry brambles (our "jungle").

Occasionally, there were the fishing trips for my brother Doug and me with Uncle Johnny to the Cedar River in south Seattle to drown some worms, and maybe once in a while catch a small trout. And, of course, there was always water, of any kind, as a last resort to occupy countless hours. We could never seem to get wet enough, often enough. Our lusts for water were satisfied by playing in Lake Washington, by getting "accidentally" wet every time we went to the Cedar River, by running through (or even sometimes riding our bikes through) the children's wading pond in the nearby park, and by visiting the Plunge at the Rainer Vista field house way down the hill from Alderwood Court.

The Plunge was an indoor pool which most of the time charged an admission to swim. But about three times a month it opened, at no charge, for about an hour to all of the poor refugees like we kids who couldn't afford to pay.

The one thing I remember about the Plunge was that the chlorine was so heavy I could smell it and my eyes burned afterwards. It never stopped us, though. We all knew when the Plunge was free, and we were there every time until they kicked us out, presumably to drain the water and refill it with clean water for the paying customers. We imagined those were rich people who lived in the vicinity of Lake Washington. I'm sure we not only left rings of dirt but also gallons of urine. I never knew a single kid, ever, who exited the pool to relieve himself in the locker room. Our thinking was "they'll never know," and so we let Nature take its course whenever the urge came. It was not until I was much older that I figured out why the chlorine was so strong.

Since we did not have sports equipment, except for our baseball gear, we had to rely on our *imaginations* to keep the summer days interesting. One of those natural occurrences that satisfied us all was the hill behind our project four-plex. The building was on a level foundation, and it had a flat yard in the front leading to the street and the coal bin. But in the back, the flat profile extended only about ten feet away from the foundation. Then the land rolled over abruptly into a downward slope which eventually terminated in the horizontal backyard of the project four-plex on the next lower court. This "stopping zone" was about twelve feet in length before one would encounter the lower project building's foundation. The length of the slope averaged about thirty yards. Also, its steepness varied and in some places could be a challenge.

Most times of the year we avoided the hill because with the proverbial Seattle rain it often was wet. However, that wetness made weeds and grasses grow prolifically on the barren ground. But 'long about the end of June the wetness disappeared and the grasses dried and turned brown. The hill became an inviting play area, and the more the grasses dried, the slicker they became. Let's see, slick grass, on a hillside slope, hmmm . . . I think we can do something with that! And, what we did was slide. The slope became the greatest slippery-slide around, and it was free!

We all learned that if we found a cardboard box, and then broke open its sides so it became a flat piece of material, then all we needed was to sit on top of the cardboard and let gravity take over! We could zip down and spin around, generally with some control by dragging our feet. Occasionally, we would hit a steep spot and the speed would pick up, along with our anxiety, until we either hit the flat bottom area and slowed, or we simply "bailed" by rolling off the cardboard, taking our chances on the bare grass for braking. Every trip down was followed by grins and laughter, regardless of how temporarily scared we may have been during the slide.

Years later it struck me how similar these experiences were to the way I snow skied as an adult, except in skiing I probably had a couple of thousand dollars invested in state-of-the-art hardware and fine clothes in which to "look good." When sliding on grass with cardboard as kids, though, we simply used what was available, and made it up as we went along. Although the thrills were the same, the simplicity of the grass and cardboard was unquestioned.

THE HUNT

As the summer wore on and the hill became more of a focal point for fun, not only by us Alderwood's, but also by the other Court gangs, "good" cardboard became a critical commodity. A fairly intact piece of laminated packaging material, which otherwise would not have drawn even a lick of interest, suddenly became a valued and guarded treasure in "sliding season." We would slide until our ribbed brown sliding surface wore away, tore, or just lost its usefulness. Then we foraged outward, scrounging for more new boxes. The back lot of the grocery store in downtown Columbia was always a first source, every morning, because everybody knew they stocked the shelves at night.

One day in early August of 1952 we happened to be the beneficiary of one of the greatest strokes of good fortune in my life up to that time. We had heard that new people were moving into one of the project units down Alderwood Court from where we lived. We didn't think anything about this since people in the projects came and went regularly. But after a full day of playing "war invasion" in the woods, and imagining all day that we were Sergeant Stryker (John Wayne) in the *Sands of Iwo Jima*, Doug and I, along with Ronnie Landers and Freddie Roberts, were walking home, expecting nothing more than another night of radio programs.

We sang choruses of our favorite playground song of the day, which went something like:

> *There's a place in France*
> *Where the women wear no pants,*
> *And the men go around*
> *With their dinkies hanging down.*

That is only the first chorus, but there were many more, which escape my memory now that I have become an "adult." However, at that time, making up various choruses to this song occupied some amount of our time and mental capacity.

As we walked home and sang, we decided to take the longer way in order to walk by the unit with the new family, just in case we might spot a new member for our gang. The ideal recruit was any boy between the ages of eight and twelve. If he looked like he had any level of coordination, so much the better. In those days we didn't have the terms "geeky" or "dorky"; our commonly used endearment to describe someone who lacked social suitability was to call them a "spazz," short for spastic. Remember, this was a time when polio was still a prevalent disease. I know this sounds cruel now, but then it was just matter-of-fact. I'm not sure we even completely understood what it meant. I don't know any of us who ever actually saw anyone who was spastic, but the word was used by all of us Court gangs. And, of course, the connotation was applied only as a measure of one's apparent lack of athletic ability, since sports and physical competitiveness were such significant measurements of our daily pecking order. If you had the ability to run, throw, climb, and jump, you were in. If you couldn't, you took your turn behind those who could. Clothes never had any impact whatsoever on social standing, because we all were pathetic. That's why we lived in the projects.

As we sidled up the street toward the new movers, we saw some grown-ups carrying pieces of barely functional furniture and other possessions into the place, along with small boxes. We sat down across the street and leaned against a coal bin. It was close to dinner time and there was not much more noticeable that held our attention. We didn't see any kids. Maybe they would come later.

After about ten minutes we were ready to get up and continue moseying down the court, when a truck rounded the corner and entered the Court. Well, this was news, because trucks didn't normally wander into our lives, on our street, by accident. They always had a purpose, and, whatever it was, they always held some interest. The truck slowly moved down the street toward us and we could see the driver and his partner in the front seat looking for addresses. Finally, the truck came to a stop in front of the movers. Both men jumped out and mumbled some verbal exchanges to those carrying junk and clothes into the unit. We watched. The guys from the truck went around to the back, opened the doors, and pulled out a ramp. We all rose and moved to the end of the truck to view the inside better. We saw the guys wrestling with a large upright container. They were trying to slide it toward the back of the truck, and then get it up onto a dolly.

"Hey mister," I said, trying to get some attention, "what's that big thing?"

He didn't answer immediately, seeing as how he was more involved both physically and mentally with coaxing an unwieldy object where it didn't want to go.

Finally, he stood back with his hands on his hips and said, "It's a refrigerator, sonny, and it's a heavy sucker. But we'll get it out, don't worry." Then he and his partner went back to pushing it toward the end of the truck. It emerged from the darkness so that we could get a better view of it, and suddenly it dawned on us what we were seeing. Here was a box ... a very tall box ... a giant tall box ... a giant tall box of ... CARDBOARD! Who cared what was inside of it!

It was the biggest, whole, single piece of cardboard any of us had ever seen. Our eyes grew as big as baseballs and our mouths opened in amazement. We looked at each other as if we had just seen the first opening of "King Tut's" tomb. We didn't have to speak; we all knew what each other was thinking—cardboard, *huge* cardboard! Wow, would you look at that treasure!

We watched the men muscle it onto the dolly and then roll it down the ramp. They continued to roll it toward the front door of the unit. We tagged along close enough to monitor the progress, but not so close as to interfere.

"Hey mister," I said again, "um ... when're you ... gonna be finished with that refrigerator?"

Much pushing and shoving with the box continued. We waited as they struggled to get it up the front steps and into the unit. At the top of the steps, at a pause, the driver reached for his handker-chief in a back pocket, wiped his brow, and turned his face toward the voice coming from the pack of us kids standing *en masse*.

"Not soon enough, sonny! Not soon enough. Hopefully, we'll be outta here in 'bout another ten minutes. I know somewhere there's an Oly with my name on it!" His partner contributed something about it being too late in the day for them to be working this hard, and the sooner they were finished with this refrigerator, the better.

I said, "Um mister . . . when you're done . . . whatcha' gonna do with that box?"

"Well, we're supposed to bring it back with us," he answered.

"Um . . . could we have it?" I asked. "Could we, huh?"

"Don't make no matter to me sonny, but you better ask the owner of the 'fridge. Maybe he wants it."

"Could you ask him for us, 'cause we don't know him. Could you, huh?"

The driver stepped inside the unit for a few moments presumably to hunt down the new tenants. We waited. He stepped back outside and said, "It's yours."

The collective excitement in all of us jumped an octave, but all I could say was, "Really??? . . . Wow! . . . Thanks, mister."

We all looked at each other with wide grins, pushing and patting each other on the backs to express our great glee and excitement in our good fortune. Now we had the largest piece of cardboard in the world! We settled down and waited . . . and waited . . . for what seemed like the longest time. Surely our moms now wondered where we were and why we were not home for dinner, but they would have to wait. This box was more important than anything. It was worth risking a scolding.

After what seemed much longer than ten minutes, the driver came out dragging the box behind him. He said, "Here you go. It's all yours. By the way, whatcha' gonna do with it?"

We all moved closer to touch it and we tried to grab the flaps.

"It's gonna be our spaceship," I blurted out before my mind could even think. Spaceship, I thought, where did that come from? The others looked at me as though they had the same question. But those questions lasted about the time for two heartbeats, and then we were consumed with the unwieldiness of getting a good handle on the box. It was not that it was heavy; it was just cumbersome, and difficult for us to control. But, slowly, three of us managed to grab hold of its opening flaps on one end, and the fourth pushed the other end. We dragged and pushed it up the street toward where Doug and I lived. After about a half block we were there.

"What're we gonna do with it?" Ronnie asked. "Aren't we gonna cut it up for sliders?"

"Naw, we're really gonna make a spaceship out of it. Why not?" I said. "Just like Flash Gordon's. It's gonna be great, you'll see!"

Ronnie insisted, "But I thought . . . Why'd we drag it clear up here? If it's just gonna be a spaceship, we coulda left it there and played in it there. And besides . . . it's CARDBOARD! Sliding's what it's good for!"

I was having a great time leading Ronnie and Freddie on because Doug knew me well enough to know that I *knew* its primary purpose from the first moment we all saw it was to become sliders. But once I had blurted out "spaceship," well, I just went with that for a while.

I said, "Yeah, I know it's best for sliding, but why cut it up? Why can't it be our slider . . . *and* our spaceship? Why can't it be our sliding-spaceship?" Now that was an idea! Why couldn't we make it our spaceship, and then all of us could get in it at one time and go on a space trip . . . sliding right down the hill! It was an idea that seemed to have a certain level of brilliance. Why not mix both fantasy and fun to double the experience of both? Once the words were out, Doug had that "I told you so grin" on his face, and the lightbulbs went on in both Ronnie's and Freddie's minds at the same moment.

"Yeah!!!" they both said in exclamation.

"Wow, this is gonna be great!" Ronnie shouted. "We'll be the only ones, ever, to have a spaceship that actually goes on a trip . . . except for Flash Gordon!"

Our *imaginations* took off.

This would work! We talked about how we could visit Mars and Venus going down the hill. It never occurred to us that these excursions to the planetary system would be one-way trips, because the "spaceship" would have a very difficult time sliding back up the hill. But hey, we knew we were going somewhere exciting, under power other than our own—we didn't need to push or pull.

All we had to do was get in, and we would be off to adventure and thrills. Our imaginations were completely stimulated and we couldn't wait.

If we had the time right then and there, we would have dragged it around to the back of the four-plex and given it a test slide. But I heard my mom yell out the kitchen window, "Jack, is that you? You and Doug get in here. I have dinner on the table."

I yelled back, "We'll be right in." Then I said to Ronnie and Freddie that we could move it behind our coal bin for the night, and hope that it was still there in the morning. We envisioned marauding bands of thieves roaming the neighborhood after nightfall looking for cardboard, that's how centrally focused we were at that moment. But we would have to risk it because we couldn't bring it in the house, and there was nowhere else to put it with such short notice. We pulled it up against the back of the coal bin and, although it stuck out on both ends, it was hidden fairly well from the street view. It was "50/50" in our minds that it was safe from marauders for the night. Doug and I bounded up our front steps, and I yelled back for Freddie and Ronnie to meet us first thing in the morning. It was doubtful any of us would get a good sleep this night.

THE TRANSFORMATION

The next morning, I awakened earlier than normal and popped out of bed with thoughts of great excursions to come. I had dreams of spaceships and sliding, and the two together tantalized my imagination. As I ate my breakfast cereal, I kept thinking about how to make the spaceship something special. Let's see . . . we needed a windshield and windows, otherwise how would we be able to see the comets and planets as we passed them by? Also, we needed controls and a dashboard to see our speed. Also, maybe we could have a radio right in the middle of the dash too, just like in our car!

Doug and I finished our breakfast and brushed our teeth—we never felt we needed to do this, but mom always made us do it before we could go outside. I'm convinced now that if it had not been for our mom always making us do this simple act of oral maintenance twice a day, we would have been toothless by the time we were sixteen, what with all of the candy we consumed. After concluding a twelve-second tooth brushing and rinse, Doug and I ran through the kitchen and burst out the front door to again see the refrigerator box—nee spaceship—resting on the back side of the coal bin, just as we had left it. The cardboard thieves had not been lucky last night! We were in! It was slightly soggy on the top side from the dew, but other than that it was still perfect, and a priceless object of our imaginations.

Doug and I dragged it away from the coal bin and into the direct rays of the morning sun to hasten its drying.

"How're we gonna put windows in it?" Doug asked.

"We need a knife," I said . . . "and then we'll cut them in. We can get one of mom's butcher's knives."

"Aw, she won't let us have it, I know," Doug said. "She's always telling me to leave her knives alone. She doesn't even like me to have scissors."

"Well, we'll just have to do a diversion. You know, like the time Hoppalong Cassidy fooled those bad guys by telling them, 'Look . . . *over there!*' Only there wasn't anything over where he pointed, and then he pulled his gun on them when they looked . . . remember that?" I could tell that Doug, being only age eight, still was smart enough to follow my description of one of the classic deceptions for which all Western movie bad guys always seemed to fall. For some reason, the good guys were always geniuses, and the bad guys—those wearing dark clothes with black hats—were complete buffoons. They always fell for the "look over there" trickery. Perhaps mom would too.

"What about the dashboard and the rocket power levers, and the other things it needs?" Doug asked.

"I was thinking we could paint them. We could use the paint set you got for your birthday."

About a month before on June 30th, it had been Doug's birthday. One of the gifts he received was a small set of cheap (wasn't everything in our lives?) poster-painting colors. There were four or five small jars in the set, each jar containing a colored powder. These powders could be mixed with water to yield some watery, colorized "paint" for coloring paper, poster boards, or . . . cardboard.

"Yeah!" Doug said. "I forgot about that. And it came with a paint brush too."

"Yeah, and dad's got some smaller paint brushes in the back closet that we can also use."

About this time Spike and Jenny Owens showed up, along with Ronnie. Ronnie had told them about the cardboard treasure after he and Freddie had left our house last night.

"Wow, it's just like you said, Ronnie!" Jenny commented. "It's amazing. I've never seen a bigger box than this. It's gonna make a perfect spaceship!"

"Yeah," said Spike. "Boy, this thing's gonna fly!"

After more talk, we all decided to move the box around to the back of the four-plex, where our actions to transform it into our transportation to the cosmos would be less visible from the street. The box would also be out of mom's view from the kitchen window. As unwieldy as it was, we somehow managed to drag it around back. Freddie had shown up by this time, and he happened to have a pocket knife to work on the windows. Except his pocket knife was so dull it was useless. I had gone into the house to try to work the "Hoppalong super deception" on mom, but she was not in the kitchen. Happily, I grabbed a big butcher's knife from her knife drawer, ran out the front door, bounded down the front steps, and scurried around the flour-plex to the back.

Now looking back, I realize I did not understand the full danger of my actions. Here I had a large lethal weapon in my hands that was so sharp it easily could have cut the head off a moose, and I didn't even consider running and jumping with it to be an issue. Talk about "running with scissors!" I guess that's what mothers are for—to constantly remind us of life's hidden dangers, even in a nagging way, when we are oblivious to them. But, at the moment, all I cared about was that I had the knife.

Doug had accompanied me into the house for my planned diversion with mom, but when I left with the knife he went for our closet. After some rummaging he found his paint set. He followed me out the front door, smacking the screen door aside as he flew through the opening. Mom yelled from the back room not to slam the screen, but it was too late; he was past the coal bin and turning left when the spring returned it to the door frame with a loud whack.

We all converged on the box, soon to become our spaceship. We became a study of concentrated effort to transform our prize. We cut an oblong opening in the upper part of the front of the box, which had previously been the topmost surface of the refrigerator. This became our "windshield," so we could see out while heading downhill. We also cut smaller, round, viewing ports in the sides of the spaceship. We figured we could also use these as hand holds, if necessary, never making the logical leap that a true spaceship in outer space never would have openings in its side.

We employed our imaginations selectively; if something we dreamed about conformed to our reality, we used it; if it didn't, we simply discarded it. **We never let our imaginations be limited by perceived reality**, another of life's simple lessons. Cutting the openings was not easy because this was not the standard cardboard. This was "industrial strength" cardboard with many more laminations. How we were able to cut through those layers without any of us incurring a sliced finger is now beyond me. Luck was definitely on our side.

Next we worked on the painting. Doug had his little paint brush and Ronnie had run home and returned with another paint brush. We decided not to go after our step-dad's brushes because we could run into mom again in the house and possibly have to answer questions that we didn't want to answer. Doug and I crawled inside the box and painted a dashboard below the windshield, complete with a radio right in the center. Doug said it was a perfect Philco, the well-known radio brand of the period. Then on the outside we painted doors and door handles. We also painted stars and red stripes down the sides.

But the crowning achievement was the name. Every spaceship

needed a name, we figured. But what to call ours? Freddie suggested "Silver Pickle" because of Flash Gordon's space ship. As much as we all understood the connection, it . . . well, just didn't seem to "fly." Doug liked "The Sky Schwinn®," and as good as that sounded, we couldn't reach a consensus. Deep down inside we knew Schwinn® was a great bicycle, but this was a machine for the stars, not a two-wheeled land cruiser. I suggested "Jack's Jet," but that also was not to be. Ronnie, in great sarcasm, asked why we didn't name it "The Refrigerator Box," but as much as that initially appealed to me too, it wasn't outer space-like. Finally, Jenny asked, "Why not call it 'The Flying Cloud'?"

The Flying Cloud. . . . Hmmm. *"The Flying Cloud."* We all looked at each other, and it seemed to fit. Maybe it was not as rough-and-tumble masculine as we guys would have liked, but it did have a certain "sky-ness" and floating appeal to us. Why not? The Flying Cloud it was! So we let Jenny paint "The Flying Cloud" down the sides, on one side with orange paint, and on the other with green paint. We also added some tail flourishes and a few more streaks on the sides to convey speed. It was done, and then we all stepped back and admired our artistic handiwork. We were pleased. While all of this occurred, we had been steadily surrounded by other kids in the neighborhood. They had either heard about the new spaceship-slider, or had roamed into the area to get in a good morning of sliding, and stumbled into this project of creation. Envy dripped from the souls of all the visitors. We had something good here, and we knew it, and best of all, we knew they knew it. We were very happy with ourselves.

22

THE VOYAGE OF "THE FLYING CLOUD"

Make voyages! —Attempt them! —there's nothing else.
—Tennessee Williams, Camino Real

"How does one become a butterfly?" she asked. "You must want to fly
so much that you are willing to give up being a caterpillar."
—Trina Paulus, Hope for the Flowers

We had to decide who would go on the maiden voyage. All of us wanted to, but we figured that someone had to remain outside in order to keep it from sliding until the rest of us could get loaded inside. Then the one person remaining outside could let go and launch the spaceship with a push. We figured that it was not a bad duty to be the launcher because every great spaceship had to have a launcher as part of the team. Plus, we would rotate positions on future flights.

But how would we determine the "launcher" from the "passengers," and also the positions of the passengers? The best way was to draw straws, and since this was a sliding surface of straw, we had plenty from which to choose. Doug and Freddie found six straws, all of unequal length, and Doug held them in his hand to conceal their lengths. We decided that those picking the longest straws would go into the spaceship as passengers, in order of length, and the shortest straw would be the launcher. We drew. Freddie, of all people, drew the longest straw and won the right to the front-most position. He thus would be the commander of the mission, looking out the windshield. Jenny came next behind Freddie, then Doug, then me, then Spike in the last position. Ronnie won the honor of being the first launcher. Freddie was ecstatic because he had never won anything before, and here he was to be the commander! Doug was happy he was in the crew, but he knew his only possible view was out the sides, since he was sandwiched between two taller people, Jenny and me. True to his form, Spike was just happy to be in the spaceship. Thus it was. The crew was formed!

We lugged the box over to the edge at just the "right spot." We then pushed its nose out over the edge until it finally dropped down into the slope. Ronnie stood in front of the box preventing it from sliding prematurely. He had his foot on a rock to the side of the ship's path as a spot of some traction. It was time to get aboard!

Freddie climbed in first with a grin on his face as wide as the sky. He took up his spot in front with his feet up against the front edge of the box. He looked out the "windshield." Next came Jenny. She squirmed in and slithered up behind Freddie with her feet outside of his. She had a more difficult time of it because she was tall enough so that it was hard for her to sit completely upright without her head interfering with the top surface of the box. This was something that had escaped us. Maybe for future flights we could cut a head hole in the top so she and I could look out the top—something like those gunner bubbles on the B-24 bombers. Next came Doug, who had no problem with height. He sidled up close to Jenny. Then I entered and scrunched up close to Doug. I also had to duck my head. By this time Ronnie was struggling to prevent the added weight from taking off on its own. He yelled for Spike to get in, which he did, and I felt Spike's arms wrap around my waist.

We then said a countdown from five. We held each other tight and counted together... FIVE ... FOUR ... THREE ... TWO ... ONE. Then, in unison, we all shouted, "BLAST OFF!!!"

Ronnie stepped aside, and "The Flying Cloud" moved, slipping down the slope. As the rear went by, Ronnie reached over, grabbed the top side, and took a few steps with us, pushing as hard as he could. Finally, our motion increased, and the inexorable acceleration of gravity took hold.

Our speed quickened with each second. Our combined dead weight pulled us down ... down ... down ... and faster, faster, faster we accelerated on the slippery reeds and straw underneath us. We squealed with delight and happiness. We were superbly, totally proud of our imagination, combined effort, teamwork, and friendship! Our little hearts beat with joy as we held each other tight in a unified mass of childish adventure. Faster we went!

We couldn't see all of what was happening, but we were totally aware we were almost falling . . . and without any control. Suddenly, we hit a bump and slewed to our left. Our anxiety quickened. I heard Spike yell, "Maybe we're going too fast!" But it didn't matter what he thought, because we all knew we were going wherever "The Flying Cloud" wanted and at whatever speed the hill and Mother Nature provided. There was nothing we could do, except ride . . . and slide. Doug's throat let out a yelp.

We continued to pick up speed. "The Flying Cloud" smashed into another bump and we now slewed to the right. Our initial joyous, carefree playfulness was quickly displaced by growing tension and fear. Now, we all were afraid. We had no control, and we were whipsawed around at will. Plus, our speed continued to increase so that each significant rock we rammed felt like a boulder smashing into our little butts.

Jenny screamed, "Jack, stop us!"

I thought, That's a great idea, and I would if I could, but it was not possible. I now wished to simply end this space ride in one piece. BAM! Another bump, and "The Flying Cloud" tilted left again and straightened. Her nose pointed straight down the hill! We held each other in a death grip of near paralysis; at least there was some comfort together. We all screamed, *"Aiiiiiiieeeee!"*

Suddenly, the nose jutted upward and we all were thrown forward, bending at the waist. The nose had struck the bottom of the slope and reacted to the flattened back yard of the downhill four-plex. Previously, when we had reached the bottom as single sliders, we always came to a quick stop. This time, however, it was not the case. "The Flying Cloud" shuddered from the change of direction, but lost no apparent velocity. I heard Freddie scream, "We're gonna crash!!!" Before I could react by aligning my head to get a better view of what was in front of us, the nose of "The Flying Cloud" made contact with the four-plex.

WHAM! We smashed into the foundation of the structure.

All of us instantly were thrown forward and compressed into each other to the extent that our small bodies could absorb the impact. My chin snapped into the back of Doug's head, ricocheted off of it, and then my whole face hit the back of Jenny's shoulders, while she was also thrown into Freddie. Spike slammed into me from behind. Doug was squeezed between Jenny and me like a boiled egg in a sandwich. His little body was scrunched into any space available.

The air vacated my lungs, and I suddenly felt intense pain in my chest and my gut. I wanted to scream but there was no air in my lungs! All I could do was gasp. And, as anybody who has ever had the "wind knocked out" of them knows, there is an immediate panic when your brain suddenly realizes that it can no longer do something, which previously it has done as naturally as . . . well, breathe. As hard as I tried, my lungs would not work. I couldn't cry; I couldn't do anything but gasp for air. I heard muffled sobs and shouting from the others, and slowly I was able to get a gulp of air. Behind me Spike scrambled out of the ship, sniffling and shaking. Jenny cried. Doug tried to cry except his voice was muffled, jammed between my chest and Jenny's back.

"My arm won't work!" I heard Freddie yell. Then he let out a scream. I've heard that scream a few times since in my life. It is a combination of pain and panic. Slowly, and with difficulty, I disentangled myself from Doug's and Jenny's arms and legs and backed myself out of the spaceship. I now breathed easier. I reached in and helped Doug out, who finally cried without restraint. Jenny leaned backwards and I grabbed under her arms and pulled. She slid out, then rolled over and slowly stood up.

Ronnie by now had run all the way down the hill and had arrived on scene. He was scared, but was the calmest of us all. He and I crawled back inside and somehow pulled Freddie out, with all of his screaming. Freddie laid down on his back and held his right forearm with his left hand. Then I noticed that his right wrist was bent downward and backwards in a strange angle. It was obviously broken. The only question was, how badly?

By now we had a crowd around us. Everyone had an opinion and a comment to share. Everyone talked but nobody listened, and it became a confusing noise in the background when I tried to think. What should we do with Freddie, who now screamed his lungs out? We decided that I should run up and fetch my mom, which I did. She took over, and we eventually took Freddie to a hospital, where his wrist was properly set and put into a cast.

Doug and I both received the "If I've told you once, I've told you a thousand times. . . ." speech from mom for our general lack of good sense. Little did she understand that we were adventuresome boys, when she expected us to be sensible young adults. To us, we were just behaving naturally, but she expected much more. This communication gap would continue for more than another decade. She was particularly irritated when she found her missing butcher's knife, and cleverly put together the details of how the holes and windshield had been carved into "The Flying Cloud."

That was both "The Flying Cloud's" maiden flight, and her final flight. She never again "flew." In fact, her nose was so smashed in and crumpled that it was not useful any more. The remaining parts of her, however, were salvaged by us and dismantled into smaller, more manageable single-slider platforms. Good cardboard like that could never go to waste. We all rode parts of her until well into September when we quite literally wore down most of the grass on the hill. By then bare dirt was again displayed, ready to receive another winter of rains, followed by another spring of grass and weed growth, leading to another adventuresome summer of slippin' and slidin'. Some things were too good not to do, in spite of the risks and dangers—something that mothers never could understand. We were just being boys.

Freddie's wrist healed and was in good shape by Halloween and the following seasonal holidays. Jenny never for a moment regretted anything, something that always distinguished her from other girls in our minds—she was more like one of us boys.

And, as time went on, for the rest of us—Ronnie, Spike, Doug, and me—the story of the wonderful escapade of "The Flying Cloud" grew, with embellishments, of course, to become one of the better gang experiences on Alderwood Court, for all time.

POSTSCRIPT

There were two very important reflections from the "flight" of "The Flying Cloud."

First, *our adventures always were driven by our imaginations.* This adventure was one of the best examples of us kids always employing our imaginations to their maximum. Our imaginations were our tools. We carried them with us, in the invisible tool kits of our minds. When needed, we simply reached in and pulled out precisely the right tool of imagination that best adapted to any situation at hand. We used these tools not only for making the best of what we had, but also for helping us become, or achieve, whatever we dreamed . . . through our adventures. *Dreams do not exist if there is no imagination.* As kids, we never imposed limits on our imaginations.

Second, *we came together as a team, and had the unique experiences that only teams can have.* Only five of us made that maiden (and only) "flight" of "The Flying Cloud," but we all understood that Ronnie's responsibilities as "holder" and then "pusher" were just as important to the team as any other position. And likewise, Freddie's glee at being Commander of the mission, for the first time in his life, although important to him, was no more important to the team than Ronnie's job.

We all were saddened by Freddie's injury, but it, too, was an outcome that we all had "achieved." We all supported Freddie through his recovery and we knew he would have done the same for us. We were a team, and that's what teams do.

Our bonding as a team grew throughout that summer and soon reached its peak with another "real life" adventure. This one was filled with intrigue, fear, and potential life-threatening peril. It involved our neighborhood "haunted house."

23

Halloween 1952—The Caper

If you don't believe in ghosts, you've never been to a family reunion.
—Ashleigh Brilliant

The Plan

As October came around every year, I looked forward to two great events, both of which occurred within a few days of each other. The first was my birthday, and the second, three days later, was Halloween. Both were joyous days of candy, cakes, ice cream, and more candy, as well as presents on the 28th. I don't know who invented Halloween, but if there is one thing that has universal appeal to kids, it is candy, and if there was a day in the year during our childhood that exemplified candy more than any other it was Halloween.

My brother Doug and I, along with other members of the Alderwood Court gang, planned for the Halloween evening "candy raid" for a couple of weeks in advance, in a way that would have made General Eisenhower envious. We drew a map of all the project's streets, complete with locations of the four-plexes. We calculated how much time we had from mission launch to return for curfew. We knew how much time we could afford for each street. We also considered how much we could carry in one paper shopping bag, and whether we needed to plan for a mid-course return home to empty our bags before making the final push.

We planned for contingencies such as rain (always a likelihood in Seattle) and the possibilities that some houses might be empty, or the residents wouldn't open the door. For such cases the "trick" part of the question took effect in the form of a bar of soap we carried to write upon the windows or the siding of the offending house. This was not a casual walk in the neighborhoods with our parents, as are today's Halloween forays. No, this was a mission that would make ninjas proud. The objective was to stuff our coffers with booty of caramelized, crystallized, "chocolatized," or jellied candy, as much as possible. We approached the evening as miners: there was golden ore out there for the taking and we were going to take it! We were not picky, either. We would take everything when offered and do the sorting later. Hershey's Kisses® were OK, but the prized and targeted possessions were Big Hunk® candy bars, or pieces of them. If we happened to be so lucky as to rake in a complete, unbroken Big Hunk®, it would reaffirm our faith that there was a god of Halloween!

The last week of the planning was bisected by my birthday. This particular year I was ten years old! My "first decade" was in the books. As I have said before, it was also my sister Cindy's birthday. I never could decide if this was a good thing or not. On the one hand, the parties were somewhat larger, having two birthdays to celebrate. But having an individual, separate party at another time was forfeited, and I couldn't figure out if we were net winners, or losers, as a result. I always tended to think in terms of total candy and cakes available.

Anyway, one of the great presents I received on my birthday that year was a flashlight, a large one with two "D" sized batteries. I'm sure it came from the Army-Navy surplus store, but that didn't bother me. It was wonderful. Now I would always have a piercing beam of light to protect me in the dark. I could even use it in our bedroom to keep the monsters under the bed before Doug and I went to sleep.

Then, all of a sudden in the middle of this euphoria, my mom said a sentence that dramatically caught my attention: "Well, Jack, now that you have a flashlight, and your sister is old enough, you and Doug can take *her* trick-or-treating with you."

I'm sure that seemed like such a wonderfully logical connection for mom—so neat and tidy. But to me it was a total surprise . . . and a dreadful thought. I instantly turned and looked at Doug, whose shocked stare caught mine. We both had stunned looks on our faces, that same look kids have when the nurse says: "It's time for your shots!"

Oh, my gosh! Where had this blindside come from? Doug and I knew this would destroy all of our plans. We couldn't be dragging our little sister around with us on Halloween, for many reasons. For one, she couldn't keep up. Worse yet, if this news ever circulated around to the other mothers, we would suddenly have a whole bunch of younger siblings to shepherd around. What would Ronnie, Freddie, Spike, and Jenny think? What would the other gangs say? We would be laughing stocks for months afterwards. "Little sister babysitters," I could hear it all now in my mind. Lastly, and most importantly, our total candy harvest would be significantly impacted! What to do??? *"Think, think, think,"* I told my brain. Doug stared at me as if he, too, was silently telling me, "Think, think, think!"

I finally said, "Uhh . . . mom . . . I don't know if that's a good idea."

"Why not?" she asked.

Darn, I realized, the "not a good idea" argument wasn't enough; she actually wanted a reason.

"What if it rains?" I asked.

"I'll put slickers and galoshes on all of you. You won't melt," she said. Chalk up another simple argument for mom.

"Mom, she'll slow us down," I pleaded. "We can't be taking a baby with us."

"She's not a baby, she's five years old. You and Doug went out trick-or-treating by yourselves when you were her age," she countered. Double darn, I thought. She was determined. This wasn't getting any easier. *Think, think, think!*

Doug said, "But mommmm," in that whine, which I had learned never carried any weight with our parents. It only made them more determined. A few more seconds went by.

Finally, I dug deep for the big guns. "Well . . . she can't go with us, because we are big enough now to go trick-or-treat the haunted house, and she isn't big enough for that!"

The words spilled out. Mom said nothing, but I thought I

detected she was thinking this over for the first time since either Doug or I had opened our mouths. I sensed the opening, and drove home another point.

"We have to cross the big street to get there. You don't want us dragging a five-year-old with us when we cross the big street do you . . . huh? In the dark? With cars coming?"

Now this was a huge risk. I had mom's attention, but she could go one of two ways. Either my logic would convince her that our sister was not safe with us, or she could now be fearful that none of us were safe, and we all would be curtailed in our wanderings. Doug and I held our breaths. Time slowed. Mom's mental gears turned.

Finally, she said, "OK, I won't send Cindy with you two. Your dad and I will take her out ourselves and you two ragamuffins can run around with your gang. But you listen good. You both be very careful crossing that big street. I'm only letting you go to the 'haunted house' because you have the flashlight. Do you understand?"

"Yes!" I said. Doug's head bobbed up and down in complete agreement as if to emphasize our unified thoughts about this promise to mom. My flashlight could prevent us from any harm, and we would be especially careful! Of course! Thanks brain, for coming to the rescue!

Our mom was only mildly concerned about us crossing the busy street at night. And she certainly was not concerned about us trick-or-treating the "haunted house." She knew the house we were talking about because she had heard Doug and I point it out in the car when we occasionally drove by it. To her it was just another run-down old house in the area surrounding the projects. There was nothing real about ghosts and goblins in her mind. But not so in *ours!*

Once that was settled, Doug and I returned to our bedroom. He shut the door and said in admiration, "Wow, that was close! . . . But we can't trick-or-treat the haunted house? Are you crazy? We can't go there? . . . I don't want to go there!"

"Why not?" I said.

"Because . . . I'm scared just listening to ghost stories on the radio, but going where ghosts really live is. . . . Man, I don't even want to think about it! What if a ghost gets us and won't let us come home? What if he locks us up in his dungeon? What if he feeds us poison? . . . What if I tried to stop him, and I put my hand right through him? *You know you can put your hand right through a ghost!!!*"

Clearly, Doug was not looking forward to the possibility of us detouring on our Halloween plan. But the more I thought about it, the more it caught my fancy. It was something we *had* to do. I don't mean for a minute that I also wasn't concerned, maybe even scared, about the unknown possibilities, but that seemed only to heighten the intrigue for me. I thought we were inexorably being drawn to the haunted house by some, well . . . ghostly attraction.

"Are you crazy???" Ronnie said when I broke the idea to the others. "The haunted house! On Halloween? We've never been there at night, ever! I can hardly go near it on my bike during the day! And you want us to go there on Halloween! You're crazy!!!"

"Scare-deeee cat, scare-deeee cat," I said, in my underwhelming brilliance.

Freddie's mouth had been wide open since he heard my first words. It was as if his mind was taking time to get over the shock before it could actually put words into his mouth. Finally, he blurted out, "Yeah, you are crazy! When I rang the doorbell that one time during the daytime, before the barrel, remember? Well, when I did that, I was scared, I'm not kidding! I thought I was gonna be grabbed by something before I could hide in the woods. Every time I went by the house after that I just knew *they* knew I was there, even when we drove by in my dad's car. I wanted to hide down under his seat."

"*Who* knew?" I asked.

"The ghosts knew," he blurted. "They know, and I don't want to give them a chance to get me by going up and ringing that doorbell again, especially on Halloween night. They might rip my skin off! And how would I explain that to my dad?"

"Oh, come on, Freddie," I said. "They're not going to rip your skin off! They might pluck your eyes out with their claws, but they won't rip your skin off!" Boy, that made him feel better.

"I don't like the sound of this, either," Spike said. "You guys know more about the haunted house than me, or Jenny, but I've *never* been near it, other than to look at it from the woods. I . . . don't know. And . . . going there will take time, and that will mean we'll have less time to cover the projects."

Now that was a sound argument, and I also realized that we probably would come home with less candy because of the time lost in going to the haunted house and getting back again. Nobody wanted not to sacrifice candy any more than I, but the attraction seemed to loom larger each passing hour, to where I now was willing to give up some candy as a price for the adventure of having said we trick-or-treated the haunted house on Halloween. That was an accomplishment that would carry significant weight on the Columbia school playground the next morning.

Jenny, finally, matter-of-factly said, "Why not? I'm not afraid. I think it would be fun. Besides, since they're ghosts, maybe they'll welcome us for coming on Halloween and give us double the candy. I bet they don't get many trick-or-treaters on Halloween."

We guys all looked at each other and instantly confirmed that **girls just naturally think differently about things**. Here we were driven by fear, and she was driven by *hospitality!*

So it was settled. We now had a change of plans. We would begin as soon as dinner was over, about 6:00 PM. We would all meet next to our coal bin. We would go directly to the haunted house: down around the hill behind our house, across the big street (using the flashlight), skirt across the woods, and there it would be right in front of us. We would then, together, cross the small street, go through the gate, casually walk up the walkway, go up the steps to the front porch, ring the door bell, say "trick-or-treat" to whomever (or whatever) opened the door, take our candy, and then casually walk away from the house and backtrack to the projects.

Then we would scurry around in the projects, up and down Alderwood Court, Cedarwood Court, Pinewood Court, and even

hit Redwood Court, if time permitted, before returning home at
8:30 PM. It was tight, but we could do it! The only thing to slow
us down would be if other kids barraged us with questions about
trick-or-treating the haunted house, after we told then we had
done it. And, of course, nothing, absolutely nothing, would keep us
from telling them once we had done it! It sounded easy and well
thought-out. What could possibly disrupt our plans? Nothing we
could think of.

How much we were to be surprised!

THE COSTUMES

After the new plan was complete, the next major planning activity
was our costumes. What to wear? This also was not a casual question. The costumes had to be sufficiently original and "cute" so as
to stimulate the "take." We had learned a simple truth about adults a
long time ago: **The cuter you looked, the more likely another
drop of candied bliss was likely to find its way into your
bag**—another of life's simple lessons applicable in so many ways.

Our decisions on costumes were complicated by the reality that
there was no money to buy pre-fabbed outfits. We had to come
up with something original that was the outcome of an extensive
scavenger hunt around the house. Our parents were utilized, as we
had learned that they also could be fairly creative in this regard.
Our moms were especially intent that their "little darlings" looked
as cute as possible before sending us out into the cold, dark air for
an evening of legitimized begging. And, although we were unified
in the overall plan, we were still fairly guarded with each other as
to what we planned to "become." Usually when we all showed up
at the designated location and time, we were surprised at how we
all had been transformed. That was part of the charm and mystery
of the night.

For weeks in advance, I had wavered between two possibilities
for my costume. One was to become Flash Gordon, one of my great

heroes and alter egos at the time. A problem with this, though, was that I did not have a legitimate Flash Gordon costume lying around, complete with ray gun. The second possibility was to become a sailor. This was much easier since one of my other favorite uncles, Mom's closest brother, Shanty, had given me some of his sailor clothes after the Second World War. I treasured those garments. As much as Flash was my first choice, a seaman I would be.

I wore clean jeans (supposed to be sailor pants) and a navy-colored turtleneck sweatshirt. Over this I wore a true Navy pea coat from Shanty. This was a heavy wool, double-breasted coat with large black buttons. It had a large collar that, when turned up in the back, protected my neck from the wind. Although it was a "small" size, it was still large for me, with the arms requiring rolled up cuffs. In addition to looking really Navy-like, I also was assured of being warm when we were out running around.

The *crème de la crème* was the white sailor hat that sat neatly on my head with a slight tilt to the right side. Uncle Shanty had taught me how to fold the canvas hat into an inside-out triangle for storage so that when it was unfolded it almost magically blocked into a square on my head. Then I partially folded two of the opposite sides of the square down slightly on each side to enhance the blocking and get a racy "devil-may-care" look. I didn't know if sailors actually folded their hats like that in the Service, but I liked the look. The hat remained one of my prized possessions well into my teens, until unfortunately it disappeared in one of our numerous family moves during that phase of my life. But, for now, my costume was set.

My brother was to become a cowboy, a small buckaroo. His stated ideal was to be Dick West, the Range Rider's trusty side-kick. Somehow our mother had come up with a small black cowboy outfit, just like Dick West's. His shirt didn't have the same pattern of buttons that Dick's had, but it was close. He also wore, tied around his neck, a red bandana that our mom had used to tie-up her hair when she worked in the shipyard during the War. On him, it was transformed into the perfect accessory item. He wore boots, which, although not actually cowboy boots, still complemented the look. On top of his head sat a very nice small Dick West type of cowboy hat, except this one was white, whereas Dick's was black. A compromise had to be made. Rounding out the whole characterization was a belt with two holsters, each housing a shinny silver "cap" pistol. I was impressed. Doug looked like he was ready to go out and round up some cattle rustlers right then. Either that, or go to a square dance. We were ready!

Bags in hand, and the big flashlight in my pea coat pocket, we said goodbye to mom, dad, and Cindy (dressed as a princess), and went out to our coal bin. It was not raining, fortunately, but it was cold and damp, typical Seattle night weather for the end of October. Our breath was slightly visible as we exhaled.

Freddie Roberts walked up out of the darkness, or at least I thought it was Freddie. I was not sure at first because his face was dark, but the gait and stature were that of Freddie. It was Freddie all right. His face looked as if shoe polish had been smeared on it. But it was not shoe polish, it was some type of dark brown cream. And he wore a baseball uniform, except for his tennis shoes. Doug and I both stared.

I said, "What are you?"

He said, "Jackie Robinson," and then turned around so we could see the number 42 on his back.

Doug and I both burst into a laugh. "But your face. You look stupid!" We continued to chuckle.

Freddie said, "Well, he is a Negro. It was my dad's idea."

Next to arrive were Spike and Jenny. Spike had on a sports jacket that came close to fitting him. He also wore nice slacks. The topper was a tie around the neck of his shirt. It was one of those 1940s ties with a big gaudy pattern that went sideways on the wide part of the tie. It was one of his father's, because I remembered seeing him wear it when the whole family came back from church one Sunday morning. Something about that ostentatious look had registered in my memory. In Spike's hand was a wooden microphone of the times.

I said, "Who are you?"

He said, "I'm Frank Sinatra!" Doug, Freddie, and I all grinned. At least he looked better than Freddie, but I think Freddie was secretly relieved that he was not the only one who looked slightly goofy. We all decided that the fake microphone had to go as soon as everybody had arrived.

Jenny was dressed in a light-blue gingham checked dress with straps that went over her shoulders. Her hair was in pigtails and she wore a heavy white sweater because of the cold. Although the sweater didn't go with the outfit, it nevertheless was necessary this night. On her feet were slip-on shoes that were red. But they were not naturally red; they had merely been painted red with glossy enamel paint.

I said, "Let me guess . . . *"Dorothy!"* . . . Right?"

She said, "Yeah. Do you like it? My dad did the shoes."

We all nodded our heads in affirmation. Yeah, it looked OK, except that it was a dress, and Jenny rarely wore a dress. We also noticed that she had full-length stockings on her slender legs to add warmth. The stockings were noticeable not so much for their color as for the fact that they sagged at her knees and ankles. But all in all, she was an eight on a scale of ten.

Last to show up was Ronnie Landers. I couldn't believe it when I saw him. He was Flash Gordon! My hero, right before my eyes! Or at least he was a reasonable facsimile of Flash. He had on a pullover shirt like Flash always wore. It had been embroidered by his mother around the chest and across the shoulders the way Flash's tunics were. He also had on tight-fitting trousers with boots over his feet. Around his waist was a holster belt with a wooden "ray gun!" I commented on the ray gun, and he said I better watch what I said or he would disintegrate me! The most outlandish part of his costume was on his head. He was wearing an *Orphan Annie* wig, except that it was blonde. It made him look like Harpo Marx in a space costume. He said he bought the wig at the dime store. We all had to laugh, even Jenny.

There we all were, a strange collection to be sure, but one that any self-respecting ghost family would welcome into their house with warmth. Right?

We were about to find out.

24

HALLOWEEN 1952—THE ADVENTURE

Curiosity will conquer fear even more than bravery will.
—James Stephens

We set out, shopping bags in hand, for the haunted house. We scurried down the hill in the back of our four-plex and came to the big street. What a rag-tag bunch we must have looked like to passing cars. The first time there was a break in traffic in both directions we all took off running for the other side. The cold autumn air kissed our cheeks as we scampered across the street, intent on achieving the far curb. Naturally, Freddie (Jackie Robinson) was the last to arrive. I thought how ironic that his character was such a great runner and gifted athlete, and yet Freddie had none of those attributes. But that's why there are alter-egos.

We dipped into the woods and were enveloped in darkness. Once our eyes adjusted, the light from the nearly full moon shining in a cloudless sky, a rarity for Seattle in October, partially illuminated our pathway. The moon helped, but neither it nor the flashlight were necessary because we all knew the path so well we could find our way with our eyes closed. Still, we stayed close together as much as possible, without stepping on each other's heels.

"What are we gonna do when we get there?" Doug asked. "Are we gonna wait outside the gate, while one of us goes to the door? . . . And who's gonna go? I think Freddie should go because he already did it once."

Freddie interjected before anyone could speak, "I'm not going to the door! I did it in daylight, the same day I found the barrel, and that was enough. Don't make me do it again!"

Ronnie said to me, "Jack, you should go, because this was all your idea. You're the one who wanted to do this."

That was true. It was my idea, and it had sounded exciting at the time. But now, here in the dark, as we neared the moment of truth, I was not so enamored with the concept anymore. In fact, with each passing moment I was rethinking this plan. We could call it off and still get back to the projects in time to do some serious trick-or-treating without worry. Who knew what we might run into here? What if there really were ghosts? What if they sucked us inside and really did put us in their dungeon?? What if they really did rip off our skin??? I liked my skin. I liked it right where it was! It occurred to me that I was beginning to shiver, and it was not entirely from the cold air.

As we neared the far edge of the woods, the old run-down house became visible. We paused to gaze across the street at it. Even from where we stood it was eerie. Doug was the first to openly admit that he was scared and would just as soon wait behind, thank you very much!

Ronnie said, "I never wanted to do this. I'm not gonna say I'm scared, but if anyone else wants to go back, I'm with 'em!"

At this, Freddie poked Ronnie in the neck from behind and let out a screech. Ronnie jumped completely off the ground and shook when his feet landed. He turned and swung an arm in the direction of the poke, not maliciously or angrily, just out of a scared reflex. He yelled something about pounding Freddie good, except it was so dark Freddie looked like he didn't have a face with that dark cream smeared on his skin. It looked like there was simply a number 42 baseball jersey walking around with a baseball hat suspended in mid-air. Of course, that didn't do much to calm Ronnie, or the rest of us.

Spike said, "That's it! I'm quitting. I'm not going over there. If you guys wanna go, fine, but I'm staying here!"

"Aw, come on," Jenny said. "We've come this far, and the whole thing will be over in a minute. I'm not afraid. Let's go!"

There was silence for a few moments except for Doug's and Freddie's teeth chattering. This was it! This was the moment. I knew I either had to back up my bravado by actually doing the deed, or forever be ridiculed on brighter future afternoons for not being brave enough to follow through. All of the others' fears now, at this moment, would be forgotten then, conveniently. The only thing they would remember would be that when it finally came to actually doing it, I had chickened out, especially after it was all my idea in the first place.

Finally, with a struggle between caution and fear battling inside my head, I said, "We're not going back. We're going to do this. It's just like Jenny said, we're here now and we shouldn't be afraid. After all there are six of us. What could a silly ghost do to all of us?"

The logic sounded OK, it's just that none of us had an answer to that question, and not having an answer, our collective worst imaginings took over. The possible horrors were too much to contemplate.

I said, as forcefully as possible, "We're going. And we're all going. Just like in *The Three Musketeers!* We're all going together! C'mon—now." Within myself, I realized: **There comes a time when you have to face your fears**. As scared as I also was, I couldn't let them think I wasn't prepared to do it.

Still, there was no onrushing movement from the others. Finally, Jenny stepped forward and said, "Let's go. Let's hold hands in case one of us gets separated or falls in the darkness."

Under any other circumstances, there is no way any gang member was ever going to be caught dead holding hands with another gang member. But, at this moment, in this situation, it didn't seem like a bad idea, and it had the logic that it would keep us from getting separated. So we joined hands in a single line and walked out of the woods, crossed the small street separating the woods from the haunted house, and approached the gate to the four-foot high picket fence surrounding the property. The fence was dilapidated and in need of repair, as were most things about the house. We huddled partially behind one of the bushes near the gate. We peeked around the bush and stared at the house, again trying to ratchet up our courage. The house appeared asleep, with no light on the porch, but perhaps that was just a trap. *The ghosts were waiting!* Again we paused and glanced at each other, everyone searching for some sign of bravery.

"OK, here we go," I said as I stepped to the gate, lifted up the latch, and pushed the gate backward into the yard. The gate rotated and squeaked on its hinges as a possible precursor to deeper doom. We slowly and deliberately walked across a stone pathway about twenty-five yards. We approached the house almost tiptoeing. My flashlight danced about with each step, throwing just enough light for us to keep from tripping, and from losing our will. With each step the house loomed larger and its presence became more terrifying. Our heartbeats raced.

The house was a two-story structure that looked like it had been built in the prior century. It was a Victorian with odd angles and asymmetrical walls in strange directions. It had a large veranda-style porch which ran the length of the front of the house. The veranda was entirely covered by a roof that sloped away from the sides of the upper floor and was supported by turned columns that dropped to the porch deck. In the middle of the veranda was the front door with a glassed transom above. There was a double glider seat on the veranda in front of a large window off to the right of the door. This large window had shutters on either side, but one of the shutters had become dislodged and hung at a skewed angle. It appeared as if the glider had not been occupied for months.

To the left of the front door was a room with a curved wall protruding outward into the veranda. This wall had a number of tall and narrow windows with beveled panes. We could see from a distance that they were backlit with a single low-wattage light bulb hanging from the ceiling inside the room. Through the glass, it was apparent how dirty the windows were. The glass was that very old style that lets light through, but distorts the images. At the sides of the windows were draped curtains, some gathered to the side, some hanging free. The hanging bulb highlighted tears in the curtains, as though cats had used them for climbing paths. Or that ghosts had purposely shredded them because they preferred them that way!

From our vantage point we could see that there were two other lights on in the house, both on the second floor, and both also of very low wattage. Whoever lived inside definitely was not in favor of well-lit surroundings. It was . . . well, spooky to be sure! One light, visible through the glassed transom above the front door, appeared to be on a landing at the top of a stairwell. It also hung alone from the ceiling. The second light upstairs came from a room to the left of the landing, and directly over the room on the first floor with the curved wall and old curtained windows.

The house overall was dirty and significantly in need of repair and maintenance. It not only looked eerie during the day, but at night looked downright scary. Years later when I saw the movie *Psycho*, Norman Bates' house up on the hill instantly reminded me of this old haunted house from this Halloween night.

There were four steps to get onto the veranda. We cautiously approached the stairs. It was eerily dark. My flashlight blazed out as much light as it could. I prayed the batteries would last. Slowly, in unison but with trepidation, we all climbed each step, eventually standing, together, on the veranda before the door. I shined the flashlight around to make us better aware of the porch. At least we didn't see rats or gargoyles. We might not have recovered from seeing any of those. As we squirmed closer together in a tightly packed bunch, the floorboards squeaked under foot. Some were missing large knotholes, and others curled and were out of plane with the surface. It was not an easy surface to navigate under lit conditions, and in the dark was not only slightly treacherous, but also frightening. We tried to extend our necks to glance into the rooms, but with our hands still held together none of us wanted to leave the safety of the pack.

The front door was very large; wide and tall. It was wooden mostly, but had a large oval shaped window in the middle of the top half. This window was similar to the others and had beveled panes of dirty and distorting glass. As we strained to look through the window, it appeared that behind the door was an entryway leading to the other rooms and to the base of the stairwell. At the right side of the door was an ornate brass knob with a brass plate behind it and a keyhole in the bottom of the plate. To the right of the doorknob on the side of the house was a doorbell button.

"Ohhh kayyy," I said. "Freddie, you ring the bell 'cuz you've done it before. Everybody get ready. I'll say 'trick-or-treat' for all of us."

I felt moisture on my left hand from Doug, and my other hand was now held in a death grip from Jenny. For someone who supposedly wasn't scared, she certainly grasped me tightly. There was no way I could break her grip should I suddenly decide to run. If so, I knew I would drag all of them behind me in the dirt. No one let go!

Freddie paused . . . but finally his hand wobbled out of the dark, and slowly, unsteadily approached the button, as if he feared 400 volts would suddenly zap him upon contact! His finger touched the button and we heard a buzzer inside the entryway. His voice squealed with an involuntary sound from deep within his throat. Doug's hand now shook in mine. We waited . . . and waited. . . . Nothing.

"Ring it again," I said.

"Do I hafta?" whispered Freddie.

"Yeah," said Spike, "one more time, and then let's get out of here!"

Freddie rang again. By now both Freddie and Ronnie visibly shook. We waited again . . . and waited. . . . Nothing!

Everybody felt very slightly better and the tension dropped a smidgen. Our collective thoughts were, Well, we did it, and if nobody's home, that's not our problem. Let's go!!!

But I didn't move. We stood there for another ten or fifteen seconds, which seemed like an hour to all of us costumed urchins. I was ready to turn and go, with no arguments I'm sure, but then . . . for some reason, I did something totally unexpected. I sloowwly reached over and touched the doorknob. It was icy cold in my hand, but I left my hand on it nevertheless. Then I did another surprising thing. . . . I turned the knob! I turned it ever so slooowwwly until it would not turn anymore!! And then . . . the door creaked and, shockingly, separated very slightly from the casing!!! It opened!!! It was unlocked!!! Oh, my gosh, now what??? I let go of the knob and jammed my hand back into my coat pocket as if that would suddenly reverse what had just happened. I was terrified inside, and my knees shook. Doug and Freddie both sniffled, and even Ronnie's body separated backwards from mine.

We all stood there stunned, frozen to the porch, scared beyond belief, not knowing what to do next. If a horde of ghosts had suddenly swooped out of the tiny crack in the door, now illuminated by the dim light inside, and enveloped us in their spirits, none of us would have been the least surprised. We expected it. The door was actually unlocked, and we had broken its seal! We had invaded the ghosts' spiritual space! As a group we stood deathly still and suspended breathing. Five seconds! Ten seconds! Fifteen seconds! Nothing!

Suddenly it occurred to us, collectively, that perhaps we were not going to be eaten by hideous monsters after all. We were still alive and together. Our fear slowly abated and momentary relief returned to our souls. We breathed again.

"OK. Let's get out of here," Spike pleaded. Even Jenny finally said, "Yeah. Let's go."

"No," I said. I was still alive, but now I was overcome by curiosity. I pulled my hand out of the safety of its pocket and put it on the door. I pushed lightly . . . and ever so slowly . . . the door spun on its hinges with a soft rusty squeaking sound. It opened to reveal an ornate entryway with wood paneling and an old throw rug in front of us on the floor. We stood very still and stared into the room, as my flashlight randomly pranced everywhere to illuminate the space. In unison we all slightly leaned forward to see within. Our petrified fear a moment ago had now been replaced with an offsetting and overpowering curiosity. If there were ghosts, and since they had not killed us already, perhaps they would not mind if we looked around, now that the door was open. After all, if they really didn't want us to see, they would not have left the door unlocked. Right? At least I think that was the reasoning at the moment. Once the door actually opened, which was the last possible thing any of us had expected, we all believed we now had a compelling invitation to look. We stared inside from the apparent safety of the veranda.

I said, "Let's go in!"

Instantly, the group's fear returned. There was overlapping whis-
perings of dire concern, which I ignored. For some reason, I was
so overly curious about the inside of the house, now that it was
exposed, that I tuned out most of their comments. But I did hear
Jenny say, "Yeah, let's go in." In fact, she didn't even wait for me to
move. She stepped toward the threshold first and pulled me along.
I in turn then pulled the others in behind us. We all stood within
the entryway. I shined my light into the room on our right and
confirmed that it was a living room, or large parlor room. It was
filled with old and worn furniture and bric-a-brac on the walls.
The room was generally messy with various things on the floor
and women's clothing strewn on the chairs.

To our left was a dining room, also messy with dirty dishes on
the table. We walked as a group into the dining room and scanned
around under the dim, single lightbulb hanging from the ceiling.
Inside the dining room was a door to another room. We cautiously
walked to the door and I flashed the light into and around this new
room. It was the kitchen. Assured that it was empty, I leaned inside
and felt around the doorframe for a light switch. Feeling one, finally,
I flicked it on. The room was lit, again by a very dim bulb.

We all slowly entered into the kitchen, which was a complete
mess with unwashed dishes scattered about. There was also dried
food on the counter tops and shriveled vegetables scattered in
clumps. A nearby garbage bin was stuffed with bottles and other
trash. The sink was piled with dishes and was half full of dirty water.
There was a smell in the air of decay and dirt that was offensive to
our noses. What was going on here? Why was the house like this?
Where was whoever lived here? Why did they live in such a stinky
mess like this?

Our great fears moments ago now were replaced by wonder and
curiosity. Even in the dim light we were more intrigued than fearful.
We even had broken our handholds, as they confined our urges to
wander and explore. Unsatisfied, we walked back into the dining
room and eventually to the entryway again. We stood in front of the
still-open front door looking at each other and talking with more
relaxed abandon. After the trip to the kitchen, we didn't seem to

be preoccupied with dungeons or poisons anymore. We were more surprised at what we had seen, and were filled with questions.

We looked in front of us and saw the stairway leading up to the second floor. Except, it was a very strange stairway, like none any of us had ever seen before. Each step was only about half the height of a normal riser, and the width of the stairs was only slightly wider than a person's body. Only one person at a time could ascend these stairs: we would have to go up the stairs in single file. And the stairway doubled back on itself not once, but twice, thus there were three riser sections and a large number of total steps in order to get from the first floor to the second floor. We all thought, how odd, and our curiosity was now completely in charge.

"Why would someone build stairs like that?" Ronnie asked.

Jenny answered, "I don't know. But let's go up them."

That was my same thought! Regardless of the poor lighting, and everything we had seen on the first floor, my interest was now directed to these unique stairs. I wanted to climb them . . . because they were different. They were like three separate passageways with two turning landings. It was a captivating maze before my eyes, yet I knew where it began and where it ended. It just seemed intriguing to climb the stairway. The others were less captivated by the stairs themselves, and had more fear of where they led.

Freddie said, "No, I don't want to go up there! We don't know what's on top. Maybe that's where the ghosts are waiting. It's a trap! We'll get up there and they'll jump on us and cut our stomachs open." Freddie definitely had an active imagination.

Ronnie chimed in with a wavering voice, "Yeah . . . uh . . . I don't know. I'm not scared. I'm not! I just don't want to go up there. We've already done more than I wanted. I say we run out of here and head back while we're still safe, and alive!"

Spike said he was with Ronnie and also wanted to leave, NOW! But he wanted Jenny to go with him. He couldn't go and leave his sister in the house. If anything happened to her, their parents would blame him.

Doug said more or less the same; he wanted to leave immediately but also didn't want to go without me. He was not so much concerned about our mom blaming him for me getting eaten by ghosts. Rather, he just felt safer with me leading the way home with my flashlight than with the remaining four of them making their way through the woods without any light.

I said, "Look, there's nothing to be afraid of. There's nobody home! If somebody was home, do you think they would have let us come this far? All we're gonna do is climb the stairs up and down, and then leave. OK? And, we can all hold hands again in a single file. We'll be like a snake going up the stairs." Oops, I thought, bad example.

"Yeah, let's do it!" Jenny said. And, before anybody could answer, she grabbed my hand and pulled me toward the stairs. Doug found my other hand faster than the others. I guess he figured since I was not going back with him now, he would rather be with me. And being in the middle of the "snake" was better than being on either end. He effectively had reserved his position. Freddie and Spike suddenly each had "dibs" on the next spot, and Spike finally gave it to Freddie. Ronnie brought up the rear.

I passed my flashlight to Jenny, now leading, and up we climbed, slowly, steadily, quietly. With each rising step it seemed as if our fear awoke from its semi-latency and revisited us. Each step was another incremental move toward an unknown destiny. What began as a curious examination of a strange upward passage became another venture into the lair of ghosts and demons. They would be waiting for us at the top, just as Freddie had said, and then they would have us trapped in the passage because they would also swoop down and seal off the bottom. We were doomed!

Every time Jenny rounded a corner with the flashlight, those at the back—those with the most agitated imaginations—again were thrown into darkness, releasing waves of anxiety and fear that vibrated all the way up to the front of the line. Freddie began to sob, even though we surrounded him. Ronnie told him to stop crying because Jackie Robinson would not be crying. That argument had no effect. Freddie continued to whimper with each step upward.

We reached the top of the staircase and stepped out into a central hallway. The foyer was poorly illuminated by the single, hanging, dim bulb we had viewed earlier. We huddled together, momentarily realizing some comfort that we had not been met by swirling spirits ready to disembowel us. We were packed so tightly that if any one of us had tried to move away, we all risked tumbling as a unit, due to the support being removed.

Jenny flashed the light up and down the corridor. Where we were standing the foyer widened, but as the hallway traversed toward the back of the house it narrowed. There were various doors off the hallway, presumably passageways to rooms. Near where we stood was a large set of double doors leading to the room that was built over the dining room. One of the doors was half open and we could see another dim light emanating from this room. This was the other upstairs light we had seen when we approached the house from the walkway. As we all stood motionless and speechless, except for Freddie's whimpers, we stared at the double doors.

For some reason, those doors "called" to me. But as curious as I was about the doors, I also began to feel that we really were pushing our limit. I could again feel shaking in my legs. We, as a group, were not sure what to do next. We treasured the dim amount of light we had above us, but still strained our eyes, and our ears were on ready alert for any sensations. I know I had promised that we would go down the stairs as soon as we reached the top, but none of us could move. We stood glued together and took comfort in each other's breathing and quivering bodies. Doug's shopping bag rattled from his shaking hand.

"What do you think," Jenny whispered, "creepy huh?"

"Yeah," I slowly replied. "What should we do?"

Spike said, "Let's go. We got up here, like you wanted, but let's go! I don't like this at all. I feel like we're being watched!" When he said that, the fine hairs on the back of my neck rose, much as my increasing concern. What a creepy thought—maybe we were being watched in the dark!!!

"I feel that way too," Ronnie said. "I'm not scared, but I wanna go too. . . . NOW!"

Then we heard a soft scratching sound within the room, near the bottom of the doors. Doug's arm circled my waist and I could hear him plea, "Jack . . . Jack!" as if begging for help. Jenny aimed the flashlight at the base of the doors just in time to catch a blur of movement as a creature scooted out the room and down the hall. We all were startled. The shock was almost too much and it broke our extended quietness.

"*Aieeee*," screeched Freddie as his fear took a notch upward. He clawed at Ronnie's and Spike's bodies trying to get inside the clump of us standing there.

Spike's voice quivered in elevated desperation, "Freddie, Freddie, it's OK! We're here. It's OK!" Freddie's clawing stopped, but his whimpering continued.

Jenny's light caught up with the creature, which had stopped halfway down the hall. The flashlight illuminated two bright red reflections shining back at us, as its eyes were totally dilated in the near-darkness. We squinted and made out a Siamese cat hunkered down in the hall, staring at us. Our breaths escaped in unison as the relief was palpable.

"I want to look in that last room," I whispered to nobody in particular.

"No!" Doug said. "Let's go!" His little cowboy hat was shaking on his head.

"I'm goin' home," Ronnie said, "but I don't want to go alone. Who's with me?"

Freddie blurted, "Me. I am. I'm going."

I said, "You guys can go back downstairs if you want, and wait for me. Or you can go all of the way home, but I'm keeping the flashlight. I'm going into that room and see what's in there. With doors like these, I bet it's a big bedroom."

"I'm staying," Jenny said. "I want to see the room too."

"Aw, come on Jenny," Spike said. Jenny shook her head; she loved her brother but she wasn't leaving me. She was too curious to miss out on whatever was in that bedroom. So now we were split equally because I knew Doug was not going to leave me. Then Spike gave in and said he couldn't leave Jenny, either. And, of course, Freddie was staying with the numbers. Ronnie, we all knew by now was not that scared, but he certainly didn't want to go away alone. So we were unified again. Scared, but unified!

We decided to hold hands again. I took the flashlight from Jenny and assumed the lead position, with my other hand holding hers, then Doug, Freddie, Spike, and Ronnie. We breathed deeply a few times. I stepped toward the doors, shining the flashlight ahead. We tiptoed as quietly as possible until we all reached the doors. We paused. I put my hand on the open door and very sloooowwwwly pushed it inward, straining my neck to see into the room as the opening expanded. Finally, the door was completely aside and we could see a large bed with four posters at the corners. On either side of the bed was a dresser and on each dresser was a table lamp. One of the lamps was on, but the bulb intensity was so low it made it difficult to see things in the room. It appeared to be no brighter than a night-light. We bunched together and squinted into the room. It was large and there was much to cover with almost no light. I moved the flashlight around the walls, to the dressers, to the lamp, to the bed. . . .

And then we saw it. . . .

There was a *body* in the bed!!!

It was a very old woman lying on her right side with her face turned away from us. She had long stringy hair that flowed loosely around her head and shoulders. She was partially covered with a blanket that crossed her back, and she had on a thin robe. Her right arm was under the cover and her left arm was extended out in front of her on the mattress. Her hand was bony and almost skeletal. She was not moving. We all gasped and held each other!

"Oh, no!!! Someone's home and we caught her in bed," Spike cried in a petrified but very low whisper before anyone else could say anything. He wanted to scream, as did we all, but we also knew that it would only make matters worse, if we startled the woman. She looked like she was asleep, and the last thing we wanted to do was wake her. Freddie really shook now and was too stimulated to even cry anymore. He tugged at me and said, "Let's back up and leave her alone. I don't want to ask her for a trick-or-treat!"

Still, we stood, though, staring and thinking. Each few seconds seemed to become minutes. The others looked around, but Jenny and I continued to stare at the woman in bed. It didn't look like she was even breathing, let alone moving.

"Maybe she's dead!" I whispered. This set off a whole new level of shaking and muted crying. Catching someone asleep was one thing, but catching them dead, on Halloween, in a haunted house, was a far greater thing! We were clearly going to pay for this! We expected the walls to open up at any moment and the ghosts to come for us. But they didn't, and we all continued to stare at the lifeless form in the luminescence of the flashlight.

"Let's go closer and see," said Jenny. "Let's see if she's dead." This was met by four voices, in unison, saying "NO" in a whispered shout. But I was with Jenny. I wanted to see if she was dead, or sleeping.

After more anxious chatter we all finally decided to go to her side of the bed, again hand-in-hand as if chained to each other. Jenny and I crept very slowly around the foot of the bed, and then up beside her. We looked into her face, which was lit by the dresser lamp. Her face seemed peaceful but her eyes remained closed and still. Then, finally, the smell was undeniable. Her bed reeked of urine and she smelled overpoweringly of body odor. She obviously had not bathed in a very long time. The others smelled it too and stepped backward in revulsion, but without breaking the chain.

Jenny and I bent over to see her face better. I carefully brought the flashlight up to shine on her hair, and her face. It was then that her left eyelid TWITCHED . . . and then . . . OPENED! Instantly, there were shrieks from all of us! I jumped back and was grabbed by Jenny who put her hand over her mouth to hold a scream inside. The woman was alive, and she had caught us in her trap! We were finally going to be killed. She was the witch from *Snow White* and she had caught us!

But no, she didn't jump up. Instead, her eye began to move around, dazed like, and finally her left arm moved slightly. Jenny bent down to see her closer, putting her hand on the bed. The woman moved her hand toward Jenny's, and softly touched Jenny's wrist. I, too, leaned down, and the others leaned in. Then the woman said, in a very soft and barely audible voice, "Help . . . Help me, please."

I said, "She's not a witch, she's sick. Something's wrong with her. Ronnie, try to find a light switch on the wall or try to turn on that other lamp."

The others, now relieved that the prospect of being eaten alive was no longer certain, relaxed somewhat. It helped when Ronnie turned on the other dresser lamp and doubled the amount of light in the room. I pulled back her gray hair and we saw her full face for the first time. She was very haggard looking with folds of age-dappled skin that drooped on her face and chin. Her eyes were reddened and watered slightly. Her pupils were large and unfocused. I turned her slightly to better prop her head under the pillow. Her breathing was now noticeable and she seemed extremely weak and not totally responsive.

"We've got to get her some help," I said. "Someone has to go get help."

Jenny very softly said, "I'll stay here with her."

Then Doug, who previously had been petrified and on the verge of uncontrolled breakdown, now was calmed and said, "I'll stay too. Jenny and I'll help the woman." It was a very remarkable change in my brother that I couldn't help noticing and appreciating in spite of the confusion. It was one of the earliest times I saw that Doug was a very sensitive and caring person. This would become apparent to me many more times in our lives, as I also came to realize how he was so naturally equipped with unique care-giving skills.

I said, "OK. I'll go and see if I can find someone to help us. Anybody want to come with me?" All three remaining "volunteered," and we took off with the flashlight, running down the stairwell, and out the front door. It felt good and refreshing to get outside in the cold, clear air and breathe normally again. We ran up the street separating the haunted house from the woods and came to another house about a half-block away that was lit with lights inside as well as on the porch. We ran up and rang the doorbell. A middle-aged lady came to the door with candy, obviously expecting we were trick-or-treating. But we had all left our bags behind with Jenny and Doug. We blurted out the story, all talking at once, about the old woman in the house down the street, and that we needed help.

She seemed taken aback initially, and was not quite sure whether to believe another hoax on this Halloween night, but she eventually came to understand the desperation in our voices. She called an ambulance and instructed them to come to her house. We waited, and after about fifteen minutes an ambulance showed up. We told our story again, and then rode together in the ambulance to the haunted house.

When we went inside the house again, we found Jenny and Doug caring for the woman. They had found some clean water and had washed her face. She was completely turned over on her back and was more animated than when we had left, although she was still frail and partially disoriented. The two attendants were able to get her onto a gurney and then downstairs and into the ambulance. It was not easy getting her down through the stairwell but they did. When we all came outside, there was also a police car in front that had apparently responded to the ambulance call. The middle-aged woman in the other house had told the policeman where we were. The frail old woman was loaded into the ambulance, and it left for a hospital with the siren blaring.

The policeman asked us questions about how we happened to find her, and we had to tell him the whole story. We were scared and relieved at the same time: scared because we were afraid that now we were really in trouble with the police for having entered the haunted house without a key, but also relieved that we didn't find any ghosts and we all were still alive. Of the two predicaments, we were happy to be alive even if it meant we were now hardened criminals, guilty of breaking and entering. After listening for a long time to all of our explanations, sometimes overlapping, he finally told us that we should not have done what we did. But, since it turned out OK, and we may have saved the old woman's life by finding her before she died, he could forgive us.

We all suddenly exploded in relief! All of the tension, fear, and anxiety left our bodies, and we noticeably slumped and relaxed. He gave each of us a big handshake, including Jenny, and commented on our costumes.

He then asked us where we lived, and did we want a ride home? A ride home!!! Wow! A ride home in a police car!!! We were beside ourselves—talk about a roller coaster evening! Here we had started out with an ambitious plan to simply go trick-or-treating, which had led to us getting scared out of our wits, more than once, and then we had saved a woman's life, maybe. Then, the absolute top, we could ride in a police car! The only thing better would be if we could also ride in a fire truck, but the police car was more than enough. Of course, we wanted to ride home with the police!!! What a night.

So before he could say . . . well, "Jackie Robinson," we piled into the car, all six of us kids and the policeman driving. We sat on each other's laps (there were no safety belts in those days) and were having the time of our lives. Off we went. He even turned on the siren for just a moment.

Then, slowly, we pulled into the projects and cruised up Alderwood Court to the end of the Court. By the time he had stopped in front of our coal bin, the car was surrounded with trick-or-treaters in various costumes and adults who were always attracted to a police car. Police cars generally were associated with trouble, or kids doing bad things. So, when we all piled out of the car, our parents were stunned with apprehension as to what we had been caught doing. Before we could say anything, the policeman addressed everybody and told the story of how we all had been brave Halloween *heroes* by saving a dying woman. Every kid's mouth was open in wonderment as the officer talked. He never called it the "haunted house," but every kid listening knew immediately which house it was.

We were in heaven, and we suddenly had been elevated to the highest pedestals of respect among our peers. Even the adults seemed to be impressed, and everybody was so happy. When he was done, everybody applauded and rubbed our heads and touched us. It was wonderful. Then the officer returned to his car and left.

Our parents still seemed surprised and wanted to hear more of the story later. We knew there would be many more tellings, and with each telling the story would receive more dramatic overtones. Years later the story had grown to the point of us deserving the Nobel Peace prize.

And we were heroes on the Columbia school playground too, for about a week, and then life was back to normal. Thanksgiving was on the way, and then Christmas. Every kid's attention was refocused on turkey, pies, presents, and Santa Claus.

But for one wonderful Halloween, when I was ten years old, life stood still for an evening.

We didn't get any Halloween candy that year, but neither Doug nor I would trade the experiences we had for any amount of Big Hunk® bars. None of us Alderwood Court gang ever saw the woman in the house again and we never found out what became of her. Truth is we never tried. Even though we escaped with our lives that night and had great memories as a result, none of us stopped believing for even a second that the house wasn't haunted. Our logic was that maybe the ghosts wanted us to come in and find the woman, and that is why they let us go free. But we all thought we never should tempt fate again.

We still curiously would look across at the house from the edge of the woods. In fact, one day we even crept across the street and hid behind the bushes near the fence to peek around and stare at the house from a closer vantage point. Getting Freddie Roberts that close again was a big accomplishment. But we *knew*—just knew— that the ghosts were staring back at us through the shredded and tattered curtains, just licking their chops for another chance to shred us too. We never again gave them that opportunity.

POSTSCRIPT ONE

One obstacle to the adventure of that Halloween night was mom's insistence that Doug and I take our younger sister Cindy with us on our trick-or-treat rounds. This was resolved when I successfully argued with her that she wouldn't want us "dragging a five-year-old with us when we crossed the big street . . . in the dark . . . with cars coming." Although my argument worked, now I am amazed at the things mom let Doug and me do at those early ages.

When I became a parent, I would not let my kids go out alone on Halloween, and we lived in a very safe and secure upscale neighborhood. And I certainly would not allow them to cross a busy street alone at night, flashlight or no flashlight! But such was parenting at the time. Our mom, and most moms in the 1950s, let their kids have much more freedom. Either mothers had more confidence in their kids then, or America after the Second World War, and the Korean conflict, just didn't seem that risky.

POSTSCRIPT TWO

That Halloween adventure was the culmination of the Alderwood Court gang coming together as a team. Yes we learned it was important to confront our fears and never give up—to hang in there against all odds, but our most important lesson was: **The team is everything!** A team always, every time, will accomplish more than individuals doing their own thing, to their own liking. Teams give each other strength and put the goals of the whole above their own personal needs. Not all members are equal. It is the role of stronger members to help weaker ones, not only by displaying determination, but also by exercising compassion and patience. And it is the requirement of all members to trust in the team and believe, as we all did that night. We understood—as petrified as we were—that we still were better off huddled together and helping each other, than if we had deserted each other. We had, without words, formed a bond among ourselves, which ultimately meant more to all of us than any other outcome that special evening.

We grew together as friends and were proud of ourselves and of each other because of our teamwork. We all knew after that night that we could count on each other for anything, and there is no more satisfying feeling than knowing you can depend on someone else, and they on you.

We all grew that evening. Afterward we knew we were different, and we were pleased with how we had changed. We each believed we had *come of age*.

PART SIX

Enjoying Pre-Adolescence

25

HIT THE SILK

Life is like a parachute jump; you have to get it right the first time.
—Margaret Mead

If at first you don't succeed, then perhaps parachuting is not for you.
—Unknown

There was another incident that happened on the sliding hill, which deserves telling. However, telling this story risks ruining the image of my brother Doug as a small child with a "young adult's brain." After this incident, he might be thought of as possibly having no brain at all.

Doug had always been mesmerized by airplanes and anything having to do with being "up in the air." Seattle, being an important military city with an established base of operations for Navy, Army, and Air Force branches, often had a visible military presence, much more than many American cities. We often saw men in uniform, on temporary leave, or "liberty" as they called it, roaming the city. Seattle also had a fair amount of civic pride about being a military city, such that men on liberty and away from their own homes often were invited into homes of the citizens. They were treated to a family environment with home-cooked meals and a nice bed for the weekend.

In some of my life's earliest memories during the Second World War, mom did that, but we never did it when living in the projects years later, because we had neither the money nor the place for someone to sleep.

But Doug and I always wished we could have servicemen around. There was nothing I wanted more than to talk to a real live sailor, like my Uncle Shanty. And my brother would have given away his yo-yo for a chance to talk with an airman.

One other thing Seattle had, which contributed to the military environment, was Boeing Aircraft, the largest maker of airplanes in the world. In fact, Boeing was so large and important to Seattle that it had its own airport in the city, and still does! Boeing built airplanes for both military and civilian (airline) use, and all of those airplanes flew in and out of Boeing Field at all hours of the day and night. Boeing Field was just over Beacon Hill from where we lived in south Seattle. When airplanes were in the "landing paths" they often passed over the projects in shallow altitude and at reduced speed. Thus we often had great long looks.

Sometimes, when squadrons of bombers or fighters flew over, we kids stopped whatever we were doing and immediately laid down on the ground on our backs. With our hands folded under our heads, we stared up into the sky in a comfortable position and watched the airplanes fly by. It was heaven when we heard the droning sound of an approaching flight of propeller-driven airplanes, or, even better, when we saw the new Boeing B-47 jet bomber fly over. This was before the advent of the now more famous Boeing B-52 bomber.

It was one of these great "flyover" experiences that "set-off" my brother on a mission to have his own "airborne" experience.

Doug and I were playing on the sliding hill one afternoon when we heard a strange sound. We looked up for the inevitable aircraft, and were shocked to see only a wing fly overhead. We were stunned because neither of us had ever seen a flying wing before. In fact, neither of us knew one existed. How could a wing fly without the other parts of the airplane? Where were the tail and the back wings?

All we knew was that we saw a large wing with propeller engines on it. It went by twice and we were forever impressed. That incident really "turned on" Doug. It was all he could talk about for days. And it was not just the flying wing; it was all airplanes. He was hooked. That day he swore he would someday become a pilot.

The second occurrence that contributed to his heightened appreciation of anything in the air was a matinee movie we saw shortly thereafter about paratroopers—guys jumping out of airplanes. After that movie, he went on and on for days about wanting to be a paratrooper because then he would get to be up in an airplane, and would also get to jump *out of* an airplane, two activities that now completely captivated his attention.

This paratrooper thing became an obsession with him. He even cajoled me to ride our bikes down to the Army-Navy surplus store on Empire Way—a very long bike ride. He wanted to look at parachutes. When he told our Uncle Johnny about his attraction to parachutes, Uncle Johnny went to the store and bought Doug a surplus parachute as a surprise. With his help, we set it up as an Indian teepee out near the clothesline across the street. It was great fun; it was a parachute, and a tent, and an Indian teepee on the Plains. For a week or two we were two parachuting Sioux Indians, another of our mixed fantasies.

As an aside, during the Second World War, all of America was mobilized in action as well as in spirit against outside enemies, probably more so than at any other time in our nation's history. One of the necessities of the period was for the general populace to sacrifice for the war effort by not having certain materials and goods available. Those items were then diverted to the war "machine" for its use. Such items, for example, were rubber, gasoline, steel, and silk.

You say "silk," what's the big deal with that? The answer is that nylon and other synthetic fabrics had not yet been invented, and at that time silk served the same purpose as nylon later would. And what were the great uses of silk during the period of the Second World War? Well, there were two. One was as women's full length stockings (today what we would call "nylons" or pantyhose). The other was as material for parachutes. Yes, parachutes then were made of silk. That's what originated the paratrooper's phrase to "hit the silk" when they referred to jumping. Years later the irony of us having that parachute struck me; here we were, two of the poorest kids in America, playing with yards of gorgeous silk, when a few years earlier every woman in America would have given almost anything to have an extra set of silk stockings!

But back to Doug. After about a week of sitting in the parachute teepee, he became even more animated about his growing compulsion to jump out of an airplane. Except that the likelihood of him, or any of us, taking an airplane ride anytime in the foreseeable future was about as remote as us meeting Walt Disney and sitting around talking with him about *Snow White and the Seven Dwarfs*. And further, the likelihood of Doug taking a plane ride, *and then jumping out of the airplane with a parachute,* was as likely as Walt teaching us all how to draw.

He had resigned himself to the reality that it was never going to happen. But, true to form, when reality interfered with fantasy, we always found another way, by using our *imaginations*, to skirt around reality. Thus Doug determined he was going to parachute, airplane or no airplane. And, he had an idea.

WHERE THERE'S A WILL, THERE'S A LADDER!

The next time Freddie Roberts came over with his almost worn-out cardboard to slide down the hill, Doug pulled him aside and the two whispered for a while. Doug recalled that Freddie's dad, when he worked regularly, was a house painter. And one of the things that painters always had were ladders . . . big ladders . . . big and tall ladders! It happened that Doug imagined a "special use" for a tall ladder. Would Freddie be able to help Doug "borrow" one of his dad's painting ladders some Saturday morning, when it was known for sure that his dad was not going to work? Freddie's dad had a work truck, but he also had an open trailer that he pulled behind the truck. Stacked into the trailer and sticking out the back end of it were his dad's ladders. They could be "easy pickin's."

Freddie said he would become an accomplice in the "Great Ladder Heist" (actually they would just borrow one for a morning) if Doug would also let him "take a turn." What "take a turn" meant at the time was not clear, but the two had a secret plan and they huddled together much over the next day or so in order to render the details more clearly.

The next Saturday morning Doug was up early, ate his breakfast, and was out the front door without telling anybody where he was going. My mom and step-dad were slow risers on Saturdays and Sundays, and especially this Saturday because we all had gone to the drive-in movie the night before and had returned late. Doug was up earlier than others this Saturday morning and was gone before anyone noticed. He headed straight for Freddie's place around the curve of the Court and down a few four-plexes. Once at Freddie's, he quietly skulked up to Freddie's bedroom window, reached upward, and softly knocked on the window glass. Apparently, this was their secret signal.

Doug then huddled down next to the foundation of Freddie's building and waited. He looked at Freddie's dad's truck parked in the front of their house. Sure enough, the trailer was hitched behind it, and also, sure enough, in the trailer were three ladders. Just like in *Goldilocks and the Three Bears*, there was a very large one, a midsize one, and a smaller ladder.

After about ten minutes, Freddie sauntered out of his house, matter-of-factly so as not to arouse suspicion. He and Doug ran around to the street side of the trailer and hunkered down behind it so as not to be seen from the kitchen window of Freddie's house.

"So, how're we gonna get away with the ladder?" Doug asked.

"I'm not sure," Freddie said. "It's gonna be scary because dad parked right in front last night instead of down by the coal bin, so he may see us gettin' it out. We're gonna hafta be really quiet because my mom and dad are still in bed. But I don't think they're gonna be comin' out for a while because their bedroom door is shut, and when I came out here I heard their bed squeaking. Whenever I hear their bed squeaking on Saturday mornings, I know they don't get up right away."

Then he asked Doug, "Why do you think their bed squeaks like that some mornings? I sometimes also hear it at night."

Doug thought for a moment and replied, "I dunno. Sometimes Jack and I hear our mom and dad's bed squeaking too. We just lie there and listen. Sometimes we whisper to each other in our bunk beds to see if the other one hears it too. It sounds really spooky, especially at night. And it's crazy, because sometimes it'll squeak for a while real slowly and then sometimes it really gets squeaking good!"

"Yeah, and sometimes it'll squeak and then stop," Freddie said, "and then squeak some more! Why can't they oil it and make the squeak stop?"

"I know," Doug said. "Once Jack and I jumped up and down on our beds to make them squeak the same and we couldn't do it. Maybe only big beds squeak like that."

Freddie thought for a moment and said, "Maybe that's it. Maybe only big beds have a built-in squeak."

Doug changed the subject. "I see the ladders are locked with a chain around them."

"I know, but I got my dad's key," Freddie said. "Here . . . see!"

He gave it to Doug, who inserted the key, and twisted it. The lock snapped open. Then they, as carefully as possible, threaded the chain out from around the ladders to free the top ladder, which fortunately was the largest, and the one they wanted. The chain was then re-threaded around the lower two ladders and the lock again snapped shut. Doug passed the key back to Freddie, who deposited it into the front pocket of his jeans.

"Can't lose that," Freddie said, "otherwise I better not ever come home again."

"Aw, don't worry. If they throw you out, you can come live with us," Doug said. He was so volunteering. I can see it now: "Um, mom . . . Freddie's gonna live with us from now on because he lost his dad's key and they won't let him come home anymore. OK mom? Thanks, I knew it wouldn't be a problem."

They struggled to remove the top ladder as quietly as possible. It had seemed like such a simple idea—just lift the ladder up and remove it—except that it was made of oak and the hinges and bracing material were made of steel. Quickly they discovered that the ladder was very heavy! They huffed and puffed and became more frustrated with every minute.

Doug was determined, but Freddie was becoming less interested.

What he lacked in strength was also complicated by his complete absence of coordination. This was no longer fun and Doug now had to forcefully urge Freddie, again as quietly as possible, to stay on the task. Eventually, they were able to free the ladder, lift it precariously, and get it lowered off the trailer and onto the ground—but not without Freddie dropping his end with a loud clang. Both snapped their heads anxiously toward Freddy's house, frozen in fear that the sound had alerted his dad to their daring scheme. But little did they know that the bed was really squeaking at that moment, and whatever Freddie was doing definitely was the last thing on his parent's minds. Freddie and Doug both waited as the seconds passed, and their fear slowly ebbed. Finally, they took deep gulps of air. Now the task was to get the ladder carried to the sliding hill.

When they lifted, they were able to raise it to their waists, but to lift and walk at the same time was a real chore. It became heavier, and as they walked it kept slipping. Plus, they couldn't seem to maintain any coordinated cadence and it seemed that often they were "out of synch" in their steps. They had to stop many times to put it down to rest before resuming.

Freddie became very tired. This "parachuting thing" was never his passion as much as Doug's. As they neared Spike and Jenny's house, Spike happened to come out his front door. After some conversation to clue him in to the caper, he was drafted to help. The three of them struggled to get it away from Spike's house, and about that time I came outside looking for Doug. I saw what was happening and ran over from our house, about forty or fifty yards away.

The "Jump"

When Doug told me they were carrying Freddie's dad's ladder back behind our house at the top of the sliding hill, I thought that was one of the strangest things I had heard in a few months. But in our world, we were accustomed to strange goings-on, so I enlisted onto the team. The four of us finally hefted it up once more. It must

have been significantly easier for Doug and Freddie now that Spike
and I were co-conspirators. We were able to get the ladder behind
our house, and then all of us dropped it on the ground with a thud.
We were exhausted, but proud of our accomplishment. Let's see—
four kids lifted and carried a dead-weight ladder about one hundred
and fifty yards for the purpose of doing what? Parachuting, you say?

What do you mean, *parachuting?*

Doug explained. Now that the ladder was here, he planned to
parachute off of it. He wanted us to help him set up the ladder with
its legs near the edge of the hill. Then he would climb the ladder,
and jump off down the hill! Spike and I looked at him and stared.

"What!!!" I finally exclaimed. I had heard some wacko things in
my extra two years of life, but this strained even my belief. "What's
this got to do with parachuting? You've got a parachute, OK, but
it'll never open before you hit the ground. Remember, those real
parachute trooper guys fall a long way before their parachutes open,
much more than about eight feet."

"I'm not gonna use my parachute because I already *know* it'll
never open in time," Doug replied calmly. "I'm gonna use something even better. I'm gonna use something that's already open
when I jump, and then it won't have to take time to open—I can
just float down. Jumping off toward the hill will let me float a long
way down the hill, like in one of those ski jump things we saw in
the sports news at the movies. Remember?"

My mind reeled. "Yeah, I get the ski jump thing, but . . . but . . . ?"
I could not make the connection in my mind with what he had so
clearly worked out in his mind over these past few days. *What* thing
that was already open? . . . *What* floating? I could not understand,
and worse, I was not sure what to ask.

Spike and Freddie also tried to follow with the little logic we
possessed. Freddie, though, seemed to be more inclined to believe
on blind faith that Doug had a plan that would work. After all, he
was promised to "take a turn next."

"What floating thing?" I finally asked.

"This!" Doug said, and then he ran over to the edge of the
house. He rustled in the weeds, and pulled up an object. Then he

spun around and showed it to us.

"It's Uncle Johnny's umbrella! I fished it out of the house last night and put it here." As he said this, he opened it, pushing the slider all of the way to the top until it snapped into a notch, and the umbrella was completely deployed. Doug held the umbrella above his head as one would when it rained . . . only it wasn't raining now.

"See. It's already open, and when I jump I'll just float with it. You'll see!"

Yes, now I did see the whole plan, but I was mystified as to why Doug thought this would work. But . . . on second thought . . . maybe??? . . . Naw!!! . . . But what if???

True, it was crazy, but what if it just might work? What if he actually could float, and slowly and softly glide on a cushion of air down the hill a long way? He was small enough, and light enough, and it was a good-sized umbrella. And no one we knew had ever tried such a thing before, so we didn't know for sure that it *wouldn't* work! Now even I wasn't certain, and I probably was guilty of significantly over-thinking it. But I wanted to believe, so much, that fantasy again displaced reality. Maybe it would work. Who knew?

"Well, I'm gonna do it," Doug said. "Help me set up the ladder," which we did.

He climbed up the ladder, all the way to the top, holding the umbrella up over his head. He spun it around and declared, "I'm ready." The ladder wobbled slightly but we held its legs steady. I would have expected Doug to look down with even some small trepidation, but no, he was totally, absolutely, completely, no-doubt-about-it convinced he could parachute and float like a bird. Then he shouted the magic words. . . .

"*Geronimo!*" (the word all paratroopers supposedly shout when they jump). And then he jumped. He jumped high up in the air and off the top of the platform, out toward the hill.

And he *did float!!!* Just like a soft cloud . . . for about one-twentieth of a second. Immediately thereafter, his umbrella inverted inside-out as though it had been exposed to a hurricane, and Doug then proceeded to float like Wile E. Coyote's anvil. A feather he was not! On his way down I reached out to grab him and break his fall, but he had jumped too far out and I missed.

He yelled, "Ohhh, nooo!"

The umbrella trailed behind in his plunge and kept his feet downward, much as the feathers on an arrow. His feet impacted the slope first. But they had no traction and they immediately slipped out from under him down the slope. Next his butt hit, followed by an immediate shout of "OWWW!" Then the back of his torso struck. He slid and rolled, screaming, first from fear, and then with a laugh. Once he stopped sliding and rolling more than halfway down the hill, he lay very still on his back.

We ran, slipped, and slid down the hill after him. When we finally caught up with him he was laughing. His initial fear had been replaced with joy from the short, uncontrolled journey, and from happiness that he was not hurt.

"Are you alright?" I exclaimed.

"Yeah, I'm OK," he said as he raised himself up and dusted the straw off his arms and legs. "That was really scary, but fun!"

"You coulda been killed if you'd hit your head first, you silly fool," I admonished.

"Well, I didn't, and I'm OK. How'd I look coming down? Did I look like a paratrooper?"

"No. You looked like an eight-year-old idiot, especially with that umbrella in your hand," I said. "I told you it wouldn't work."

"Nooo . . . you liar!" Doug said. "You said *maybe* it would. And if it had worked, now you'd be saying how great an idea it was. You know you would!"

I thought for a moment with my mind still racing from my initial panic at seeing him fall, then my fear when he tumbled down the hill, then my relief at him being unhurt, and now arguing with him as to who was right. My heart still pounded and I was not at my mental best. Deep down I knew he had an argument, that I probably would now be convinced that it was a pretty smart idea if it had worked, but I was not going to admit it. All I could say was, "Baloney! You're really lucky, you know it! If you'd been hurt, mom would've been really mad. She would've whipped me too just for being here and letting you do it."

We looked at each other and knew we were both right. Mom would have reacted that way, and Doug would have felt badly that I was spanked. We knew that I would have felt terrible if he had been hurt. But the more we looked at each other and touched each other, the more we both were relieved—as much for Doug's safety, as well as for ourselves. It was one of those moments when our words spilled out in frustration with each other, but that frustration was also motivated by concern and love for each other.

I put my arm around his head and said, "Let's take this ladder back before anybody finds out, and let's never tell anyone about this, OK?"

"Yeah," said Doug, "but first . . . Freddie, it's your turn. You want to take it now?"

"Nooo way," said Freddie, shaking his head for emphasis and backing a step down the hill to confirm it even more. "Nobody's gonna get me up on that ladder. I never thought it would work!"

Doug, Spike, and I looked at each other and we all thought, Yeah, right. But none of us said it. We all knew that Freddie would have demanded to be the next jumper in line if Doug had floated all the way down to the lower four-plex.

Since Freddie had lost all appetite to "hit the silk," we needed to return the ladder. This was to be more of a challenge since it was later in the morning and more people were up and about. Presumably, all of the beds had stopped squeaking by now.

We four lifted up the ladder and eventually lugged it back over to Freddie's house, resting a few times for deep breaths. A couple of cars passed us, but no one stopped to say anything. The drivers probably wondered why four kids were carrying an (obviously) heavy ladder at this time of the morning, but nobody interrupted us. We kept moving, trying to look as invisible as possible. Once at Freddie's, we worked the chain to get it unlocked and then locked again. Done! Except, just as we climbed out of the trailer, Freddie's dad came out of the house with only his pajama bottoms on.

"Hey kids, whacha doin' on my trailer?" he said as he stretched both arms to the sky. Apparently he was getting a late start this particular morning.

We all looked at each other, and paused.

"Um . . . " Freddie answered. "Jack was saying he maybe wanted to be a painter when he grew up, and so I was showing him some of your ladders," which even we thought was lame. But those were the first words out of Freddie's mouth, and now that they were out, that was our story and we were all sticking to it. I nodded my head.

Freddie's dad had that "whatever" look on his face as he scratched his bottom with his left hand. It was a good scratch, the kind that roots around for a while and covers all of the territory. Clearly, his mind was not yet sharp enough to pick up the stupidity of Freddie's response. Or else he chose to ignore it because it was still too early for him to get locked into a debate with a bunch of kids. His only words, as he turned to return inside were, "Well, don't hurt yourselves."

We all breathed easier.

Such was Doug's first adventure with parachuting. Nothing similar to it was ever tried again by any of us, and none of us talked much more about it afterward. It was not the kind of captivating news that swept the Columbia grade school playground. As time went on, Doug's fascination with jumping out of a plane waned, and he never in life (so far) achieved that goal. However, true to his continued fascination with flying, he did become a private pilot, and over the years owned many of his own airplanes, which he used for both business and pleasure. He eventually accumulated over 2,000 hours in the air piloting his airplanes.

Experimental "Flying Wing."

26

STICKS AND STONES

Girls . . . and . . . Boys

By the time I was ten years old, it had become apparent to me, and other members of the various project gangs, that girls naturally were different from us boys, and at that age we were not yet attracted to the difference. The grown-up's description was that girls were "feminine." I never understood the word feminine, I just knew that girls didn't like to be rough and tumble, didn't like sports (other than jump-rope, if you call that a sport), and were not interested in Western movies or Flash Gordon. They preferred music, liked clothes, played with dolls, actually *cared* about whether they were clean, and generally spent more time with their mothers, being trained in domestic and social skills. Remember, this was the 1950s.

But worst of all, girls had *feelings*.

Oh, I don't mean we guys didn't have emotions too, because often it was emotions that caused the scrapes we had. But emotions were *different* than feelings. Emotions were created when someone purposely ran into you on the base paths, or stole your skate key, or moved your bike without permission and didn't tell you. Those emotions were worthy of a punch or two, or a wrestling match in the dirt.

In the code of our neighborhood gangs, when two guys had "emotions" toward each other which had to be "worked out," they did it without thinking about it for hours or days. It usually was all spur of the moment. And the manner in which all of these were settled was to have it out, one-on-one. In such skirmishes, all things were within limits except sticks and bites.

You couldn't hit the other person with something hard, like a stick or a baseball bat, and you couldn't bite. Biting not only hurt like sin, much more than any of us considered acceptable in war, but also risked opening the skin, thus drawing blood and leaving marks. This was not done because it meant moms were then involved. Tincture of Iodine and Band-Aid®s were sure to follow, along with the hundred questions such as, "Who did this to you? I'm gonna talk with his mother and give them both a piece of my mind!" And the question we always heard, "Why can't you act more *civilized*?"

One of the codes was not to rat on the other guy. He could bloody you with his fists in a moment of anger, but you couldn't rat on him, no matter what. Another unwritten rule was you couldn't kick the other guy in the groin. Anybody trying to do so was considered to be "fighting dirty" and that was against the code. Even then, we treasured our privates.

Interestingly enough, throwing rocks at each other was *not* against the code. As strange as that may seem now, it was OK to throw a rock at someone and actually inflict a fair amount of pain if successful with a hit. The code for throwing rocks was that you had to give the other guy a warning first; surprise ambushes were not acceptable. The reality of the warning was that it naturally produced some separation between the target and the accuser. I mean, who wanted to stand close to someone who had just told you he would pelt you with a rock?

The separation always seemed to be self-equalizing, meaning that you couldn't allow yourself to be too close to the thrower for obvious reasons, but if you were too far away then you didn't stand a chance of making a retaliatory hit either. So, although we never understood the dynamics of it at the time, a good rock fight was the best example of balance between naked aggression and the natural defense of protecting yourself. Mostly, rock fights allowed all parties concerned to work out those "emotions" without any real danger to anybody. I don't remember anybody ever meaningfully getting hurt in a rock fight because it was so difficult to hit someone, except by pure accident.

We Alderwood Court guys once had a serious rock fight with the Pinewood Court guys. It was a real war, complete with swearing and vile name calling. It was during one obscene-laden tirade that Ronnie Landers shouted back the memorable phrase, *"Sticks and stones can break my bones, but names'll never hurt me. . . .* Naa-naa, naa-naa-naa!" This pronouncement was always spoken by someone at least once during the heat of every battle. I doubt that it ever changed a single thing, but it *had* to be said, every time, by someone.

This particular rock war went on for two days. Late into the first day, we all decided it was time to stop for dinner. We then resumed the next morning at the predetermined time. How many true wars can call a "time out," all go home peacefully because it's dinner time, and then resume later at a predetermined time because all participants knew that things had not yet been "worked out?" After it was finally over, when the mental and physical energy had run its course and the adrenaline had also given out, for all of the hundreds of rocks that were launched, as I recall, not a single participant was hit, even once. Oh, there was a window broken in one four-plex, and someone's car received a large dent in a fender from a stray missile, but none of us on either side were even scraped.

The satisfaction was never in the result—it was in the process. We all felt good about the fact that if you really were mad at someone, you could roll around in the dirt scuffling with him, trying to get in a good poke or two, or you could declare a rock war. Both effectively allowed everybody to "work it out" of their systems.

After this two day rock war, when all were satisfied that the emotions were gone, we then went to the ball field and played baseball together for the next three hours. That's how boys dealt with emotions: don't think about them, react immediately, sock the other guy or throw a rock or two, and then be friends again because who wanted to waste a single hour when we could be playing? Actually, reflecting now on mom's question above about,

"Why can't you act more civilized?" it would seem that we were quite *civilized* in our aggression, relatively speaking.

Girls, however, were different. They could get very upset with each other—from our perspective, for no apparent reason. And the other girl might not even be aware of it! What's with that? At least with guys, when someone was upset, everybody knew about it immediately. But with girls, one could be offended and upset for days, without anybody being the wiser. And then, once discovered, the offense could be something as serious as, "Well, I didn't like the way she looked at me!" or "Well, she just hurt my *feelings.*"

There's that word: "*feelings.*" Girls had feelings, and they always seemed to get in the way of something more important with deeper meaning. We guys were much more transparent. We either were friends or enemies, a simple dichotomy, and the status could change in an instant and/or be cured in an instant, with no apologies needed or demanded. But, with girls, there seemed to be an invisible protocol whereby the most insignificant slight could blow up into an issue of huge importance, and not get effectively resolved for days.

Guys didn't carry grudges, but girls majored in them. We guys never understood, not then, and not even later when we grew up and dealt with girls in real "relationships." We still often were clueless.

Also, girls could cry at the drop of a hat, for reasons that were never understood by us guys. Guys never thought about crying. That doesn't mean we didn't cry, but usually the tears came when we were in the safety of our own bedroom. In the heat of a battle, no matter how hard it hurt, we guys tried not to cry, or even rub where it hurt, if we could possibly avoid it. There were times when we took a blow and every sensation of the affected area was transmitted to the brain as PAIN, but we guys just asked our tormentor, "Is that the best ya got, huh, is it, is it? Didn't hurt, didn't hurt!!!"

We all knew the claim was pure baloney and the affected area probably stung like a raging fire, but we also all appreciated the code, and the code was, **Don't give the other guy the satisfaction; instead earn his respect.** We all understood, and that's how we guys did it.

But girls thought nothing of showing *all* of their feelings. They could be smiling and apparently totally happy one moment, and the very next moment they could burst into tears for reasons known only to themselves. Girls, to us guys, were an enigma and we knew it. We tolerated them, especially if they were sisters, but it was very difficult to take them seriously in any deep level of play in which we were involved. They never responded the same as we boys.

Furthermore, if we were involved in social interaction with girls, and one of them suddenly burst into tears, the first reaction of grown-ups was to ask the nearest boy, "What'd you do to her? Huh?" We guys always thought, I didn't do anything. She's a girl and they do that sometimes. I just happened to be standing here. We guys tended to give girls great latitude because we never knew what they would do at any given time. We just didn't want to be the unfortunate guy standing near one of them when they "blew."

The fact that girls had "feelings" was true of every girl we knew, with one exception—Jenny. She was the only girl who was a full member of any of our neighborhood gangs. She was unique, and what made her so in our view was that she played, and most of the time—not all of the time—but most of the time, she also *thought* like us boys. She eventually earned the respect of all various gang members as someone to be reckoned with on the playground in any athletic competition, or in any other "boy" type activities. The highest unspoken compliment for her at the time was that she was "just one of us guys."

Still, if I truly admitted it to myself, I had a special sensitivity to Jenny all of the time I knew her. Call it an appreciation, but certainly not an attraction. She was never a "girlfriend" because that potential position was held by Sally Donovan, who truly acted and behaved as a real girl. But there was something about Jenny that made me like her very much, something that went beyond admiration for her athletic skills and her affinity for being one of us boys. I never understood it at the time, but looking back, I know it was that, in spite of all of her roughness and "boyness," she still had a hint of something different—a softer skin, a cuter look, a twinkle on occasion. I now know that was a latent charm which could someday stimulate my then latent attraction to such aspects of girls.

When I was eleven to twelve years old I was on the verge of a radical change in my thinking and actions toward the opposite sex —puberty. But being almost age ten, it had not happened yet. I still was oblivious to its coming and its effects. Subtly, my unconscious mind was onto something about Jenny. When the time did arrive, and my glands did begin to work, I knew I could feel very differently about her. But in the late spring of 1952, all that meant was simply: I liked her.

It was after the aforementioned two-day rock war, in which Jenny participated, with a vengeance I might add, that she and I had a conversation.

We were sitting on the ground, leaning against a coal bin, and softly pitching rocks into the street. This was the position we kids always settled into when nothing else was happening and we had idle time. The coal bins occupied central locations on the Courts and it was a place to hang out for a while, observe, and talk. Also, since the streets themselves were surfaced in gravel, a handful of good pitching material was only an arm's length away.

She said, "I've been thinking about the rock fight. We ran around a lot and threw so many rocks, but we didn't *hit* anybody. We tried, but it's hard because they move and hide. If those Pinewood guys would've just stood still and not hid, I bet we could've hit 'em."

There was a long pause. I pitched a couple of stones before I said anything.

"Yeah. . . . But who wants to get hit? I know I don't! I got hit a couple of years ago and it hurt bad! But I never told on the kid."

"Wow!" Jenny said, impressed. The code was intact. "I don't wanna get hit either, because I *know* it'd hurt . . . but still I wanna hit someone. Not hittin' someone . . . it just isn't *right*. If we're gonna try to hit someone, we should hit 'em."

"But you can't expect to hit someone and *not* be scared that you'll get hit yourself," I argued.

There was another long pause, and a few more stones were skipped across the street by both of us. She searched for something. I waited.

"I know," she finally said. "But being scared is funny. It's like when we trick-or-treated the haunted house. I was really scared . . . we all were. And, the more scared I got, the more I didn't want to do it. But I *did* it—being scared didn't stop me! Then, after we did it . . . well, being scared made it better! It made it something we could brag about." She paused again, and then continued. "The Pinewood guys . . . they needed to be hit because they're snots . . . and we're better'n them! But nothing happened. If I'm gonna be scared, I need to hit someone."

Now it was becoming clear. If we were to fight, we also had to be *scared*, and the more scared we were, the more deeply committed we were. Plus, something else had to come out of it, which was *satisfaction* from overcoming the fear. Also, it was important that we could brag about the adventure to our peers later! The redeeming virtue had to be that we had *achieved* something by *overcoming* our fear, just like with the Halloween adventure.

If there was no achievement of purpose, in this case actually hitting someone, then all of the fear that drove the whole effort was expended in vain. And all that was left, as a residual, was irritation . . . at both the effort and the danger, without *reward*. This was what was bothering Jenny! For it all to be worthwhile, there had to be fear *and* reward, and the reward was missing now—we hadn't hit anybody!

"Yeah. I know I'd like it better if we'd hit somebody," I said. "But still, I wish I didn't have to worry about getting hurt."

We sat in silence a long while and tossed a few more rocks. We were locked in thought. I turned over my last statement in my mind,

"I wish I didn't have to worry about getting hurt." I thought about the meaning of those words. Jenny must have also.

Finally, she said, "You're saying it's OK to be mad at the Pinewood guys, and scared about being in a rock fight, but you don't want to get hurt? Me, too! . . . Wouldn't it be great if we *knew* we wouldn't get hurt! Then we could really go all out, and not have to hide."

More deep thought.

Then Jenny perked up, turned, and looked directly at me. "I know what! What if *we* did somethin' together that was scary, but we knew we couldn't be hurt? What if we did somethin' that was really scary—because just *doing* it was scary enough? What if we did somethin' that nobody else has ever done before? What if we did somethin' that nobody else would even *think* of doing? What if we did that?"

Now she had my attention. "That would be great. And, if it were really scary and crazy, that would make it even better, right?" The thought had great appeal—adventure without fear of being hurt. What a concept! But what to do? I didn't have an answer, but my mind churned.

THE PLAN

"I've got it!" Jenny finally spouted. "Listen to this. Why don't we throw rocks at somethin' that can't throw back at us? At somethin' that's moving, because then it would be hard to hit? At somethin'. . . that would be so *crazy* that the other guys would really be impressed?"

"Yeah," I said. "Yeah!!!" I paused for a brief inhale. "Like the trains?"

Jenny said, "Naw. We could do that, but it wouldn't be scary. The trains move too slow, and they're so big, they'd be easy to hit. And, if we hit 'em, so what? There's no danger in that."

I saw her point and agreed.

She brightened, and leaned a little closer so as to share her thought with more emphasis.

"Um . . . I know. . . . What if we throw rocks . . . at cars . . . driving down the street?"

"At *cars!!!*" My first reaction was shock. That was just too out-landish to even consider, which was why nobody in our known world (those of us at Columbia grade school) had ever done such a thing. It was just too extreme to even think about, let alone do. Why would anybody throw a rock at a moving car? I mean, cars had grown-ups in them who could get really mad if they knew you had thrown a rock at them. And, how could you hit one of them? After all, they were *moving*. It would be hard to do. And, what if you did hit one of them? What then? Who knew what would happen?

It was, at first, too "far-out" to even think about. But after the thought was out of her mouth, we both considered it. It was like when we first thought about trick-or-treating the haunted house. It really was a crazy idea, but the more we all thought about it, the more it grew in our imaginations to become a possibly great adventure.

Such was the case here. The prospect of throwing rocks at mov-ing cars became more acceptable, and, as it did, the reward *vis-à-vis* the risks became more attractive. Here was an adventure which met all of the criteria! It had not been done before. It was daring. It was scary. It was certainly not without consequences if we were caught by our parents or some other grown-up, and it was hard to do. We could brag about it later, and we could envision the great awe such a story would create in our schoolmates we sought to impress.

And, here's the best part, we couldn't get hurt! Nobody would be throwing rocks *back* at us! It was an idea that had everything. We could throw rocks at moving cars. And maybe we even could hit some! We both were good throwers, two of the best. The more we thought about it, the more excited we became, and the more committed we were. We could do something unthinkable and dar-ing, that none of our peers had ever done before, and we would be proud later! We would be heroes. It was a done deal!

But where? As we talked, we determined the correct place would be where the cars would have some speed, and thus be more difficult moving targets. Also good would be if we would not have much time before seeing them. Thus we would have to wait in anticipation, and, when they suddenly appeared, we would have a very short time to get off our throws. We imagined it was as if we were hunting pheasants, although neither of us had ever done that before.

The big street we crossed to get to the "woods" was the ideal place. It was where we kids ran across that Halloween night. The street came down a slight hill. At the top of the hill to our left was a big sign that would block most of our view. Since cars moved at a fairly good speed, they suddenly would emerge from behind the sign and head down the hill. This hill bordered the back sides of some of the four-plexes on Alderwood Court. Since these back sides were all on level ground, they were increasingly above the street as it went down the hill. We couldn't see the cars until they surprised us, then we had a shot at them from above. We decided this would be the *perfect* location to enact our next great adventure.

27

FREE TO PLAY ANOTHER DAY

In comradeship, is danger countered best.
—Johann Wolfgang von Goethe

Once Jenny and I had convinced ourselves that we were onto one of the potentially greatest adventures ever known in our neighborhood—and that was saying something—we were filled to the brim with the glee of expectation. Our *adventure that had everything* was almost too much to bear. We couldn't wait. But we had to prepare, and it had to be done with proper care.

Both of us filled our pockets with gravel. We had to search for just the right rocks. You might think that rocks are rocks, but we knew you couldn't throw just any old rock. The rock had to be just right. And what made it just right? Well, it had to be the right size—not too big and not too small. And it had to fit our hands . . . and have the right shape. It had to be thinner in one direction and slightly elongated in another. This allowed us to hold it between our thumb and the middle finger and then curl the first finger, which we called "pointer," around it to give it that snapping action when we let it go. This was great for making very flat rocks skip across water, and also for making all rocks spin properly when thrown for distance.

Grown-ups probably thought all rocks were the same and that none of them should ever be *thrown*, but we knew that kind of "thinking" just showed how little they knew. Jenny and I had rock selection and rock throwing down to a science.

Now we were about to test our knowledge and skill. We were excited as we partly walked and partly ran over to the perfect spot for an ambush. Once there, we walked along the back yards, atop the hill abutting the street. Sure enough, the cars swooshed by after emerging from behind the large sign. Some were going faster than others, so that gave us opportunities to pick our best targets.

This was also the section of the hill where Doug and I had crawled in the grasses when we had set the trap for the thief of my bicycle, who turned out to be Jackie Richey. The grasses and weeds now, as then, were about waist high. We thus had some protection in which to hide, in case we really wanted to pretend we were stalking wild animals—the famous "automobilus" creatures, which we would take down with our precisely delivered missiles to their most vulnerable spots.

"OK. Are you ready?" Jenny asked.

"Yeah. I'm good," I replied as I found the right spot and dropped down on one knee. Jenny followed.

"You go first," I said.

"No, you go first," she said. "You were the one who didn't want to get hurt."

"Well you were the one who wanted to hit something. You go first!" It occurred to me that we were now at that final moment of last chance, the moment when all of our previous planning and bravado was put to the test, the moment when we had to back up our mouths and our planning with some action. This was the moment when paratroopers need to take that last small step, with such ominously large consequences. My senses were on high alert. The adrenaline was flowing. This was it!

"You go," I said one last time.

"Nope, you," she replied shaking her head.

Hmmm.

A car emerged from behind the sign. My eyes bore down on it. The artillery computer in my mind subconsciously calculated range, distance, speed, and points of intersection. Suddenly, I rose up, drew my right arm back, stepped with my left leg, and brought my arm forward in a powerful throwing motion. As soon as the stone left my hand, I dropped down and partially hid in the tall grasses. The rock arced under the influence of both gravity and forward momentum . . . and fell to the pavement slightly behind the passing car. Darn, I thought. Missed! The intended victim continued down the hill completely unaware of its good fortune.

"Your turn," I almost whispered.

Jenny paused, and let five or six cars pass innocently. We also had to pay attention to the cars coming up the hill in the far lanes, and we decided not to throw when one of them was approaching. Our best opportunity to keep from being detected was to only throw at the cars going down the hill in the near lanes. Finally, Jenny jumped up and let go a heave. She then dropped down and we both watched her rock also arc to the pavement behind its target.

"Darn," she said. "How can it be so hard to hit one? They're big, and they're not moving that fast."

This was a question without an answer because we both threw a few more times, again without success. Either we threw in front of the car, or we threw behind it. Sometimes we overthrew and the rock skipped over the car, landing in the far lanes. Finally, I was able to get a very good throw off, and we watched as the rock, although thrown short, still managed to hit the pavement at the side of the car and then skip into its back wheel.

A hit! I did it! I hit a moving car with a rock! We both were excited, and grins covered our faces. This was proof that it was *possible*, and now we knew it also was *fun*. Jenny, feeling more confident now, after watching the master at work, stepped up and let a stone fly. We watched as it slowly converged on its lumbering target, a '52 Ford sedan. The rock suddenly impacted the back fender in front of the trailing bumper. There was a distinct loud whack of hard rock meeting metal. As we crouched, we saw the driver react with a snap of his head. The shock created by the sound was in his mind, but he had no clue as to what had happened! He didn't know a rock had been thrown, or even that he had been hit. His mind simply registered a loud bang behind him and he was confused, but not sufficiently alarmed to stop and investigate.

The Ford continued down the hill. We both slapped each others' shoulders and momentarily jumped around on the ground. I slipped and fell and she jumped on my back laughing. We were having so much fun, and were so pleased with ourselves. We were doing something nobody else had done and were having a ball. What could be more fun than that?

SUCCESS . . . AND CONSEQUENCES

After a few moments of laughing we again rose and took our positions. I said, "Watch this. I'm gonna cream the next one."

We were now on high alert. Our confidence soared. I stared at the sign.

Suddenly, a late model Chevy emerged from behind it and sped down the hill. I jumped up and let go a hard toss. But just as I completed my throw, and before I could drop down, I saw that the driver of the car had seen my motion. I saw his head stare upwards, and I saw him make eye contact with me and my outstretched arm. He also had seen the rock soar. Now the three of us watched it arc upwards and then downwards toward his car. I dropped down into the semi-protection of the weeds, but it didn't matter because I had been seen, and the driver knew something hard was converging on his vehicle. He stepped on his brakes and slowed almost imperceptibly before the rock crashed into his front grill with a smashing sound.

Both Jenny and I gleefully let out yelps of success! We almost were ready to begin our backslapping and roll-around-on-the-dirt routine again, when suddenly, to our shock, the driver slammed on his brakes. All of the car's tires skidded on the street. The tires screeched and the car slowed almost to a stop. Then the driver maneuvered over to the curb, parked, and exploded out of the vehicle all in the same instant.

The driver's door flew open and a tall, lanky, and somewhat athletic looking man emerged into the street. He rotated so as to look directly up at us, and raised his right arm up in our direction.

"HEY!!!" he shouted at high volume. Then another, "HEY!!!"

We froze in shock and couldn't move. We instantly tried to become less visible, and at that moment would have traded all summer's admissions to the movie matinees for a magic wand that would have made us disappear. But it was no use. Clearly, he had seen everything and was on to us. He had seen me throw, had seen the flight of the rock, and had clearly heard its sickening impact into the front of his prized possession. He had overcome the surprise of being struck, and now was livid. The rage burned from his collar.

"I'M GONNA GET YOU MONSTERS AND KILL YOU!" he shouted upwards, shaking his outstretched arm in both defiance and emphasis. We were stunned. All of the glee and happiness which we enjoyed a few minutes ago had now vanished, and been replaced with intense fear for our lives. And it paralyzed us. We couldn't move. We did not know what to do. We couldn't hide and we couldn't run. Every sense in our minds told us to move quickly for our self-preservation, but our brains were in disbelief. We couldn't put any part of our bodies or limbs into motion. How could this be? How could this guy suddenly stop, and seriously threaten us? How could this happen because we were having so much fun? The questions flowed like water downhill, but the answers were not forthcoming. We stared back at this raging fury now wanting to punish us. If his intent was to scare the living daylights out of us, it was working. We began to shake.

Suddenly, he slammed his door shut and rounded the front of his car. He took large strides and moved across the pavement, fully intent on carrying out his threats. Jenny and I, with our eyes as large as saucers, both tried to jump up. Now, finally, our bodies moved. We half scrambled to our feet and half clawed the ground at the same time. We tried for any traction and speed we could attain, in whatever direction we could move. The man reached the lower part of the hill and did not pause for even a partial second.

His legs and arms carried him forcefully in our direction, up the hill, against the gravity trying to retard his progress. When he was about halfway up the slope, Jenny and I finally were in full run, only there was not much choice for our escape. We were bounded on the one side by the hill, which would bring us to him quickly, and on the other side by the backs of the four-plexes. We lurched forward in the high grass, and his presence loomed closer. The less the distance between us shrunk, the more our fear increased. His angle was cutting us off, and even running uphill he could run faster than we could on flat ground.

"YOU NASTY PUNKS ARE GONNA WISH YOU WERE DEAD!!!" he screamed.

Jenny yelled, "Jack, he's gonna catch us! Oh, no!" She was ready to break into tears. My own fears had not yet triggered the cry, but I knew it was coming.

"YOU MISERABLE TWERPS!!! I'M GONNA SKIN YOU!!!" he screamed again, now so close I could almost feel the heat of his breath.

Jenny and I ran as fast as our legs could move, but it was no use. Suddenly, I felt a strong push on my back as his swinging arm made contact. He hit Jenny about the same time knocking us both off our stride. We fell to the ground and slid on our stomachs as he stopped and towered over us. I could sense his anger through his shaking and flaying arms. He kicked at my side, but I managed to roll slightly before his shoe impacted my rib area. My side stung. I fully rolled over, and as I did he reached down and grabbed my shirt below my throat. He jerked me upward with his strength and I could see his eyes were filled with anger and malice. I feared that I would be beaten and maybe skinned, who knew?

"YOU ROTTEN BRATS!!!" he screamed once again as he drew back his other hand, ready to slap me with an open palm. I feared the worst from his apparently six-foot long arm making a round-house slap across my jaw. I now shook and almost cried. I couldn't say anything other than tearfully plead, "Don't." I closed my eyes and expected to perhaps be knocked unconscious.

Jenny had also rolled over and pushed herself up with one arm on the ground. Between her sobbing she pleaded, "Stop. Please mister. Don't hit him!"

I did not feel anything when I fully expected to be clobbered, so I snapped open my eyes. As I struggled with both arms, and with my legs only occasionally touching the ground, I saw that his cocked arm was still in the back position. He had not yet let go with the slap to perhaps knock my head off my shoulders. I braced. Still, he did not move, but he stared at Jenny lying on the ground, now fully aware that she was a girl and not another BRAT-TWERP-PUNK like me.

"You're a *girl!*" he exclaimed, fully surprised that a girl could be an accomplice in such a despicable activity, of which he had become the victim. Imagine his shock if he had known that she was also a perpetrator and co-schemer! But with her wearing jeans and a pullover sweatshirt, and with his anger overriding any observations to the contrary, he had assumed she was a boy, up until that moment of his surprise. In his angry chase, he had never noticed her bouncing pigtail braids. Now realizing that she was *not* a boy—meaning the worst sort of devil scum imaginable—completely unnerved him. He lost his concentration on trying to knock me silly. He was so shocked that he stared at her, not believing his eyes.

"A girl!!!" he said again, incredulously.

His grasp on me loosened somewhat and both my feet again touched the ground, but he still held my shirt in a death grip. Jenny continued to rise until she stood. She sobbed and asked him to let us go. He continued to stare at her.

"What are you doing here with this monster?" he asked, while staring at her, obviously implying me as the M-creature. "Huh, what are you doing? A girl shouldn't be doing this kind of thing—nobody should—but certainly not a girl!"

So that was it: It was OK for me—a guy—to have his block knocked off for throwing rocks at cars, but it was absolutely unthinkable that a girl—*a girl!*—should ever be caught in the presence of someone doing such a foul deed.

"WELL, WHAT ARE YOU DOING HERE, HUH?" He shouted at Jenny for an answer, never letting loose of me.

Jenny continued to cry, but to my surprise I had yet to break into a sob. I detected for the first time that perhaps I was not going to be beaten within an inch of needing paramedics.

Finally, Jenny squeezed out between gasps and sobs, "He's my

best friend," gasp, sob. "We were just having fun," gasp, sob. "We
didn't mean to hurt anything," gasp, sob. "Please, let us go," gasp, sob.

There was a pause as the man slowly digested Jenny's words
and seemed to calm ever so slightly. His grip on my shirt loosened,
although he continued to control me.

Finally, he said sternly, "OK. I've a mind to take you both to the
police, girl or no girl, but I'm gonna let you go. Maybe I shouldn't,
but . . . you both better understand good . . . listen to me! I drive
by here often, and if I ever see either of you again . . . EVER . . .
I'm gonna catch you again and beat *both* of you into next week—I
don't care if you are a girl, I'll do it! And then, I'm gonna take you
to the police. Neither of you will ever throw another rock again,
ever! Do you understand? WELL, DO YA?" he screamed at us as he
swiveled his head in both of our directions for emphasis.

His raise of inflection at the end worked because we both were
startled at the volume. I sniffled out the words, "Yeah, I understand.
. . . We both do. We won't throw any more rocks. I promise!" My
head hung down.

He let go of my shirt with a push backwards for good measure.
"OK then! See that you don't. And remember, I'll be on the lookout.
If I ever see, or hear, either of you doing anything like this again,
you're both in the trouble of your lives, I'll tell you that, brother!"

With that he reached down and dusted his pant legs slightly,
more as a nervous reaction to his abated fury than out of true need.
He straightened and turned his body to move back down the hill
to his car. However, his head and eyes rotated and stayed fixed on
us. As his legs dropped him lower, he watched us, and said one last
warning, "You better do as I say, ya hear?"

We both nodded as we wiped our noses. We stood there, thank-
ful to be alive and drained of energy from the fearful experience.
Neither of us could move nor speak for a moment. We watched him
climb down the slope. He occasionally swiveled his head around to
glimpse up at us, presumably to verify that we had not loaded up
another round and were set to let it fly. But we had not. We were
as contrite as choir boys at that moment. We had escaped. Somehow,
we had been set free to play another day.

He reached his car and bent over the grill to check the damage, which thankfully was minimal from what we could see.

We heard him mutter to himself, "I can't believe she was a *girl!*" He then opened the driver's door, threw one last menacing glance upward at us, slid inside, closed the door, and slowly drove down the street.

Jenny and I both expelled the last air in our lungs in relief, and then drew in fresh. We were exhausted.

"Whew," I finally said. "That was a close . . . I thought we were dead for sure. I was scared he was gonna smack me good . . . and he woulda too, if it hadn't been for you. *You* did it, Jenny! He let us go because of you. If it was just me, or if I was with Doug or Ronnie or Spike, we'd have been beaten up, I'm sure. But because you were with me . . . we got away."

At that moment I felt very appreciative for having her with me, not just because she was my ticket for escape, but also because **there is a bond that forms among friends,** even when they're only eleven years old. **When both parties endure hardship and difficulty, and somehow get through it because of their attachment and dedication to each other, it has meaning.**

It was true that we had only ourselves to blame for getting into this situation, but it was also true that getting through it *together* gave us both a strength and a closeness that we otherwise would not have had. I looked at her and smiled, and she looked back, without words. We turned and slowly walked side-by-side along the edge of the four-plex. We stumbled along purposefully, each lost in our own thoughts, occasionally swishing the high grass with our hands.

"So . . . what'd you mean by: *'He's my best friend'?*" I asked.

Jenny turned her head slightly to look into my face. She squinted from the sun, and, with a slight hint of the faintest smile, said impishly, "None of your beeswax."

We continued to amble along, quietly and deliberately, until we were back in the front of my coal bin. We slumped down on the ground again, leaned back against the bin in the same position as when this whole experience had begun, and took some long breaths. I picked up a couple of rocks and drew back my hand to pitch one into the street, when I caught myself. "Well, I don't know if we can do that any more, huh?" I said.

Jenny picked up a stone, looked at me with a devilish smile that made everything so enjoyable, and said, "Don't bet on it!" Then she let it fly across the street, hitting the coal bin on the opposite side.

We looked at each other and grinned.

This story circulated on the playground within a day because we *definitely* told it. We both were treated with awe and admiration for such a daring escapade. But Jenny and I never again threw rocks at cars, and so far as we knew, nobody else in Columbia Elementary School ever did, either. However, we still had an occasional rock fight among us Alderwoods and the other Court gangs. Some things were just too good to give up.

Also, none of our parents ever knew any of this.

28

THE CLAMORAMA: GETTIN' READY

Imagination __and__ protection . . . preparing for adventure

In February of 1954 I had been in the Cub Scouts for almost three years. I had worked my way up to the rank of Lion Cub, with one gold arrowhead and one silver arrowhead. Only one more silver arrowhead to go and I would be ready to transition my scouting career out of the Cubs and into the really big world of . . . Boy Scouts, when I turned twelve. But that was to come later.

For now, though, I was feeling pretty cocky; I was big man in the Pack, three years into the Cub mainstream, had fought the big wars, had made the Plaster of Paris logs, and for the most part could tie a square knot behind my back with my eyes closed! I had done almost everything, but I had never been to the "Clamorama."

What the heck is that you may ask? Well, it was just about the *biggest* thing to happen in Seattle Cub scouting. Boy Scouts had their national "Jamboree," where they all came together in a huge conclave for a week or so, did good deeds, camped, and generally reaffirmed their values, morals, and commitment to America and her way of life. But the Cub Scouts in Seattle had the Clamorama, which was a weekend affair of similar intent, only much smaller. It was for Cubs to have a good time, learn something from group fellowship, and demonstrate what Cub scouting was all about to those who came to see the show (mostly parents and family who already knew it).

The highlight of the whole event was a show Saturday night where the theme was the "Settling of the Prairie." There were to be "settlers" and "cowboys" and "Indians," and lions and tigers and bears, oh, my. . . . No that's not right, we did *not* have Tiger cubs in the Cub Scouts. So substitute wolves for tigers, and there you had it—Lions and Wolves and Bears! Anyway, the idea was to demonstrate how the cowboys and the settlers came out West to settle America, against all odds and adversities. Various action skits would demonstrate our history, and our prowess as Cub Scouts, in demonstrating history. Presumably, we would have many Plaster of Paris logs around in case it had never occurred to anybody in the audience that trees were cut down along the way to build log houses. However, I could never imagine settlers building houses with Plaster of Paris logs.

Cub Scouts from all over Seattle were to play all of the roles. When we had our monthly pack meeting to discuss the upcoming Clamorama, we learned that we, Pack 231, were to be Indians in the big play. Darn, I was crushed! I wanted us to be cowboys; those were the glory roles. In spite of my love for Tonto, I felt there was more adventure and excitement in being one of the cowboys. But for some reason when I learned that there would be no horses, I figured it didn't matter. If both the cowboys and Indians were on foot, then it somehow evened out. Indians we were, and we decided that Pack 231 would be the best darned Indians on the whole Prairie! We wanted future Clamorama attendees years later to talk about the legendary "Pack 231 Indians of 1954," or at least the Den 5 Indians of Pack 231.

Mrs. Bronson, our den mother, was energized and motivated. The den meetings became intensive craft sessions to create and make everything we needed to set a good impression. We made Indian braves' breast plates. In the Western movies the Indians always wore dangling and rattling armor-like plates over their chests, presumably to keep arrows shot by enemy tribes from penetrating their hearts. Real Indians made their breast plates from buffalo ribs, deer leg bones, or something tough like that. But we made ours from uncooked pasta. Yes, I know it's hard to believe how strung-together rigatoni, macaroni, and penne would stop an arrow, but trust us, our *imaginations* did wonders! For two weekly meetings we all sat on the floor of Mrs. Bronson's house and strung together pasta. Then we painted it various colors with Easter egg dyes and poster paints. The breast plates looked darned good when finished, and we then believed we could take anything those poor unprotected cowboys from the other packs could throw at us.

Next we made "braves' bags." Mrs. Bronson's husband made leather handbags and decorated saddles for a hobby. He had all of the tools needed to work with leather. With Mrs. Bronson's help, we cut out leather patterns and sewed them together to form sacks. These went over our shoulders, with rawhide thongs as the shoulder straps. Initially, we Cubs were not too hot for the idea of the bags, because we thought they were too similar to purses. But The Duchess called them "braves' bags," which we accepted. We figured every real Indian brave needed a bag to carry his wallet, pictures of his girlfriends, and his spare arrowheads. Braves' bags it was! And Mr. Bronson helped us decorate them with his tools. We made a bag for each brave and we had our names impressed into our bags by Mr. Bronson—not our real names, but our Indian names.

Which brings me to our names. We all felt that since we were Indian braves, we couldn't run around the Clamorama with our true names. We needed Indian braves' names, which conveyed our true bravery and Indian-ness. I knew immediately what name I wanted. There were two Indians we all revered. One of course was Tonto. But nobody would self-proclaim himself as Tonto, any more than someone studying Eastern religions would call himself Buddha. Respect would offset adoration. The other Indian we all loved was Little Beaver®, Red Ryder®'s friend. For some reason, the juxtaposition of "Red" and "Beaver" seemed to fit for me, and once it appeared, my mind immediately adopted it. I became "Red Beaver," a great and courageous Indian brave.

When Ronnie Landers and Spike Owens heard that, Ronnie proclaimed with pride that he wanted to be called "Little Ryder!" That left Spike with the onus of coming up with something new. After much thought and many discarded names, he finally settled on "Brave Eagle." The other braves in the den thought that was a super name and they all were envious. Even Mrs. Bronson gave "Brave Eagle" high marks.

My friend Sally Donovan and her whole family came to know about the upcoming Clamorama, and that I was to be an Indian brave in the evening's big "Settling of the Prairie" production. Sally had two sisters and a brother, Jack, who was twenty, going on thirty. He worked at Boeing on an assembly line after barely getting out of high school. He thought he had the world by the tail. He had money (relative to anybody living in the projects), girlfriends, more girlfriends, and even then some girlfriends—you could definitely say he was interested in women. Sally's dad, Ed, also worked at Boeing, in a machine shop, and was the person responsible for getting Jack his job. Father and son were at that stage where the son thinks the father is not very smart, so occasionally they had some tension in their relationship, but Jack still lived at home. How this impacted his ability to mingle with the ladies was not a question I understood at that time. It was not until I also became twenty that I then looked back and wondered how Jack had managed it.

Ed was a crusty guy who rarely smiled, so initially I was leery of him. But after being around him for a while, I dropped my guard because he loved building things with wood. He had a tool called a "Shopsmith" and with it he could do almost anything with wood. I found I also had a natural attraction for woodworking, and I liked to stand in the background and watch him work.

After much discussion, Ed announced he would help us braves make things. He always looked for any excuse to go into his wood shop, which was a spare bedroom in their project unit. The Donovan's unit had four bedrooms: one for the parents, one for Jack, one for Sally and her two sisters, and one for the Shopsmith. It was all about priorities, and the "wood shop" was right up there with his children.

Ed crafted various wooden things for all of us in Den 5. He was very excited about it. He let us watch as he turned lance shafts and arrows on his lathe. Wood shavings were everywhere and he was in seventh heaven. He rounded the tips of the lances, though, so nobody would hurt themselves. These lances were not your basic smoothed pieces of wood. No, he turned intricate patterns and ridges into the wooden shafts, so every lance looked like it had been purchased at the Indian's home improvement store, rather than hand-whittled by each brave out of birch saplings. We were all very excited about our lances and arrows. Add this to our braves' bags and our colored macaroni breast-plates, and we were an Indian force to be respected.

We also absconded with some pigeon feathers from my Uncle Johnny's fly fishing tying materials. We held the feathers in place around our foreheads by tying shoelaces around our head. We looked formidable. I was certain Cochise and Sitting Bull would have been enormously proud of each one of us braves.

A Man's Protection

The last detail came from a conversation I had one evening with Sally's brother, Jack. I was in his bedroom talking with him about the upcoming Clamorama. I showed him all of our Indian paraphernalia and the things his dad had made for us. He humored me, but didn't get too excited about his dad's lances. Clearly, he was not interested in woodworking at that time in his life.

"What you guys need is some *protection*," he said with a big smile on his face.

"I got some," I said. "See my breast-plate. It's got different sizes of macaronies and they're all different colors. This'll stop anything from the cowboys or the settlers."

Jack stared at me, and I didn't understand his look. He had a sly grin that seemed to start behind his ears and sweep across his mouth, but it actually came out of sheer devilishness.

"That's not the kind of protection I mean, Geronimo. What you need is a real man's protection."

There was a long pause as I looked at him in complete bewilderment, and he looked back with that teasing sneer, as if to draw out every bit of suspense he could muster.

A man's protection! What could that mean? I wondered.

My brain turned. What had I missed? We had everything The Duchess and Mr. Bronson had made, along with the gear from Ed's wood shop. What was this "protection" thing that apparently was so essential to our complete survival, the last accessory that every Plains Indian needed?

"You need some rubbers!" Jack said.

He just threw it out there, into the room, with the words hanging out of his mouth for a few seconds for emphasis, before they each invisibly fell to the floor.

Rubbers? What does he mean rubbers? My brain labored.

Finally, I said, "Rubbers? That's crazy. Why would I wear my galoshes?" I thought, Why would *anybody* wear his galoshes indoors, especially any self-respecting Plains Indian brave? Besides, they didn't have galoshes; they wore moccasins; everybody knew that, even people Jack's age. I couldn't figure it out, and I thought it was the stupidest idea I had heard in a while.

I must parenthetically explain for those not from Seattle, or other wet winter climates, we kids all had galoshes, which we wore when it was raining. These were rubber boot-like things that fit over our shoes and had a row of buckle snaps up the inside of the ankles and lower leg. However, everybody I knew never snapped the buckles, we just walked in the rain with the tops open and with the snaps clattering with each step. Cat burglars, or Indian braves for that matter, could never wear galoshes! They would be professionally unsuitable. Also, instead of calling these items "galoshes," which grown-ups seemed to prefer, we kids always called them "rubbers." So, when we went outside with our rubbers on, that was apparently a completely *different* circumstance than when Jack Donovan went out with his rubbers on.

Jack threw his head back in a laugh. The fish had taken the bait! I had swallowed the line whole.

"Not your galoshes, you donkey. I'm talking about rubbers. The kind of thing a man wears for protection. Don't you know what I mean?"

I thought I did, but I didn't. I just looked at him. I hoped that some brilliance would enter my brain, but I was stumped. I didn't have a clue. Time stopped.

"Haven't you ever had a boner?" he asked.

Well now, finally, that was something I actually *did* understand because being eleven, I along with the other guys all talked about boners, and hard dinkies, and stiff soldiers, and erections (that term always made me think of my Erector® set), and things like that. In fact, it was a topic that had come to occupy a fairly large part of our thinking, because now that we had begun to have them on occasion, they were both a marvel and a curiosity to us. Why would that appendage that at pre-ten years of age we knew as our "wee-wee," "wiener," or "peter," and which up to then always was flaccid, suddenly become stiff and unmanageable on occasion when we were now eleven? For some boys it was earlier, for some later, but once it began, everybody knew about it. It was the dominant talk of every gang's play, and when we were not talking about it, we were thinking about it quite often.

Sometimes, we discovered, we could even make it happen by rubbing our pants. Once, I shinnied up the metal pole where our school basketball backboard was mounted, and I discovered when I made it to the top . . . that I had a boner. And it felt good! And, when I slid down the pole, well, that felt good too! I then decided to go *up and down* the pole again. I even went a *third* time before my arms finally were so tired they had no strength. But I was mesmerized by the feeling in my groin, which was all new to me. What was going on? I wasn't sure, but all of us guys were experiencing it too and we all bragged about ours. Yes, boners had intruded into our consciousness by age eleven and definitely now occupied a good portion of our attention.

"Well . . . haven't you?" he asked again.

"Sure I have," I replied with conviction and pride. How old did he think I was, nine or ten? "I have 'em a lot, and they're big too!"

"Yeah! I bet they are," he said, again in that leering look. "You're not using them on my sister are you? Huh? Are you trying to show your 'big' boner to Sally? You're not trying to 'make it' with Sally? Are ya? Huh?"

Make it? I thought. Make what? Again, at first I was not clear on what he meant, but as I continued to stare at him with no words leaving my lips, it finally occurred to me what he meant by "make it."

Let me say that by this time in my life I was not completely stupid about either the behavioral or physical differences between boys and girls, or men and women. After all, I had seen the "naked lady" at the drive-in a few years before and I still remembered the hairy triangle. I had figured out that she, and presumably all women, had that triangle for a reason, and I also knew that sometime in my life I could explore that triangle area in more detail. But at age eleven it was not in my immediate vision as to when that would be. I knew men and women came together and did certain things which boys and girls didn't, so it was not like I just fell off the hay wagon when it came to relations between the opposite sexes. I really did have some awareness of what was coming.

Saying this, however, does not mean that I, and all of my friends then, had even an inkling of how much children would know about sex today. Remember, this was the 1950s and sex then was not nearly as pervasively talked about in society as it is today. People acted more "proper," and sex was more hidden, or protected. It was not overt in the movies we saw, or in the radio shows we liked. Plus, we didn't then have access to books, magazines, and the Internet where anyone of any age could be exposed to extraordinary levels of prurient material. At age eleven we just knew that one day we guys would probably begin to have an interest in actually kissing girls, even though *why*, was still puzzling to us.

At age eleven, going on twelve, we were in that awkward transition—not yet active and drawn to girls, but nevertheless beginning to be quite curious about the whole matter. After all, our boners were there for a reason, and we suspected they had a purpose. The physical sensations we were beginning to feel were big clues, although the picture in the puzzle had not yet materialized for any of us.

Also, I have to say that I was becoming very curious about Sally, as well as unclear in my own mind as to why I wanted to be around her more as I grew older. I recognized that I had far more interest in her now that we both were eleven, than I had when we first met at eight. I guess I had an attraction for her that I was not yet ready to fully acknowledge.

As I stood there with Jack staring at me and asking me questions, I recalled an incident a month before that had aroused me toward Sally.

We had gone ice skating together at the rink in downtown Seattle. Sally and I were skating side-by-side when she happened to lose her balance. She grabbed me to keep from falling. However, she also pulled me off balance and then both of us were slippin' and slidin' in all directions trying to stay upright. But it was to no avail; we both went down.

Sally happened to fall sprawled on her back. I was right behind her, and I came down on top of her . . . and, my right hand just happened to come, palm down . . . right where that *triangle* was! It was a complete accident, but my hand was pressed on her lower stomach between her thighs! And it felt soft! I immediately removed my hand and acted as if nothing unusual had happened.

Except, something had happened. For the first time in my life I had my hand on a girl's very private area, and as much as both of us tried to pretend nothing of it, or me to ignore it, in my mind I couldn't do that. I was now intrigued by what I had felt there between her legs. As much as she and I had friendly chit-chat for the remainder of the day, and even though my words and outside behavior tried to act as though my hand had never touched her private triangle, my mind knew it had, and it couldn't forget.

I wondered what she thought. We never talked about it; we always kept that formal ignorance of the moment. But I always wondered if I would ever get another chance to do that again with Sally—only when we both knew it was not by accident.

My reverie was broken by Jack's voice intruding. "Well, are ya? Are ya making it with my sister?"

"No." I stammered. "I haven't done anything, I promise!"

"Well, you better not! Ya better keep your dick in your pants, ya hear! If I catch you makin' it with my sister, I'll box your ears. You understand?"

"Yeah, sure. Sure, I will . . . I promise!"

"OK then," he said. "So . . . you want any protection or not?"

I thought, I'm not sure where he's going with this, but what could it hurt?

"Sure," I said. "I want all the protection I can get. I want some rubbers."

Jack turned and went to his dresser. He opened one of the drawers, rooted around his underwear, and finally pulled out a small flat package. He handed it to me.

"Here's a rubber," he said. "Whatta ya think?"

I took it and turned it over in my hand. Printed on the outside of the paper wrap was the word "Condom."

"Con . . . dom," I read out loud. "What's that?"

"It means 'rubber,' that's what they're called. Rubbers! You know what they're for, right?"

"Sure," I said. Only I didn't.

I tore the paper wrapping and saw that it held a piece of rolled up rubber sheath material. I slowly unrolled it from itself, until it was completely unrolled. It looked like a small rubber mitten with no thumb hole. I stared. My mind was curious, but I was not sure what I had.

"Yep, that looks just like all of the other rubbers I've seen before," I lied.

Jack knew I was fibbing but he let it pass.

"So, mostly you just put those on your dick when you're making it with someone, but they have other uses too, right? Can you imagine what else you can do with them?"

I was not to the "other uses" part yet, because I was still trying to figure out the first use. Oh, I *now* understood that it was something you used when you explored a woman's triangle area, but why? What purpose was it?

"Why do you need this?" I finally asked.

"So you can keep all your swimmers in the pool . . . if you know what I mean."

I didn't.

Swimmers in the pool, I thought. What does this rubber thing have to do with the Plunge? My mind just couldn't connect any dots.

"Ah, well, never mind," Jack said, knowing that he had lost me completely and he apparently didn't want to further explain. "Let's just say that they offer protection, like I said before."

OK. I'm good with that, I thought. Maybe someday I would need to be protected, but not today.

"So, what else could we do with them?" I asked.

"Well . . . they make really good balloons," Jack said. "You can blow them up, or fill them with water. They're great when filled with water." Again he had that devilish half smile. ". . . You could do something in your Clamorama with them. It would be the last thing anyone would expect."

Now *that* was an idea! We could make water rubbers out of them, and then when nobody expected anything, when the cowboy packs came in to save the settler packs, we Indians could let fly a few of our water rubbers and surprise everyone. Who knew what the outcome would be?

It was daring, it was unexpected, and it was just the kind of inventiveness and cleverness that Tonto would have appreciated. The Indians of Den 5 of Pack 231 would have a trick up their sleeves, well . . . actually in their braves' bags!

"Yeah!" I said excitedly. "Would you get us some rubbers? That would be neat!"

"Sure, I can do that. My friend's in the Navy and he can get them by the boat load. I'll get you a bunch of 'large' ones. Any bigger than that and they're too heavy and too hard to throw." Here was a man who obviously had some experience with such matters.

"How about smaller than 'large'?" I asked. "Why do we need large?"

"Because 'large' is the smallest size," he said.

What? I thought. Why is "large" the smallest size? Obviously, I knew nothing about condoms, or the male psyche, regarding such matters. Large it was to be.

A few days later, Jack Donovan, true to his word, gave me two dozen condoms. I waited until I had them in my possession and then told Little Ryder and Brave Eagle about them. They were intrigued, and it took some explaining by me to bring them up to the maturity level I now enjoyed after my man-to-man talk with Jack. But instantly they agreed with the devilishness of a plan for the Clamorama. Once they were convinced, we let the other Den 5 braves into it. It became our private secret.

We never let Mrs. or Mr. Bronson know. I had a suspicion that outwardly she would have been negative on the idea because that's how den mothers were supposed to be, but inwardly she would have appreciated its originality. But we couldn't risk her finding out, so we couldn't say anything to anyone.

A pair of jacks: me with Jack Donovan.

The cloth Clamorama badge sewn onto our Cub Scout uniform.

Ready for the Clamorama.

29

THE BIG EVENT

Life is either a daring adventure, or nothing.
—Helen Keller

As the buildup continued to the big show in the Clamorama, we learned that the program called for the settlers to be the first groups to come into the arena. They were from packs in north Seattle. They would be riding wagons looking like Conestoga wagons. They would circle around inside the arena for a few laps, finally parking the wagons in some semblance of a circle. Then they would get out their camping stuff and set up some tents and do settler things so they could demonstrate their Cub Scout craftiness.

Then we were to enter the arena. Our Pack 231 and other Cub packs from south Seattle were the Indians who would come in and lay siege on the settlers. We were supposed to run around whooping and hollering and making those TV and movie Indian-type sounds with our hands and mouths. We were supposed to be doing Indian dances, and some packs even had Indian drums to beat. Our job was to threaten the settlers and make them scared. We were to wear all of our Indian paraphernalia and have war-paint makeup on our faces, applied by The Duchess and other dutiful den mothers. We were to be, well . . . just a bunch of wild Indians. We could do that!

Then, the big climax, after we had made everybody fearful, was that the cowboy Cub packs from west Seattle were to come in and engage us Indians in a mock battle, helped on by the settlers.

Eventually the cowboys and settlers were to capture all of us Indians —again, this was not history from the Indian's perspective. After our "capture," we all would have a good Old West celebration— cowboys, Indians, and settlers in harmony, thanks to Cub Scouting!

The day of the event came. We braves in Den 5 were excited. We all gathered late in the afternoon at Ronnie's house. It was selected because nobody was home at his place and would not be until dinner. We made the water rubbers by filling them with water and tying off the ends with string that Spike (Brave Eagle) had found. We called them "rubber bombs," thinking that only we knew what that meant, and if anyone accidentally heard us talking about them, they would mistakenly think we were talking about rubber *bands*. At least that was our logic. They came out to be small oblong pro- jectiles somewhat larger than our hands.

We didn't fill them as much as we could, because we wanted them to be easy to throw. We made twenty of them, two apiece, and packed all of them inside our braves' bags. We were ready for condom surprises!

I had an early dinner with my family and then put on my cos- tume. I wore a sweatshirt to keep warm, and put my breastplate over that. We all knew real Indians never wore sweatshirts, but even Chief Seattle would have frozen in the winter nights if all he had to wear was a costume like ours. I also put on some Indian-like pants, and of course my Indian headband with the feathers tied into it. Lastly my handmade lance and my brave's bag made up the whole costume. I was awesome looking.

True to my step-dad, he didn't like to go places with crowds, so none of my family was going to the Clamorama. They drove me over to where the Pack met and dropped me off. I met with all of the other braves in Den 5 and we shared that secret look that communicated among ourselves that we had a surprise coming later. We then boarded buses and were driven to the Clamorama arena. Once there, we staged into one area with all of the other Indian packs of south Seattle. There actually were quite a bunch of us. I have to say we all looked like braves with whom to be reckoned! Mrs. Bronson beamed.

The show began. There was music and the Pledge of Allegiance to the Flag. The settlers came in and, well . . . settled. We couldn't see any of it because we were outside of the main arena. But we could tell it was big. The wagons were driven by the scoutmasters, and the den mothers of the settlers were dressed as Prairie moms. The wagons were pulled by jeeps, go figure, but maybe another motto of the Cubs was "Be Resourceful."

Finally, we Indians were cued. We all huddled by the entrances. Our Pack 231 scoutmaster was also dressed as an Indian chief with a long headdress. He looked good too, except that he was the largest and most out of shape Indian I had ever seen—about 250 pounds with a big belly. He also held up his pants with big suspenders, which somehow didn't seem like regular Indian issue. But it was OK with us. If the settlers could pull their wagons with jeeps, he could wear big suspenders. Mrs. Bronson looked like an Indian woman with Mukluk Eskimo boot moccasins on her feet. She looked pretty spiffy and we could tell she was fairly pleased with herself. She too looked like a formidable Indian—one who could throw a tomahawk through a teepee if needed!

The music rose, and we were off and running. We sped down the ramp and out into the arena whooping and hollering as if we tried to wake every old Indian spirit from the dead. I could not imagine that the real Indians who had attacked General Custer had hollered like that, but hey, this was show biz. We were some tough Indian braves, and tough Indian braves made noise.

When we came in, the music was dramatic, and the audience in the arena clapped and made much noise too. Everybody was into it. We ran toward the wagons and then circled them. We shook our lances and did the Indian "hot-foot" dance. The settlers shook their fists at us and hollered back.

After about ten minutes of this, I was tired. I mean, how much can you whoop and holler and "hot-foot" dance? Then . . . we heard the music change, and trumpets blared the cavalry's charge. There was not supposed to be any cavalry, but the bugles accompanied the cowboys anyway. The cowboys ran in, *en masse*, and tried to make as much noise as we Indians had previously. They hollered and fired cap pistols. They were all dressed like cow-punching buckaroos with scarves around their necks and cowboy hats on their heads. They ran through our Indian ranks. They also ran into the areas where the settlers were camped. We chased them.

Soon everybody ran everywhere, and hollered and yelled. I thought it looked more like a mob riot than an organized drama, but everyone had a great time! Some cowboys tried to run up to Mrs. Bronson and capture her, but we rallied around her and pointed our lances at them to run them off. I really think Mrs. Bronson could have fended for herself, though, if the truth be known.

All of us Den 5 braves were together now. We looked at each other and decided it was time. We dug into our braves' bags and each of us came out with a rubber bomb. A couple of them were immediately launched into a crowd of cowboys—with *perfect* results. They broke, and drenched a group of them! Some of us took off running into the middle of the settler's camp circle. I threw my first rubber bomb at a jeep. It splashed against the windshield and water went everywhere. Wow, a direct hit! Other braves now in the middle of the campground heaved at will. Ronnie (Little Ryder) let one fly, and with his great athletic skill made a perfect toss onto the back of one of the north Seattle scoutmasters. *Kersploosh!* The man let out a huge yell, turned, and chased us. We ran and darted in and out of the melee of people, whooping and yelling more. Now this was really fun!

We re-armed with our last bombs. We now ran into the center of the camp circle, and I could see the wagon of the Grand Scoutmaster of the Seattle Cub Scouts. It had banners to signify an official's wagon. I let my last bomb fly and made a direct hit on the side of his wagon. There was much shrieking as the bomb burst, throwing water over a few of the occupants. It was not a full drenching, but it certainly was more water than they ever expected. Now they were irate, and we braves were all on the move. We ran for our lives, and were chased by most of the grown-ups who huffed and puffed behind us. I finally was grabbed by someone and held down. The other braves eventually also were subdued. There was much shouting and screaming by all of the participants on the arena floor, and it was complete bedlam.

Of our twenty bombs, I believe seventeen or eighteen were smashed. But, to our surprise, the audience *loved* it! It certainly was not representative of Cub Scouting, but it was, apparently, good comedy. Now I can appreciate why, whenever clowns throw pies, it's just *funny!* And this totally unexpected and delirious show we had put on was *funny* to the audience, such that when it became apparent that the anger from the scouting representatives was about to be directed at us poor little defenseless braves, the audience became raucous and demonstrative.

Even though I was solidly in the grasp of a six-foot settler scoutmaster with anger in his eyes, when I put my arms in the air to play to the crowd, a huge *cheer* arose. That alone made it all worthwhile. I could have been skinned and beaten later in the dungeons of that arena, but that one cheer was redemption! The people—the paying customers—were "with" us, the "bad" Indians! It was sweet.

Eventually, we Den 5 braves were all rounded up and turned over to our pack scoutmaster, who after much scolding, admonishment, and threats of great punishment, then turned us over to Mrs. Bronson. The Duchess acted not pleased. She had a very stern look on her face as she herded us out of the arena and into a backstage dressing area. We thought, Oh no! Now we're really going to get it!

When the door closed, and we were alone with her, she stared at us. Then, slowly, her stern look crumbled. First, there was a look of resignation, which was followed by a slight smile that grew broader and broader with each second, although she fought it.

She said, "Look at you all! What am I going to do with you?" She smiled more, but still tried to contain it and not show complete acceptance of our misadventures.

But we could tell she was cracking. We knew she was beginning to laugh inside, especially since she had found that out the rubber bombs actually were condoms, and not balloons, filled with water. This was funny to her, and we knew her attitude was, yes, we were scamps and scoundrels, but we also were *100% young boys!*

And, we really were braves too, because she finally said that for us to do that, was brave of us—stupid, but brave. We all relaxed knowing that she was understanding, if not completely forgiving, and would not be beating us. Our scoutmaster was not quite so forgiving, and when he finally came back he gave us a tongue-lashing that was memorable. But even though we had our heads down, with our most contrite poses, we could still see The Duchess standing behind him with a smile on her face. That too made it all worthwhile. Jenny would have been proud of us too.

My Cub Scouting career didn't exactly prosper after that incident. There were no more gold or silver arrowheads, and I left the program soon after the Clamorama. I was not kicked out, but Mrs. Bronson decided to give up the Den 5 and I didn't feel like breaking in another den mother at that late stage. I hung up my blue twill uniform, and my mother mothballed it for the next three decades before mildew finally consumed it. The patches and awards, though, were saved.

After sitting on the sidelines for a few months, I did go on to become a Boy Scout and this led to a whole new level of stories and escapades. I eventually achieved the rank of "Life Scout." I diligently collected merit badges and was on my way to becoming an Eagle Scout, until, at about age fourteen and a half, my hormones finally kicked in "big time." I then discovered I had more interest in girls than I did in merit badges and community good works.

After the Clamorama, I was still a good friend of Sally's and her family for a couple of years more. Although Sally and I shared many fun times together, we never became boyfriend-girlfriend, and I never, even remotely, touched her triangle area again, contrary to my curiosity about doing so.

Jack Donovan went on to pursue his lifetime ambition, which I'm sure was to "make it" with every girl in America.

When he heard about what we braves had done at the Clamorama, he was beside himself with glee. I'm sure he vicariously enjoyed the whole escapade as much as we braves, and The Duchess.

30

CHANGES AFOOT

All things, even the most longed for, have their melancholy;
for what we leave behind is a part of ourselves;
we must die to one life before we can enter another!
—attributed to Gail Sheehy

Some months after my scouting mischief at the Clamorama had become nothing more than a memory, my brother Doug and I once again enjoyed unrestricted play, sunrise to sunset, in the wonderful period of long warm days and generally rainless skies that was summer in Seattle. Unbeknownst to us, though, financial changes were occurring within our family. My step-dad had achieved more meaningful work and we kids were now old enough that mom felt she also could work, at least part time. We kids never thought anything about it, and were oblivious to any impending consequences. But one evening over dinner, mom dropped a bombshell!

"Dad and I have a surprise for you," she said. ". . . We are going to move!"

It was delivered as such a benign utterance, as though she had observed that tomatoes had appeared on the scrawny plant outside our entrance stoop. It almost went completely over our heads as I pestered Doug for a shaker of salt he withheld from me, out of sheer devilishness. But slowly the fuse to enlightenment burned down in my brain . . . four . . . three . . . two . . . one. . . . *Move!!!*

The word sunk into my mind, Doug's too.

"MOVE!!!" I almost shouted. "Whatta ya mean, move? We're gonna move?" I mouthed, before Doug or Cindy could say a word.

325

Doug was as stunned as I was.

"Yeah . . . where mom, where?" he said excitedly, while I took a breath. If the conversation had ceased at that moment and someone had asked us both to answer Doug's question, with our best estimate, we both would have believed we were making a big step out of the "old" projects to the "good" projects, those luxurious duplexes with electric heaters. In our minds, at that moment, it was a likely probability we would move right next to the Donovan's because mom liked Sally's mother.

"We're moving out of the projects completely! We're moving to a real house! . . . A few miles from here. What do you think of that?"

Our first reactions were of unbridled excitement. "Wow! We're gonna live in a house, our very own house! Does it have a lawn . . . and a heater? Huh . . . does it?" I blurted with enthusiasm. Doug's head nodded in agreement with my questions.

"Yes. It has both of those things. Not a big lawn, it's small, but it has a heater . . . yes it does," mom answered with a large smile on her face. Dad didn't say much, but then he never did; mom always did most of the talking. But to mom, this clearly was an answer to her prayers. This was more than that; this was a step upward to respectability.

We no longer would need a coal bin, one of those things that in her mind was associated with "lower class." We now were to have real heat, like respectable people!

"And it also has a washing machine in it," she purred, "with an automatic cycle."

This meant no more rollers to manually wring out the water, or trap her arm. Clearly, mom was in heaven. How she could hold this news inside of her, and then deliver it so matter-of-factly, even now is a mystery to me. And we didn't even try to follow her lead. We almost cheered as if we had won a free shopping spree downtown at Frederick & Nelson's!

But then it began to sink into my mind. All of the questions, and the consequences, began to worm their way into my consciousness. See, we kids were all for moving. We could move in a heartbeat. . . .

"Um . . . just give me a minute, mom, to get my baseball mitt and a couple pieces of underwear, and I'll be ready to go. We don't even have to eat dessert . . . we can get it along the way. . . . "

But then the reality slowly became obvious.

Yes, we were moving, *but our friends were staying behind!* They were not coming with us to the new "promised land." OH NO!!!

Initially, I was disappointed, then distraught, and then, finally, devastated as the true depth of this development sunk in.

The Alderwood Court gang members were more than my friends: they were my closest companions. We had shared everything together for years. Nobody, other than my brother and my other direct family, meant more to me than Ronnie Landers, Freddie Roberts, and Spike and Jenny Owens. Yes, we were only moving a few miles away, but it might as well have been to Alaska. Walking a few yards to pick them up at their houses was not the same thing as riding our bikes miles to visit them. The first was an everyday occurrence with no thought involved; the latter was a trek that wouldn't happen often.

This move was a development of major importance.

Within a few weeks, we had moved a few miles away, as mom had said, into a rented three-bedroom house, still in the Columbia section in south Seattle. We now had defined streets with curbs and sidewalks, and our little house had a meager front lawn with real grass! But best of all, as mom had said, we had a gas furnace to heat the house, and an electric stove in the kitchen. We had escaped the coal burning stove, and I never again in my life shoveled coal. We might as well have moved to the Hamptons. We now were a short distance away, but in a different world, from the "old" projects.

Moving was as traumatic as I expected! For all of the newness and the excitement of now being able to explore new territory, there also was the separation from my dear friends for whom I cared deeply. Many times it was us, united against everybody— the other gangs and even grown-ups—which bonded us together.

We often could not understand the strange world of older people, including parents, but we had each other to share our miseries, our tribulations, our triumphs, and our fantasies. We grew up together and came to depend upon and trust each other as more than close friends, almost as kin.

Such relationships are difficult for anybody to break, perhaps to never again experience, even for ten- to twelve-year-olds. We were used to other kids suddenly moving away from the projects, but when it finally happened to us, to Doug and me, it was just, well . . . painful. Gone were the days of playing baseball with Ronnie and envying his athletic skills, of teasing Freddie about his complete lack of ability yet appreciating his total effort every time, and of enjoying Spike's adaptability to every situation—never a problem.

We had our last gang meeting in the woods. I swapped baseball cards with Ronnie and Spike, and shared one last Big Hunk® with Freddie.

However, separating from Jenny was especially difficult, because we each felt a kinship that never came from, or was affected by, her being a girl. We just happened to click together and we appreciated each other in ways that neither of us fully understood with our then limited emotional development. *We were the best of pals;* I can't describe it any more thoroughly.

We faced each other that last time, staring without words, neither knowing quite what to say. Finally, she softly kicked my shin. I put my arm around her neck and gave her a side-by-side hug. Then both of us said, "Bye," and that was it. My heart hurt. As much as we all wished otherwise, and promised to each other, I never saw her, or the others, again—because of the move, but also because we all were changing.

Doug and I saw Sally Donovan and her family again, though, because of our parent's friendships. We occasionally had dinner together as families through the next school year.

In September, I settled into the seventh grade at Sharples Junior High School, and had a fairly uneventful year. I stopped going to the Saturday afternoon movie matinees because seventh graders didn't do that "juvenile stuff" anymore. I continued with my Boy

Scouting, and was heavily involved in collecting merit badges, at least for another year. I was focused on sports, cars, grades in school, scouting, and I was becoming more interested in girls.

I was not chasing them, but I was slowly realizing I might have some interest. I was in that awkward stage where I had not begun to shave and thus become a real adolescent, and yet I was too old to still be considered a young boy.

By the time school was out in the summer of 1955, I was skinny, gangly, occasionally pimpled, and a few months short of thirteen wanting to be sixteen so I could drive; I was just marking time.

Looking back, the seventh grade was eminently forgettable. Although Doug and I adjusted to life beyond the projects, and were happier in many respects, in other ways we never made a successful transition.

Both of us missed our gang friends, and the camaraderie we left behind.

31

SLO-MO-SHUN

Life is change. Growth is optional. Choose wisely.
—Karen Kaiser Clark

When my seventh-grade school year was over, in June 1955, Doug and I settled again into the pleasures of summer. Mom and dad worked, mom still half-time. Cindy spent mornings with her friends and then the afternoons with mom. Doug and I spent our time in never-ending baseball games with our new neighborhood pals.

We also covered more distance on our bicycles. My old rusty red bike with the missing front wheel fender had been "down-gifted" to Doug, and I now had another bike. This newest one was a full-sized Schwinn® with 26" tires, also red. It was not the "Phantom" model with the white sidewall tires, the ultimate bike of my dreams. It was not even new when my step-dad brought it home, but it certainly fit me better now that I had begun to "stretch out" with added inches everywhere. I was now into my early adolescent growth spurts.

This newer "speed demon," as I called my new bike, was adequate transportation for another summer or two until social pressures would lead me to put it aside permanently. By age fourteen, I walked, because I'd rather be caught dead than riding a bicycle.

But in the late summer of 1955, I did ride, and Doug and I thought nothing of journeying as far as the shores of Lake Washington. I should say that every August a temporary insanity overtook Seattle.

That was in the form of the month-long city-wide celebration of "Seafair," the Seattle equivalent of New Orleans Mardi Gras. Seafair was an excuse for Seattleites to come out of their homes, throw off their galoshes and rain gear, and finally enjoy that burning ball of fire in the sky. It was a time of celebration with parties, dances, civic events, and marauding bands of "pirates" in costumes who kidnapped office-working damsels on their lunch hours in downtown. The pirates rampaged through the city on boats on wheels—trucks constructed to look like pirate ships. Everybody picked up the spirit, and Seafair over the years grew to become an excuse to party and enjoy the outdoors. In the early 1950s it was a city-wide celebration almost akin to when the Second World War ended.

The showcase event for Seafair was the unlimited hydroplane boat race on Lake Washington. In August this race, and the events for two weeks leading up to it, were similar to what Indianapolis enjoys for the Indy 500 auto race on Memorial Day weekend. The whole city went crazy for the sport. The race was called the "Gold Cup" and it was a traveling race depending on who was the prior year's winner. Contenders came from various water locations across America and the winner claimed not only the trophy, but also the right to take the race to their city for the next year.

Seattle was the reigning champion of unlimited hydroplane racing—with two boats that were owned by a gentleman named Stan Sayers. He had become a city celebrity. They were both called "Slo–Mo–Shun." There was Slo-Mo-Shun IV and Slo-Mo-Shun V, and they were the fastest things on water!

These were big boats, over 28-feet long, with open cockpits where the drivers were plainly visible and rode without seatbelts. They were powered by large Allison or Rolls-Royce piston engines, the same engines that had driven the great propeller fighter aircraft of the Second World War—the Corsairs, the Hellcats, and the P-51 Mustangs, to name a few. They were loud, temperamental, exciting, and fast! Slo-Mo IV was capable of 185 miles per hour on a straightaway on a calm day, at "no sweat" according to one of her crew members. She wasn't quite as good in the turns as Slo-Mo V. But "V" didn't have the top end speed in the straightaway as "IV."

Above 165 miles per hour Slo-Mo V tended to wobble in the front, a characteristic referred to by her crew as "kiting." They were sister boats but with different personalities. When screaming at high speed, both boats left in their wake a large "rooster-tail," or plume of white water spray, as a signature of their authority over the water. The rooster-tail reached thirty or more feet in height and thirty to forty yards in length, and not only was a thing of beauty, but also a problem for any trailing boats. Clearly, this was a race with a strong incentive to be in the lead.

Seeing a bunch of such heavyweight boats, each with engines of greater than 1,500 horsepower screaming at maximum RPM's, stirred every Seattle boy's (and man's) passions and imaginations. Prior to the actual race on Sunday, all of the boats practiced the week in advance. The "pits" for the boats were in a sheltered cove area on the western shore of the lake. Doug and I rode over to watch every day of race week. We watched all of the action—the boats, the drivers, and the going's-on as the boats were lifted in and out of the water by large cranes and then deposited on specially designed cradles for support. Everything about the atmosphere was exciting, and visiting the hydroplanes was the only thing that suspended our baseball activities.

On Sunday race day, estimates were that between 300,000 to 400,000 people (a large percentage of the city's population) would show up to line the lake along the three-plus-mile oval course to watch and enjoy the three "heats," each of 30 miles, which in total comprised the race. It was great fun, but again, it was mostly a good excuse to party-hearty in the warm days of Seattle's short summer. At the conclusion of the Gold Cup, which Seattleites expected either one of the Slo-Mo-Shuns to win, Seafair came to an end, and all Doug and I could look forward to was another school year.

One of the vivid memories I have of race week that year was standing on the shore on Saturday, the day before the race, on a gloriously sunny afternoon, watching Slo-Mo-Shun V make a qualifying run.

She came up the backstretch at her maximum speed, throwing plume and screaming with horsepower—and yet she was all elegance and beauty at the same time. She flew across the water, until . . . quite literally, she decided to *fly*.

As with most accidents, especially those happening at 170 plus miles per hour, it is impossible to know what happened.

But I remember that even the immaturely developed computer in my mind instantly *knew* that something was wrong when the front sideboard sponsons of the boat—the two stabilizing hull members upon which she rode the water—began to lift up and *off* the water. She perceptively raised her front, and the sponsons wobbled side to side, each time lifting one side free of water and into the air. With each wobble she allowed more air to flow under her hull, until eventually the whole front of the boat separated from the confines of the water contact, and freed itself by launching upward into the air. She literally took *flight*.

The front pointed upward, climbed, and rotated until it was now vertical. Upward she went, continuing to rotate until finally she was completely upside down, with the engine screaming at its top-end red-line, and the propeller totally freed from the resistance of fighting through the liquid. At this point in the rotational apogee, the driver, a well-loved gentleman named Lou Fageol, separated from the boat and fell toward the water with arms and legs splayed in all directions, but still traveling forward with the momentum of the boat, at well over 100 miles per hour. He struck the water and skipped a couple of times like a flat stone thrown across the surface, and then settled into the liquid with a huge cannonball spray.

The boat continued her rotation and also fell back into the lake, miraculously finally smashing onto the surface with her bottom side, pre-flip orientation. She had done a complete "360 head-over-heels" in the air before she hit the water again.

The surface exploded with spray as the boat also skipped and then dug in her front edges, shuddering to an explosive shower of spray absorbing the deceleration. Also miraculously, the boat never hit the driver. Both now floated completely spent on the flat surface of the water.

The screaming sounds of horsepower, and then destruction, were now totally replaced by an eerie and desperate silence as observers everywhere, my brother and I included, gasped for air. The stunned silence lasted for a second or two before screams of shock pierced the air. Eventually, people cried from the anguish and disbelief of it all. There was as much concern for the boat as for the driver, because both were viewed as beloved icons and local heroes. Both Slo-Mo-Shuns were our Seattle treasures. The two drivers, Lou Fageol for "V" and Joe Taggart for "IV," were heroes of the same magnitude for Seattleites as Joe Montana would become many years later for San Franciscans. Every viewer was completely stunned.

Eventually, rescuers reached the scene. The driver, Lou, still alive but semi-conscious, was plucked from the water and hospitalized. He survived, but never raced again. The boat, leaking and listing, was towed back to the pits and also saved. She required extensive rebuilding but was never the same—much as a great Thoroughbred who suffers an injury, then never again recaptures her form, and retires early.

The Gold Cup was run the next day as scheduled with all of Seattle's hopes now riding on her sister ship, Slo-Mo-Shun IV, the "Grand Old Lady" as she was known. With Joe Taggart at the controls, she led for most of the race, until two laps short of victory she slowed and drifted off the course with a cracked exhaust manifold.

Joe prevented her from exploding and sinking by shutting her engine down, but the race was lost. Although the outcome of the race was less tragic than the damage to Slo-Mo V and her driver, both were stunning developments to a whole community—the effects of which were relived for months, if not years. The whole city reacted as though their beloved grandfather had suddenly died. The grief was palpable. And both events affected not only Doug's and my moods, but also our psyches.

You may say that merely a race was lost, but to Seattleites, the winning boat, Gale V, was from Detroit and represented the evil empire. The Gold Cup would not be held in Seattle the next year. The city was crushed.

In spite of the disappointing finish, my brother and I shared images and stories of that hydroplane season for months. To us it represented the epitome of sport and emotional involvement.

And, it also represented the second of three legs of a major transition in our lives.

The third leg of that transition occurred within a few weeks of the finality of Seafair that summer in 1955, when mom and dad informed us we once again were *moving*—this time more seriously—to *Northern Colorado!* We were leaving Seattle, forever, to return to the farmland of our roots, to live surrounded by our large family, in a place that supposedly would be more to our liking—a place where we could feel more *at home,* and achieve our dreams.

That was the plan and the hope; it remained to be seen if it would come true. Ahh . . . but that is the subject of my *next book!*

To Doug and me, that major move was the final blow in a series of changes, none of which was of our making. In the short span of slightly over one year, we had gone from unbridled happiness and close friendships, to uncertainty and newness. Our immediate viewpoint was that our lives had taken turns for the worse. We would have loved to enjoy our friends endlessly. We could have gone to Columbia Elementary School forever, or to the Saturday movie matinees every weekend for the remainder of our lives. But we learned that **life forces changes upon you, often when you least expect them, or want them, and you have to move forward, with no choice.**

The realization was upon us of the abruptness and sometimes brutality of change. Suddenly, in just an instant as with Slo-Mo-Shun V, nothing is ever the same again. Events force you to redirect and adapt to new awarenesses, new circumstances, new directions, and new lives. You have to find new friends, new playgrounds, new solutions, and—always—new adventures.

You have to grow, there is no alternative!

For me, in addition to all of the above, I was fast approaching major changes in both my body and my mind. My internal chemical factory was coming to life, and adolescence was approaching. I would never again be the eight- to twelve-year-old boy I had been while living in the projects.

For a while after our move from the projects, and certainly after our move to Colorado, Doug and my lives were disrupted. But eventually we came to understand, from the distance of time, that life does not come to an end when changes occur.

Yes, it is a cliché, but **life is a journey.**

And, as you move forward, you always leave some of yourself behind. That cannot be avoided. But you gain memories, and the residues of those become the foundations for your future. Eventually, time filters out much of the pain, the misery, the difficulties, and the unhappiness—and positions you for your future.

You realize that the good memories which remain are rich treasures to build upon and to enjoy always.

COURTESY OF THE HYDROPLANE & RACEBOAT MUSEUM, KENT, WA.

Slo–Mo–Shun IV cruising at about 50
miles per hour on Lake Washington.

It's a pleasure to share one's memories.
Everything remembered is dear, endearing, touching, precious.
At least the past is safe—though we didn't know it at the time.
We know it now. Because it's in the past;
because we have survived.

—Susan Sontag

PART SEVEN

SEATTLE REVISITED

32

SEATTLE — FIFTY YEARS LATER

Take only memories, leave nothing but footprints.
—Chief Seattle

In May 2006, more than fifty years after our family had moved to Colorado, my brother Doug and I, along with my wife, Jaio (pronounced Yi-oh) returned to Seattle. Our mission was to relocate the environs of our youth. If we could also re-discover some of the innocence and joy of those years, that would be an added blessing. I never had been back, not once. Doug, however, had unsuccessfully tried to find the inner city of Columbia about fifteen years earlier when he had a couple of hours to kill during a business trip. We were anxious with anticipation, but uncertain. Would those old projects still exist? Would Columbia grade school, with its cherished hardwood-floored classrooms and hallways still survive? Would its playgrounds still be filled with gleeful children, who had no concept of time, or of growing up—all of them modern-day *Peter Pans?* We wondered.

Upon arrival we picked up a street map of Seattle, but nowhere did the words *"The Old Projects"* blink back at us. The graveled streets we remembered from our youth—Alderwood, Cedarwood, Pinewood, and Redwood Courts—were not on the map. We recognized that as a potentially bad sign.

We drove though suspected streets of our past, looking for clues behind the murky cobwebs in our brains. We became frustrated with our inability to recognize any familiar landmarks. Finally, by chance, we approached an intersection I vaguely recalled. Something struck me! Immediately off to our left was a collection of dilapidated old single-story buildings with flat roofs.

My memory exploded and my mouth followed, "Doug, that's Rainier Vista School! That's where we first went to school, *before* Columbia!"

Doug exclaimed with great excitement, "You're right! And the projects *were* just around the next corner, to the right!" He jabbed the air in a pointing movement.

We immediately pulled to the side, parked, and sprang from the car. Our hearts leaped with excitement! We had found a familiar site! Now we could look for *all* of the old landmarks because we had a point of reference! This *was* our old neighborhood!!!

Doug and I chattered without restraint, and without waiting for replies. We were almost manic in our words and our movements. Neither of us could remain still as we paced, almost jumping with happiness. Our arms followed our feet with herky-jerky motions. Our glee at finding our home grounds had made us little boys again. We were so excited we could pop.

Finally, Jaio said, "Whoa guys! Do you see yourselves? Do you see how you are? You're both speed talking like you're in hyper space! I've *never* seen either of you like this. Settle down and we'll make it through the day. If not, you'll both burn up within ten minutes!" She laughed, but more with us than at us.

Doug and I looked at each other with smiles and realized she was right. We were so consumed with surprise and excitement that we were almost out of control.

We approached the curb. I took pictures, laughing and talking. I continued a dialogue until, after a minute or so, it occurred to me that only my wife and I were talking. I glanced around for Doug. He wasn't there. Then I saw him running down the street.

"Why that bugger..." I exclaimed. I laughed again because I knew him. I knew he couldn't contain himself any more. He was simply so spontaneous that he couldn't wait for me to finish with the pictures. He had to go look for the projects NOW, he just *had* to!

"HEY!" I shouted. "Wait up, darn you . . . you. . . . ." I couldn't think of the word I wanted because I was laughing too hard. I watched a sixty-one-year-old boy running before me. He turned his head and waved his arm with a pointing motion. He said something but I couldn't make it out. His arm motion said it all—"I'll see you at the projects!"

"C'mon," I exclaimed to Jaio, with urgency. We both ran back to the car and jumped inside. I accelerated, but Doug had already turned the corner. We followed, turned right at the corner . . . and immediately our fears were confirmed.

I parked the car and we both exited. We walked toward Doug who stood in the street. He waited for us, and then we all strolled toward our vision.

As we suspected, the "old" projects were nowhere to be seen. Instead, erected in their place was a campus of buildings, maybe twenty years old. If it were not for our memories, and the few pictures I still have of those days, there would be no proof to anybody today that those old projects, nee that poor life we once lived, ever existed. It was a chilling thought. It struck me that only fifty years had passed, and here an environment had been completely erased and now was invisible. I had an appreciation for archeologists who try to understand supposed civilizations that have been history for thousands of years.

The elation we had felt a few moments before now dissipated. We stared at the buildings, and Doug and I tried to collect our thoughts. We were disappointed, but not despondent. We were *here!* We were standing on the same grounds where we rode our bikes five decades earlier. We looked at the same gray sky we remembered. Mother Nature had not changed a thing for us. Only Man had determined that our old homes were no longer appropriate and had replaced them with something that also would be replaced in another twenty or thirty years.

"Well . . . let's go see if Columbia school is still there," I said finally. "It should be down this street and then a turn or two."

Reinvigorated by this thought, we reentered the car. We rounded the corner, drove a little further, and then...*there it was!* In front of us and stretching over the whole block frontage was Columbia Elementary School! It was just as the picture in our memories.

We parked our car and exited. We stared, laughing with almost tearful joy at how nice it was again to see this treasure. If seeing Rainier Vista was exciting, finding Columbia grade school was hitting the Mother Lode. Being late afternoon, the school had disgorged its students for the day, but children still played on the grounds, as we did when we were their age.

We wandered around the grounds, taking pictures and happily reliving memories. I saw the very same spot where Freddie Roberts ran up to tell me about finding the "mysterious barrel" in our woods, much as spies passed codes in crowded town squares.

We found an entrance to the building. Should we enter? We debated it for a few seconds. After all Doug and I were sixty-year-old men. What if anybody should catch us wandering the hallways? My wife reminded us that we had had come for this.

We carefully grabbed the handle and pulled the big door open to stare down a hallway. Children's drawings were taped over the walls, and various paraphernalia were scattered here and there in its length—a jacket, a soccer ball, and other things I could not distinguish in the dim light.

We quietly walked in and down the hallway, almost tiptoeing as if we didn't want to awaken old spirits. We turned right and immediately saw the Principal's Office.

"Doug, look at this! Remember Mr. Robison? Huh? Remember how he sat in that back office and we kids always thought it was like the cave of doom? To enter there was a fearful journey to the unknown, not knowing if we would ever return...alive...with all our limbs? Remember?"

He looked in. "Yes, I do, although there doesn't appear to be anything fearful about it now, does there? It's just a tiny, cramped administrator's office! Amazing!"

Immediately across the hall we saw another door with the words "Boys" printed on it. "Doug! How about this?" I said. "Let's go in." We did, and then called Jaio in also, when we verified there were no lingering boys in it. It was comical and we all laughed at the same moment. We found urinals against the wall that were so tiny it would have been difficult for a man of normal height to use. Even the stools were small. These fixtures never struck us that way when we tinkled in them, but now they were—quaint and cute, all made for little boys, the little boys still in our minds. We stepped out and strolled down the hallway further. Finally, flashes came back to me.

"Doug! This is the hallway to my fourth grade classroom, I know it! As we approached the room, I almost had tears in my eyes, surprisingly. It was more than I expected. I tried to say something and choked on the words. I slowly and carefully pushed open the door as if I expected a lion on the other side to snare me with its claw. Actually, I merely was uncertain of the memories I would discover, and my reactions to them.

We found a young man sitting at the teacher's desk shuffling papers. The desk was in the same location as Miss Dillon's so many years ago. He looked up, and we went through an explanation of being travelers from the past. He smiled and invited us to make ourselves at home. We could stay as long as we liked.

My eyes slowly scanned the room as though I were looking at an old crypt. It was the same room, but it was different. The old rows of oaken desks were gone, now replaced with large tables with metal legs. Four little chairs were arranged at the corners of each table. There were seven or eight such tables in the room. Some of the blackboards were still present, but most had been replaced with modern "white" boards with markers.

I felt overjoyed sitting at one of the short tables, but also awkward. Silently I sat and scanned. I wondered to myself, My gosh! If only these walls could talk. I could sit here all evening and converse with them. I closed my eyes and imagined my left arm propped on my desk holding up my chin, my right hand fingering the ink well lid, and my eyes staring at Sally Donovan's long ponytail flowing down her back in front of me. It was so vivid.

Finally, we thanked the teacher and left, solemnly and peacefully, as though leaving an old family grave. Back in the car, we were reinvigorated.

"The town of Columbia should be that way!" I pointed. "Just a couple of blocks. I wonder if the old movie theater is still there?"

We drove to the city's main street. It rekindled our memories of when we had bicycled up and down these same sidewalks. Finally, we found the entrance to the old Columbia Theater, but its marquee was missing. We peeked through the glass of the door, squinting as we shielded our eyes to better pierce the semi-darkness inside. We tried the knob and the door slipped open. We stepped into an empty corridor that was a passageway for time travel.

This was the lobby of the theater. Here they took our tickets, and there they sold all of our treasured candies, popcorns, and soda pop which we ate, drank, or threw. Doug, with a glowing smile on his face, said he remembered. We now were almost at a fever pitch of excitement.

A young woman approached from a new doorway on our left and offered help. We explained our objective. She said the theater had ceased showing films "many years ago," but it still existed at the end of the hallway, if we wanted to look. Did we! She threw a switch on the wall and the theater's interior suddenly illuminated, as though it once again was intermission.

We strolled with trepidation through the empty lobby, toward the light. With each step our heartbeats rose. As we walked, it all came back. At the end of the hallway we imagined the curtain, through which the theater manager had erupted after he had stopped the movie that one time. Ah, we were devils! Now I saw it all from his perspective and wondered how I could have kept even his state of "coolness" if I had to deal with us kids then!

We stepped though an archway and entered the old theater. It was elongated with a high ceiling and all of the walls were very old brick. We were instantly shocked. Yes, it was the same room, but again, it was so *small!* We remembered a large theater, and here we could have bounded from side to side with a number of large steps. Both of us were truly stunned. How could this be? How could our memories play such tricks on us? The rows of seats had been removed, but this ex-theater, the darkened location of our weekly escapes from reality, now seemed like nothing more than a decent-sized cave.

Once we recovered from the initial shock, we saw where the screen had been. Its location was hidden by the original draperies, but they also were *small*. We climbed the stage steps and peeked behind the curtains. Yes, the screen was still there. And it was square shaped! It was right out of the '20s or '30s. This was a theater built in and for that era. Thankfully, almost nothing had been changed. Only our memories had altered reality.

We stayed for about fifteen minutes reliving the many afternoons we had spent in that same space. Finally, we walked outside into the late afternoon sun. We took deep relaxing breaths of fresh air, and paused in our thoughts. We silently looked at each other; words were not necessary. I put my arm around Doug's shoulder, and my wife put her arm around my waist. We walked back to our car together with large smiles on our faces and contentment in our hearts.

We then drove up and down the main street looking for old landmarks. The buildings still stood, with their now antiquated façades, but now there were different tenants. The old "dime" store looked exactly the same from the outside, but now it was a day care center. Our grocery store, where we had scrounged for cardboard, was now an empty shambles, just waiting for a stiff breeze to blow it over. The Plunge, our indoor community swimming pool, also existed now only in our memories.

We left the main street and again drove up the hill on the big cross street. About midway up, I received a brain tingle and suddenly turned left into a driveway. I drove twenty yards or so, and parked the car. To our right we looked upon a hill with the backside of the relatively new campus above us on the high ground.

"Doug, do you realize where we are?" I asked in wonderment.

He thought for a moment, trying to digest the landscape and match it to the old and faded mental map in his mind.

"YES!" he finally said. "It's the hill we slid down on cardboard! It's the bottom of our sliding hill!"

"You're right," I said. "And, up at the top was the backside of our project's four-plex, the place where we lived! And, about over there (pointing with my left hand), is where the bottom row of four-plexes stood, where 'The Flying Cloud' came to a stop, breaking Freddie Roberts' wrist. Do you remember that?"

"'The Flying Cloud!' Wow! I haven't thought about that in ages. My gosh! You're right."

He covered his chin with his palm as if to help himself recall. "I barely remember 'The Flying Cloud's' only 'flight,' but I remember the countless times we slid down this hill finally wearing out the cardboard under our butts . . . and the grass too!"

He laughed slightly, then suddenly laughed even harder. "Do you remember the time I stupidly tried to parachute down the hill . . . ?" He now burst out laughing so hard that he couldn't finish his sentence. I also laughed.

". . . Remember . . . when I jumped off that ladder with Uncle Johnny's umbrella . . . and (more laughter) . . . I darned near killed myself . . . (belly-shaking laughter now from both of us)? Man, was that stupid!"

"Yes . . . I do remember," I said between breaths and additional laughs, "and yes, you were stupid for that. But just think of the *innocence* we had then! Think of the funny, crazy, scary, and just loony things we did. Wasn't it *fun?*" I poignantly asked.

Our lives and activities then had been all of those things and more. Yes, we were poor as anybody in all of Seattle, but all of those boyhood adventures had now left us with priceless treasures. Those treasures were the vivid memories of the fun we had experienced and had shared with others like us—our band of similarly poor scruffy ruffians who populated our lives during those years.

It all came back to us then, sitting in that car, staring at that hill, with the same grasses on it now as fifty-plus years ago.

Jaio obviously was not with us back then because she had not even been born until more than a decade later, in the middle of the 1960s. But, as we all laughed, she offered: "You know, I can relate to this too because—and you're probably not going to believe this—but we had a sliding hill also, near my house in northern Spain, where I grew up. And, we all—my brother and sister and

I, and the other kids in our neighborhood—well . . . we used to slide down *our* hill too. We used slickers and sleds . . . and cardboard also . . . anything that was slippery. Sometimes, we just laid on our sides and rolled down until we laughed so hard we almost couldn't stand it. But it never stopped us. . . . It was so much *fun!*" Teary now, she continued, "*I* remember all of those times, just like *you* do now, with your sliding hill in front of us! Isn't that something?" She blinked at moisture in her eyes.

Doug and I looked at her. We were touched and surprised with her disclosure, but yet not surprised. There are some childhood experiences that apparently are universal with time and location. Young boys and young girls are what they are, wherever they are, and dry grassy hills are the same wherever they are. And, if the two happen to come together, it's understandable the same things happen. It made perfect sense to all three of us sitting in that car laughing, and then almost crying, with each other.

Finally, we dried our eyes and chuckled even more. This was a great day we all agreed, but it was not over yet.

"There's one last thing we have to find—the haunted house," I said.

"Oh, I doubt if that still exists," Doug said, "or the woods, either. I'm sure they're both long gone."

"Well, let's go see," I said.

I made a "U" turn. We exited the dirt driveway, and crossed the street at almost the same place we costumed beggars had run across on that fateful Halloween night in 1952. We drove to the location of the old fabled haunted house, but sadly Doug was correct. It no longer existed. Surely it had been razed years before, as had the adjoining "woods," to make way for small houses which now dotted every space of ground in the area.

"OK. I guess that's it for the Columbia area," I said. "Let's head back."

We again drove up the hill. I immediately looked off to my left, and a memory flashed into my mind of the area where Jenny and I had thrown rocks at cars. I stared at the spot where she and I had launched the missiles, one of which had struck that old Chevy. I recalled our fears in the ensuing chase and capture by the irate motorist. I felt the hairs on the back of my neck rise again, just remembering his anger. I chuckled at how stupid Jenny and I had been that afternoon and how lucky we both had been to escape with our lives.

I looked at the launch site again, mindful to preemptively seek out any other such modern day replicas of Jenny and me, crouching semi-hidden in the same tall grasses. But luck was with us today. Our rental car labored up the hill, unaware of the apparent danger and its passing—much as the years.

We turned onto a larger thoroughfare and after a couple of blocks suddenly on our right we saw some of the "good" project buildings, the duplexes! I pulled the car to a halt, and again we erupted from the vehicle. We stared in amazement at the old condemned buildings, now slated for demolition. *They still existed*, although their remaining lifetime was short. We saw wrecking machinery chewing up and scattering another such duplex only a few hundred yards away. What amazing timing and luck, I thought. These buildings have stood for all of these years, and now within a few moments of their destruction, we show up to see them before they are gone forever.

We returned to the car and continued to drive up the thoroughfare. I suddenly remembered an intersection with a tug at my consciousness, but I was not sure why. However, after a few hundred yards I looked off to my right and was again struck with a bolt of memory. I pointed and exclaimed, "This is the location of the old Seattle Rainiers' ballpark! This is where Sick's Stadium was! Oh, my gosh! Look, now it's a home improvement store! Darn!" We slowed to a crawl, incurring the wrath of drivers behind us.

"Some of my most enjoyable memories were spent inside that park watching pro baseball. Man, I still remember the day I got Jimmy Rivera to sign the *ball* I caught."

My eyes almost glazed over, but I kept driving. Soon we were back at our hotel.

The next day, with a feeling of peaceful accomplishment in our hearts, we all returned to California. Doug and I had found what we came for. The visions of our youth were revived, and the memories now again danced in our minds with all of the freshness imaginable. All of it once again was real and alive.

For Jaio, our journey back to another life was also enlightening because she came to understand Doug and me better. She saw and now understood the glistening twinkles in our eyes on occasions. She saw the youthful and almost boundless energy which returned to us from over fifty years earlier—a time when it all came naturally to us.

She saw the *joy* in our hearts. She also saw the memories come alive, because, with only a tiny bit of her own imagination, she, too, saw all of us poorly dressed young boys happily running on the playgrounds, riding our bikes on the sidewalks, playing jungle wars in the woods, and skidding down the sliding hill. She, too, envisioned our innocence and imaginations, which allowed us to set aside our poverty and enjoy our lives to the fullest. She understood and appreciated how all of our fantasies and adventures added richness to the fabric of our boyhood lives. She also saw her *own* youth again: Our boyhood memories had rekindled memories for her too, and her own nostalgia made her happy and content.

That is what memories do.

POSTSCRIPT

Through the journey to Seattle, I was able to revisit an era in time—the early 1950s, and the old neighborhood we called "home."

I am neither maudlin nor naïve enough to believe those years were *"the good old days."* Instead, even then, we thought they were *"these hard times"*—our parents always told us so. But for all of our issues then, post World War II, in our culture, in our city, and in our very own home at 3232 Alderwood Court, we still had many things that made our life more than passable, they made it enjoyable.

Our parents had their family—their brothers and sisters, our aunts and uncles. And they had their friends too, also coping with life. Their friends were backbones of support and sources of enjoyment for them. And, of course, they had us, their sons and their daughter, who in spite of all of the problems and predicaments we created for them, were still their life, their *hope* for the future, and the main reason why they persevered against the formidable difficulties they faced, poor and uneducated as they were. In this regard, nothing has changed. Family is still critically important and children are still the manifestation of parents' love. This is true whether we discuss the 1950s or the 21st century.

More importantly, I was able to revisit, relive, and re-experience a period in my life—which was as important and significant to me as any other I have so far enjoyed. My mind and my senses were able to come alive again with the youthful exuberance of my childhood. I saw the earth, the streets, the buildings, the sky—the complete environment of that time. The linkage was perfect. I could close my eyes, take a breath, and once again smell the smokiness of the coal-burning stoves permeating our atmosphere in the projects. I could listen and hear the radio programs in our living room, the buses we rode, the hawkers at the baseball stadium, and the playing cards flapping against our bicycle wheels as we careened through the neighborhoods. I could see the popcorn and candy flying through the flickering images during an especially raucous moment at the Saturday movie matinees. I could even see a rundown, old (haunted) house which scared the very life out of us kids, day or night. It could have been a completely benign old house, but our imaginations then made it otherwise.

It all exists again for me, in my mind and in my memories. Those images elicit contentment within me, and that is all that matters.

Chief Seattle said it best: *"Take only memories, leave nothing but footprints."* For me, the footprints are quickly gone, but the memories remain forever.

The old Rainier Vista School—my third grade classroom.

Columbia Elementary School, the playground of my youth.
My 4th grade classroom is to the right of the entrance doorway.

The old Columbia Theater where we spent so many Saturday afternoons watching our heroes escape from every possible cliffhanging dilemma.

Our sliding hill today. The flat pad on the left has been cut into the original hill making the down-slope very short now. The parking area on the right is where the lower four-plex existed, where the "The Flying Cloud" slammed to an abrupt stop. But the weeds and wild grasses remain today as memories of those endless summer days, when our quest for fun and adventure was fulfilled on this hill—and it was all free!

354

The "good" projects, waiting for the wrecking ball:
a front view above, a side view below.

Sally Donovan lived in a unit like this one.

Doug and I enjoying our visit back to Seattle,
after rediscovering our youth.

EPILOGUE

Our lives as young boys in the projects, in the 1950s, were in most respects no different from lives of other boys, in other times and other places. We had regimens and routines, we had chores and responsibilities, we had things to live through, which were difficult and which led to unhappiness. We had school, which was not always fun, and we had competition for everything, often with defeats as a real life outcome. We had to struggle with the pecking order on the playgrounds, and deal with the bullies and the nasty ruffians. Life at our level, within our small world, was a microcosm of life everywhere, at any time. Sure our lives were maybe different from those of the faceless kids of our dreams who grew up in the rich sections of Seattle. Although we didn't realize it at the time, those kids had problems too, some the same as ours.

But for all of us, everywhere, our passage through those youthful years was made easier by our imaginations. They enabled us to dream about more satisfying lives where our wants and needs were fulfilled, about winning at whatever was important to us, and about having the things that mattered—love and care from our parents and other adults in our lives, plus acceptance and respect from our peers. *Affirmation and appreciation are so important to kids, always!* We needed to understand and believe that we were OK.

Our imaginations were the catalyst that allowed us to overcome the daily drudgery in our lives and escape into worlds of fun and adventure. The adventures stimulated all of our emotions, sometimes to the extreme, and provided the crucibles for our development through pre-adolescence. But the last critical ingredient that made it all possible was our heroes, our ready-made examples to lead us in those escapades and exploits. Through them we realized we could *live* our adventures, and ultimately *catch our dreams*. It was from our heroes we learned that success and happiness *were* possible, but were achieved only by overcoming—often against great odds. **The greater the danger, the sweeter the victory; the larger the risk, the greater the reward** were early life's lessons repeatedly delivered by our heroes.

It is my hope that this book will be an example to children everywhere—to you—that you *can* achieve your dreams. Don't let anyone say it can't be done—we boys in these stories did it, against all odds. We grew up almost as poor as one could be, with dysfunctional surroundings, and with people around us who sometimes frightened and threatened. But we engaged the *magical mixture* that both defined and enriched our childhoods . . . *our active imaginations, our wonderful adventures . . . our larger-than-life heroes, and our cherished dreams.* By employing and enjoying all of them. . . .

We realized the importance of having fun.

We discovered paths out of the blackberry brambles of life.

We learned how to invest in treasured friendships, and the benefits of doing so.

We learned that education and hard work are keys to everything.

We realized that opportunities come along, sometimes when least expected.

We appreciated how important it is to recognize when they appear, and then to hop aboard for a ride to our destiny.

We learned the value of patience, of believing in ourselves, and of having determination and tenacity regardless of occasional slips backward. We learned that if we keep moving forward, eventually we *will* get to our dreams.

Lastly, we learned the most important lesson: good deeds somehow, magically, come back, not to haunt us, *but to assist us* in our journey

—that success in life is about treating others well, even when they sometimes don't treat us well. Forgiveness is hugely important, and separates us from everybody else.

In closing, and as a helpful hint, I believe it *always* helps to have some spiritual faith in your life—to believe in something larger than yourself and to trust that He will help you, if you merely commit and ask for guidance. You'll be surprised how often that guidance will show up.

To boys and girls of *all* ages, I encourage you to *live the lives of your imagination, have your adventures, enjoy your heroes, and catch your own dreams.* Not only are they possible... they are *waiting* for you!

GIVING BACK

The Author's vision is to use a portion of proceeds from this book to further his philanthropic and nonprofit endeavors to help children everywhere employ their imaginations, pursue their dreams, overcome their problems, and find their own success. The "Dream Cards" following page 374 are tools for this objective.

The greatest gifts to children are love and hope.

"Giving back" with orphans and homeless children.

The joy from having *hopes* and *dreams*.

Three "makers of mischief" having fun.

LESSONS WE LEARNED

The difference between school and life?
In school, you're taught a lesson and then given a test.
In life, you're given a test that teaches you a lesson.
—Tom Bodett

Throughout the pages of this book I have emboldened Lessons We Learned that my brother and I came to understand as important, even way back during our boyhood years. These lessons were so simple, and so pervasively true, that even as children we grasped them. But their ultimate beauty and reward were that, once learned, they had great value if we simply continued to live them and apply them. These lessons have been with us most of our lives, and have contributed to who we have become.

I offer a simple review of these lessons here. For a more in-depth discussion, please go to my website, www.makersofmischief.com, and download the document titled, "Lessons We Learned."

INTRODUCTION

It is very difficult, without help, to rise above what you do know or to migrate into something you don't know.

CHAPTER

1 Miracles do happen.

2 If intelligent people associate with idiots (or fools), the idiots will be forgiven, but not those who "should have known better."

2 If you were not born with it, you may never excel to match your dreams, and the best thing would be for you to find another "ball game" which suits you better.

3　You should pay more attention to your "sixth sense" and let it override the other emotional aspects of your mind.

5　It is unfair to pre-suppose anybody can, or cannot, do anything. It is unfair to categorize people for any reason.

8　Success sometimes requires "give and take."

9　Dreams are wonderful, but they are not *always* achievable.

10　Fear is contagious, but bravery stands alone.

11　You should never underestimate anyone, especially when they are strongly motivated.

11　Always treat others the same way you want to be treated.

20　If you miss a bus, another will come along soon.

20　As long as you don't overspend, you can do most of what you want.

20　If you are properly positioned, and can grab a little luck, anything can happen.

21　Never let your imagination be limited by perceived reality.

23　Girls just naturally think differently about things.

23　The cuter you looked, the more likely another drop of candied bliss was likely to find its way into your bag.

24　There comes a time when you have to face your fears.

24　The team is everything!

26　The satisfaction is never in the result—it is in the process.

26　Don't give the other guy the satisfaction; instead earn his respect.

27　There is a bond that forms among friends. When both parties endure hardship and difficulty, and somehow get through it because of their attachment and dedication to each other, it has meaning.

31　Life forces changes upon you, often when you least expect them, or want them, and you have to move forward, with no choice.

31　Life is a journey.

EPILOGUE

The greater the danger, the sweeter the victory; the larger the risk, the greater the reward.

How This Book Came About

An attribute I have always enjoyed is an ability to remember certain events or periods of my youth with exceptional crispness. In my life I have been both a daydreamer, and a dreamer, not entirely similar things, but I never expected to be a writer. This book has happened almost with a mind of its own.

During one particularly enjoyable time spent reminiscing with my brother, we recalled a specific childhood event that was so "alive" to both of us, even after fifty plus years, that we laughed uproariously. Stimulated, I wrote about the event. Interestingly, it became a well-defined story. I titled it, "Mystery in the Woods"—our story of finding the barrel. That first composition also contained the background of what became the first two chapters in this book—"The Projects" and "The Alderwood Court Gang"—as well as Chapter 4, "The Last Straw."

I decided to share that first story with Doug and our very close cousin, Ann Everitt, in Colorado. They both provided encouragement, but Ann further suggested that the story, along with the descriptions of how we lived in the projects, could be of value to our other family members. She asked, "Do you have other stories?" I thought about that. Perhaps if I wrote more, it could serve a valuable purpose to our family, beyond my own enjoyment.

Stimulated by both her and Doug, I found that I recalled other vignettes from my childhood. I then wrote, "A Magical Afternoon," which appears as Chapter 5. Some weeks later I wrote an essay about the entertainment we kids enjoyed then—the radio programs, early television, and the Saturday afternoon movie matinees. This essay also described many of our "heroes" of the times.

Ann continued to suggest that I compose a book as a gift to our immediate family.

My thought, however, was to give these writings to my own daughters because I had never told them any of these stories when they were growing up! I had never shared with them any of my early childhood experiences of life in the housing projects, or anything personal about those times—the early 1950s. Thus that period had no more meaning to them than any other formless, emotionless period from their classroom history books. In addition, by my not sharing with them, it occurred to me that I had not only failed to give them some understanding of that era, but also of their dad's childhood. I had missed that opportunity.

To my daughters Amy, Erin, and Lindy, as well as my step-daughter Haizea, hopefully you will now have a better understanding of the times in which I grew up, and the life I enjoyed as a pre-adolescent boy. Also, I hope you will finally have an appreciation of what impish *Makers of Mischief* your dad and your uncle were, so many years ago. Perhaps this will help to explain some of the things we all did as a family when you were being raised. Wasn't it *fun!*

THANKS

Writing is a solitary activity. The romantic images of "artists" in smoke-filled enclaves sharing creative concepts and constructing words to "change the world" are prevalent. Reality is, the writer must seclude himself... put aside all distractions... approach a keyboard... stare wantonly for sometimes long periods... and wait for inspiration. Rarely is there a fire-hose stream of brilliantly composed prose.

However, assuming the writing happens, somehow, making that output into a finished book is a team effort. Many play a role and all are valuable—from seemingly simple conversations of encouragement at the right moments, to the committed help of skilled professionals over long periods. All are necessary, and appreciated.

Without my dear cousin, Ann Everitt, this book never would have begun, and she remained an inspiration throughout. Thanks Ann, more than I can say.

Thanks to all who read parts along the way and offered praise as well as honest criticism. These friends are Neil Cernese, Beth Clifford, David Everitt, Connie Finch, Kathryn Gibney, Nanci Grady, Elizabeth Hutt, Judy Lawrence, and Carol Van Wyk. Thanks also to other friends, too numerous to mention, who for months listened to my passion for this book and always provided encouragement.

Special thanks to Don Hammond, my pastor, with whom I shared enjoyable discussions about both of us growing up in the 1950s. I thank Mikala Woodward of the Rainier Valley Historical Society in Seattle for all of her joy and help with my reconnection to Columbia, the inner-city small community of my youth. I also very much appreciate my discussions with Patricia Vaccarino of Seattle regarding content of the book, as well as marketing and promotional activities. Additionally, I wish to draw special attention to the insightful and helpful suggestions I received from author Phillip Yancey, as well as the wonderful inspiration I received from author Debbie Macomber.

A heartfelt thank you to those who provided skilled professional services: Victoria Pohlman for the cover design, Ed Kamholz for the interior design, and Paula Hendricks for her support and encouragement along my path to independent publication.

Deep appreciation is extended to Desta Garrett who did all of the layout—text and covers—and who was the monitor of all proper English usage, to Minette Siegel for her amazing resourcefulness, thoroughness, and perseverance when it came to photo research and securing permissions, to Wendy Williams for permissions help, and to my editor Vicki Weiland, who contributed so much more than editorial review through seemingly never-ending drafts—along the way she became my very dear friend, prayer partner, and most ardent advocate. This book never would have happened without her efforts.

To each who follow, you all have changed my life and made me who I am today, and I am grateful.

Thank you Naomi Osborne, the mother of our children. Our friendship and your encouragement were so meaningful.

To Siena Foxx, my dear sister, who was "Cindy" until she changed her name. Thanks, Sis, for all of the joy you gave me—not only during the creation of this book, but also in our lives together.

In a similar vein, thank you brother Doug. Without your presence beside me throughout all of those sometimes difficult, but still enjoyable years, there wouldn't have been many of these stories. And without your discussions in our later "adult" life, there certainly never would have been the genesis for this book. You were the spark that set it all aglow. Thanks brother!

To Haizea Alemany, my stepdaughter, thank you for your good humor and curiosity about my childhood.

Above all, my most special thanks and deepest gratitude are to my love, my wife, Jaio. You continually inspired my creativity, supported my tenacity, and stimulated me endlessly to not only bring this book to conclusion, but also to produce it with the best of my abilities. Hopefully I have done that—all because of you by my side.

Lastly, I wish to thank my wonderful God. You have been a powerful force who has empowered me and carried me, at times when nothing, or nobody else, could. Thank You, Lord.

CITATIONS

QUOTATIONS

FRONT MATTER

John Greenleaf Whittier, from *The Barefoot Boy,* www.QuotationsBook.com

Gilbert K. Chesterton, www.QuotationsBook.com, www.QuotationsPage.com

Nadine Stair (attributed to), www.QuotationsBook.com, www.QuotationsPage.com

CHAPTERS

1 Benjamin Franklin, www.QuotationsBook.com, www.QuotationsPage.com

   Jackie Mason, quote used by permission of Jackie Mason

   Quotation by Linus from the comic strip "PEANUTS" by Charles M. Schulz (May 29, 1981), PEANUTS © United Feature Syndicate, Inc. Used by permission of United Media

2 Mohammad Ali, quote reprinted by permission of Mohammad Ali Enterprises LLC

3 Satchel Paige, www.QuotationsBook.com, www.QuotationsPage.com

   Ellen Parr, www.QuotationsBook.com

5 Yogi Berra quote excerpted from *The Yogi Book: I Really Didn't Say Everything I Said,* ©1998 L.T.D. Enterprises. Used by permission of Workman Publishing Co., Inc., New York. All Rights Reserved.

6 Will Rogers, www.QuotationsBook.com

8 Mark Twain (attributed to), www.QuotationsBook.com

   Mary Jean LeTendre, www.QuotationsBook.com

9 Johann Sebastian Bach, www.QuotationsBook.com

10 Irwin Sarason, www.QuotationsBook.com

12 John Reeves, quote used by permission of *Motley Fool*

13 Bill Watterson, *Calvin and Hobbes,* quote used by permission of Universal Press Syndicate

   Howdy Doody, phrases used by permission of MediaNet Group Technologies, Inc.

18 Quotes, phrases, and Creed from THE LONE RANGER, copyright ©Random House, Inc. Used by permission of Golden Books, an imprint of Random House Children's Books, a division of Random House, Inc.

19 Roy Rogers and Dale Evans, phrases used by permission of Roy Rogers Family Entertainment Corp.

   Roy Rogers Rider's Club Rules, used by permission of the Roy Rogers-Dale Evans Museum

20 Dwight D. Eisenhower, quote used by permission of John S. D. Eisenhower and the Dwight D. Eisenhower Presidential Library and Museum

   Jim Rivera to President John F. Kennedy, Baseball Opening Day, 1961, www.BaseballLibrary.com

21 Rupert Brooke, www.QuotationsBook.com

22 Tennessee Williams, (excerpt) from *CAMINO REAL,* by Tennessee Williams, copyright © As "Ten Blocks on the Camino Real" (a one-act play), copyright © 1948 The University of the South. As "Camino Real," revised and published version, © 1953 The University of the South. Renewed 1981 The University of the South. Used by permission of New Directions Publishing Corporation.

   Trina Paulus, excerpts from *Hope for the Flowers,* written and illustrated by Trina Paulus, Copyright © 1972 by Trina Paulus. Paulist Press, Inc., New York/Mahwah, NJ. Reprinted by permission of Paulist Press, Inc., www.paulistpress.com

23 Ashleigh Brilliant, quote used by permission of Ashleigh Brilliant

24 James Stephens, www.QuotationsBook.com

25 Margaret Mead, www.QuotationsBook.com

27 Johann Wolfgang von Goethe, www.QuotationsBook.com

29 Helen Keller, www.QuotationsBook.com

30 Gail Sheehy (attributed to); also attributed to Anatole France

31 Karen Kaiser Clark, quote used by permission of Karen Kaiser Clark

   Susan Sontag, www.QuotationsBook.com, www.education.yahoo.com

32 Chief Seattle, www.QuotationsBook.com

LESSONS WE LEARNED

Tom Bodett, quote used by permission of Tom Bodett, www.bodett.com

NOTE: All quotations were found on multiple Internet websites, including the sampling above, and are believed to be considered "fair use." However, additional requests for permissions were pursued as able and verifiable.

Quotations

Special Thanks to:

Martin Berns, CEO, MediaNet Group Technologies, Inc.

Ashleigh Brilliant

Maggie Campbell, Assistant to Roland Scahill, William Morris Agency, LLC

David Chaudori, Creative Director, Muhammad Ali Enterprises LLC

Karen Kaiser Clark, The Center for Executive Planning, St. Paul, MN

Laura Davis, PEANUTS Licensing Associate, United Media

Joanne DelloRusso, Harcourt, Inc., Paralegal, Copyrights & Permissions Team Lead, Harcourt, Inc., publisher of *Satchel Sez: Don't Look Back*, ©2007 by David A. Adler, an illustrated biography

John S. D. Eisenhower

Thomas W. Branigar, Archivist, Eisenhower Library

Dominique Giammarino, Administrator, Copyright & Permissions, Random House, Inc.

Patricia Flynn, Director of Licensing, Random House, Inc.

Betty Graber, Director of Copyright & Permissions, Random House, Inc.

Cheryl Gordon, Paralegal, Legal Department, Brown Shoe Company

Ian R. Gross, Contracts Manager, Workman Publishing Co., Inc.

Robert Hirst, Curator, Mark Twain Archives, Bancroft Library, University of California, Berkeley

Ron Hussey, Permissions & Quotes, Houghton Mifflin Company

Kim Anthony Jones, Licensing Manager, Classic Media, Inc.

Shannon Speck, Business & Legal Affairs, Classic Media, Inc.

Dennis O. Palmore, Permissions Manager, New Directions Publishing Corporation

Permissions Department, Paulist Press, Inc.

Krystle Scott, Executive Director, Intellectual Property, MGM Studios

Mary Suggart, Permissions Director, Universal Press Syndicate

Photos

NOTE: Unless otherwise identified, pictures are from the Osborne Family album or have been found on numerous online locations and difficult to ascertain ownership.

Special Thanks to:

Karen Ackerman, Whirlpool Corporation Community Relations

Kristine Vernier, Carmichael Lynch Spong, Whirlpool Corporation, Maytag Brand

S. Victor Burgos, Photofest, Inc., NY

Tom Gordon III, Gemstone Publishing, Timonium, MD

Susan Karl, CEO, Annabelle Candy Co., Hayward, CA

Jeff Kramer, President, Roy Rogers Family Entertainment Corp.

Tony Lobue, Owner, www.flashgordon.ws/

Mike Mattes, www.flashgordon.ws/

Carolyn Marr, Museum of History & Industry, Seattle, WA

Roy "Dusty" Rogers, Jr., Trustee for the Estate of Roy Rogers, Roy Rogers – Dale Evans Museum, Branson, MO

Dave Koch, Roy Rogers – Dale Evans Museum, Branson, MO

Mikala Woodward, Rainier Valley Historical Society, Seattle WA

DISCUSSION QUESTIONS FOR READERS

PART ONE

- What are your fondest memories from your childhood?
- What are some of the "mischievous" things you did?
- What hardships did you face?
- Who in the Alderwood Court Gang were you most like?
- Do you remember boys and girls like them? (including Sally)
- Did you have a "woods," or a special place, where your imagination could soar and you could find adventure?

PART TWO

- What are some of the "pranks" you played at school?
- Who was your favorite teacher? Why?
- Do you remember your own school assemblies? Were you in the audience or on the stage?
- Can you relate to the school environment in the 1950s, as described in this book?

PART THREE

- Who was your favorite TV hero? (or heroine)
- Who was your favorite movie hero? (or heroine)
- What was your favorite radio show?
- How important are heroes or alter egos to kids, in any era?

PART FOUR

- What do you remember most about the Lone Ranger and Tonto?
- What do you remember most about Roy Rogers and Dale Evans?
- When did your family get its first TV? (Or when did you see your first TV show?)

- Did you ever have a "dream" come true?

- Did you get an allowance? What did you spend it on?

PART FIVE

- Did you have a "sliding hill"?

- What did you learn about having friends and being part of a team?

- What was your favorite Halloween costume? (Or what costume do you remember most?)

- How do you think you and your friends would have reacted during the Halloween Caper and the Halloween Adventure?

PART SIX

- What did you want to be when you grew up?

- Did you ever try out an "experiment"?

- Did you ever do anything dangerous? Or did you do anything that turned unexpectedly dangerous?

- What event or change in your life showed you that you were "growing up"?

PART SEVEN

- Have you ever revisited the favorite spots of your childhood? How did you feel?

- What experiences did you have that taught you lessons you have kept with you all of your life? What were the lessons?

LESSONS WE LEARNED

- Which of the lessons Jack and Doug learned do you identify with most?

- If you could tell current day "makers of mischief" anything, what would you most like to say?

- Have you filled out your "Dream Card?"

- Have you given a "Dream Card" to anyone else?

About the Author

Jack Osborne is an author, businessman, husband, parent—having raised three daughters to adulthood—and grandparent. Born to "dirt poor" sugar-beet sharecrop farmers in Northern Colorado, his family was relocated to Seattle during the Second World War. He was raised in poverty in government housing projects in south Seattle during the 1950s.

Leaving home at age seventeen, he joined the Marine Corps. After service, he moved to California and put himself through college—the first of his ancestry to do so—by working nights, graduating in Mathematics and Physics from San Jose State University. He then lived in and around the San Francisco Bay Area and fashioned a thirty-year career in "Silicon Valley's" high-tech industries.

He is a successful engineer/businessman-entrepreneur, having been an executive or founder in six start-up companies. One company he founded, and served as President and Chairman of the Board, became a multinational public company.

Mr. Osborne is an avid outdoorsman, sports enthusiast, and sailor, having coastal cruised and sailed over 8,000 miles on the open ocean. He is a devoted (now second) family man, who with his wife is raising her teenage daughter. He stays active in business as an executive management consultant.

He is a man of spiritual commitment, and a keen observer of life and people. His love, beyond helping people develop their potential, is writing heartwarming and enjoyable stories which touch upon the human experience with humor and poignancy.

This is his first book, and he has two others nearing completion.

ABOUT DOUG

Despite having the learning disability dyslexia, which was not known when he and Jack attended Columbia Elementary School, Doug attended the University of Washington medical school. He became an expert in the field of prosthetics and orthotics—the design, fabrication, and fitting of artificial limbs. Additionally, he became notably skilled in creating and implementing "halo's"—the braces used to stabilize broken backs and necks.

He, too, formed his own corporation, later in his career, and provided such services to clients of all ages, primarily to those of lower economic means.

"Both Doug and I employed the lessons we learned as young boys. As we grew, developed, and became adults, we studied hard and 'applied ourselves'—as was our mom's dream—to eventually capture many of our own dreams. We both became people we wanted to be.

"We now look back and enjoy the journeys which have brought each of us to this point in our lives. We still have our dreams, even today—neither of us is finished yet! But we both remember those wonderful days when we had nothing, and we had everything—those days of our boyhoods in the projects and surrounding neighborhoods of south Seattle."　　　　　　　—Jack Osborne

To Order This Book

For ordering instructions via online, telephone, fax, or mail order
—or—
For current pricing and author's special promotions,

Please visit our website:

www.makersofmischief.com

Makers of Mischief may be purchased in bulk for education, business, non-profit, or fundraising use. For information, please contact the publisher:

Dream Away **Books Inc.**

P. O. Box 5457
San Jose, California 95150-5457
E-mail: makers@dreamawaybooks.com

To Contact Us

If you enjoyed this book, or have suggestions, or other comments,

We would love to hear from you.

Please send your comments to the Publisher.
Or visit our website and pull down "Contact Us" on the menu.
Or send e-mail directly to makers@dreamawaybooks.com.

DREAM CARDS

Children, *of all ages,* need dreams as destinations to fulfillment, happiness, and self-worth. But for dreams to be captured—to become real—they must be more than simply idle diversions: *they must be focused objectives.*

Here is a set of your own "Dream Cards." Tear out a Card, write your dream on that Card, and then carry it with you always. Regularly take out your Dream Cards and review your dreams, especially during difficult times.

Use these Dream Cards as simple reminders of your dreams. Add imagination, hard work, perseverance, and some good luck and opportunity whenever they come along. All of these ingredients can enable you to catch your dreams.

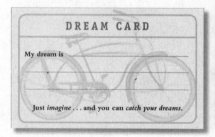

"It is my present dream to use this book—and the attached Dream Cards—to inspire children of all ages to employ their imaginations, to seek their dreams, to follow their hearts . . . and to become the best they can be."
                                                        —Jack Osborne

To order more Dream Cards, visit our website:
www.makersofmischief.com

DREAM CARDS

It is my present dream to use this book—and the attached Dream Cards—to inspire children of all ages to employ their imaginations, to seek their dreams, to follow their hearts . . . and to become the best they can be.   —Jack Osborne

Children, *of all ages,* need dreams as destinations to fulfillment, happiness, and self-worth. But for dreams to be captured—to become real— they must be more than simply idle diversions: *they must be focused objectives.*

Here is a set of your own "Dream Cards." Tear out a Card, write your dream on that Card, and then carry it with you always. Regularly take out your Dream Cards and review your dreams, especially during difficult times.

Use these Dream Cards as simple reminders of your dreams. Add imagination, hard work, perseverance, and some good luck and opportunity whenever they come along. All of these ingredients can enable you to catch your dreams.

To order more Dream Cards, visit our website:
www.makersofmischief.com

 **Books**

E-mail:
makers@dreamawaybooks.com

DREAM CARD

My dream is _____

_____

_____

Just *imagine . . .* and you can *catch your dreams.*

DREAM CARD

My dream is _____

_____

_____

Just *imagine . . .* and you can *catch your dreams.*

DREAM CARD

My dream is _____

_____

_____

Just *imagine . . .* and you can *catch your dreams.*

DREAM CARD

My dream is _____

_____

_____

Just *imagine . . .* and you can *catch your dreams.*

I + D + E + A = S

Imagination+Dreams+Energy+Adventures=Success

IDEAs lead to SUCCESS!

I + D + E + A = S

Imagination+Dreams+Energy+Adventures=Success

IDEAs lead to SUCCESS!

I + D + E + A = S

Imagination+Dreams+Energy+Adventures=Success

IDEAs lead to SUCCESS!

I + D + E + A = S

Imagination+Dreams+Energy+Adventures=Success

IDEAs lead to SUCCESS!

To order more Dream Cards,
visit our website:
www.makersofmischief.com

DreamAway Books

E-mail:
makers@dreamawaybooks.com